Islamic Law

Claiming the American Wilderness: International Rivalry
in the Trans-Mississippi West, 1528–1803 (2006)

The Pursuit of Learning in the Islamic World,
610–2003 (2005, paperback 2006)

Medieval Justice: Cases and Laws in France,
England and Germany, 500–1500 (2004)

Four Paths to Jerusalem: Jewish, Christian, Muslim,
and Secular Pilgrimages, 1000 BCE to 2001 CE (2002, paperback 2006)

Fort Bridger, Wyoming: Trading Post for Indians,
Mountain Men and Westward Migrants (2001, paperback 2006)

The India-China Opium Trade in the Nineteenth Century (1999)

Islamic Law

*The Sharia from Muhammad's
Time to the Present*

HUNT JANIN *and*
ANDRÉ KAHLMEYER

McFarland & Company, Inc., Publishers
Jefferson, North Carolina, and London

LIBRARY OF CONGRESS CATALOGUING-IN-PUBLICATION DATA

Janin, Hunt, 1940–
    Islamic law : the Sharia from Muhammad's time to the present /
Hunt Janin and André Kahlmeyer
        p.   cm.
    Includes bibliographical references and index.

    ISBN-13: 978-0-7864-2921-9
    (softcover : 50# alkaline paper) ∞

    1. Islamic law — History.   2. Jihad. I. Kahlmeyer, André, 1978–
II. Title.
KBP50.J36   2007
340.5'9 — dc22   2007005335

British Library cataloguing data are available

On the cover: Cairo's al-Azhar University and mosque, founded in 971
(photograph by André Kahlmeyer).

Manufactured in the United States of America

McFarland & Company, Inc., Publishers
  Box 611, Jefferson, North Carolina 28640
  www.mcfarlandpub.com

Acknowledgments

In this book, we are aiming at an ambitious goal. We want to present the *sharia* in impartial terms which are simple enough to catch and hold the attention of the general reader but at the same time are sturdy enough not to buckle under the weight of scholarly scrutiny. If we have made some progress toward this goal, it is largely due to the help of numerous scholars and friends. To them we extend our warm thanks.

Listed alphabetically, they include Abdullah F. Ansary, Annelies Boogaerdt, Jeff Bridges, Ary Budiyanto, Sharon Chadha, Lateef A. Choudhri, Geoff Craig, Mary Douglas-Bate, Wael B. Hallaq, Noga Hartmann, Toby Huff, Elizabeth Iskander, Ulrika Mårtensson, Christopher Melchert, Rudolph Peters, Paul Sherrin, Mary Speer, Muhammad Isa Waley, Dennis Wolff, and Sami Zubaida.

Very special thanks are due to Ria van Eil, who brought to this project the editorial and proofreading skills we sometimes lack, being too close to the text.

If there are any errors or misjudgments in this book, the responsibility is ours alone. Any work of scholarship, even a general survey such as this one, is necessarily provisional. Old explanations must be abandoned as new facts and new interpretations come to light. In this spirit, we welcome scholarly corrections from readers. Comments can be sent to us care of the publisher.

And now We have set you on the right path. Follow it, and do not yield to the desires of ignorant men; for they can in no way protect you from the wrath of God. The wrongdoers are patrons to each other; but the righteous have God Himself for their patron.

Quran, *sura* 45:18

Table of Contents

Introduction

This book is an introduction to the *sharia* (pronounced "sha-REE-ah")—the religious law of Islam and one of the most important aspects of this far-flung world religion. The *sharia* is an extremely complicated legal and academic system with a long, revered tradition. Indeed, Islamic culture as a whole can be characterized as being a "legal culture."[1]

Books dealing with the *sharia* tend to fall into two categories. The first consists of academic studies that require a considerable prior knowledge of Islam. Such works are too specialized for the general reader. The second category consists of books written by devout Muslims who want to defend and propagate their faith. These publications are designed more to persuade than to educate.

In contrast, this book is written with three objectives in mind. It tries to be, at the same time, accurate in scholarly terms, interesting, easy to read, objective, and even-handed in assessing the *sharia*'s achievements, shortcomings, and future prospects.

To keep this book short and simple, we have purposely ignored many of the academic controversies and finer points which scholars of Islam like to explore at great length.

In Arabic, *sharia* literally means the "way to water" or "the path leading to the watering hole." By extension, this meant, in the unforgiving climate of the Arabian desert, that it was the only sure path to survival. In religious terms, it was the sole path which, if followed devotedly and unswervingly, would lead the faithful to a blissful heavenly afterlife. It was, moreover, God's own idea about what life should look like on earth. Following the dictates of the *sharia* thus put the faithful on the path toward a life on earth which could be marked by security, good governance and stability.

1

Atlantic Ocean

North Sea
Moscow
Kazan
Baltic Sea
Vienna
Black Sea
Caspian Sea
Aral Sea
Lake Balkash
Venice
Genoa
Tabriz
Samarqand
Peking
Cordoba
Granada
Damascus
Bukhara
Kashgar
Tunis
Baghdad
Fez
Jerusalem
Basra
Isfahan
Kabul
Cairo
Herat
Lahore
Canton
Pacific Ocean
Medina
Delhi
Timbuktu
Lake Chad
Red Sea
Mecca
Persian Gulf
South China Sea
Kano
Arabian Sea
Bay of Bengal
Malacca
Java Sea
Jakarta
Zanzibar
Indian Ocean

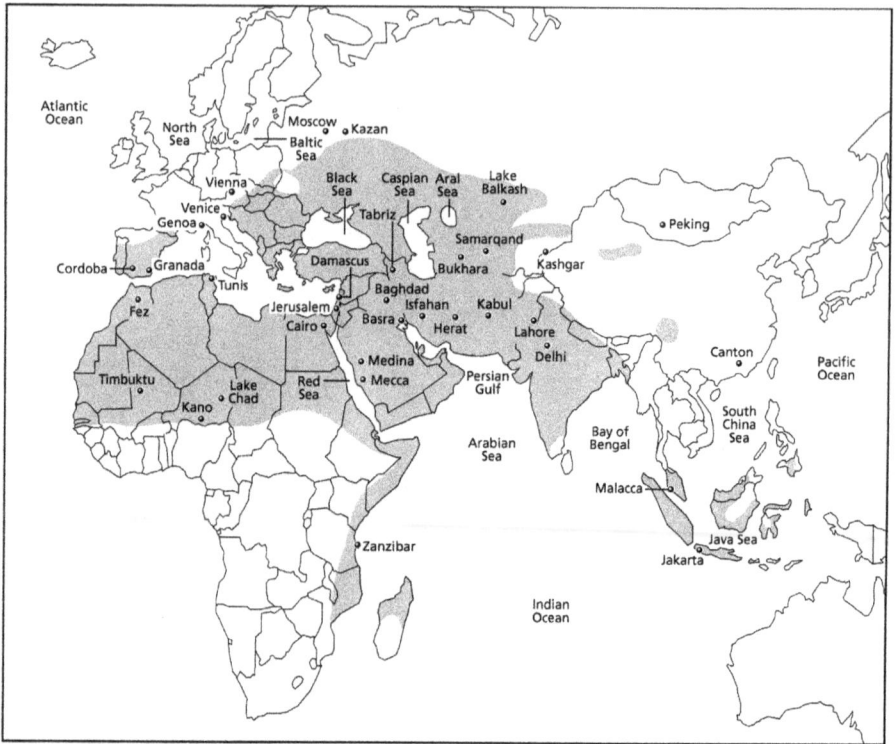

The shaded areas of this map show the expansion of Islam at its greatest extent. This expansion was never a uniform, unbroken process but was marked by major ebbs and flows. Muslim power in Spain, for example, arose in 711 and ended in 1492. (Map by Graeme Bandeira, adapted from Lapidus, *A History of Islamic Societies*, p. 199.)

The *sharia* is solidly based on two theological foundations: first on the Quran, which is considered to be the word of God Himself, and then jointly on the *sunna* and *hadith*. Because of the cardinal importance of these sources, they will be discussed frequently in the pages that follow.

In short, the *sunna*, which is based on the life and teachings of Muhammad, consists of the religious, legal and social obligations of Islam. *Hadith* (the plural in Arabic is *ahadith* but for the sake of convenience only the singular form, *hadith*, will be used here) are the traditions, habits and sayings of the prophet Muhammad, as preserved and transmitted by his favored Companions. This last word is often capitalized in English to draw a distinction between the prophet's closest associates — his Companions — and the many other people he knew and with whom he worked.

Hadith and *sunna* are often so intertwined that it can be difficult to separate them conceptually. The essential difference is that *hadith* are based on Muhammad's own life and thus constitute a biographical basis of Islamic law. The *sunna*, on the other hand, is the entire system of religious, legal and social obligations derived from the *hadith*.

The British Arabist N.J. Coulson reminds us that, from the classical Muslim point of view, Islamic law has some unique characteristics. He describes them as follows:

> [The *sharia*] does not grow out of, and is not moulded by, society as is the case with Western systems. Human thought, unaided, cannot discern the true values and standards of conduct; such knowledge can only be attained through divine revelation, and acts are good or evil exclusively because God has attributed this quality to them. In the Islamic concept, law precedes and moulds society; to its eternally valid dictates the structure of State and society must, ideally, conform.[2]

It is important to understand that the *sharia* is not a well-defined set of specific rules and regulations that can be easily be applied to life situations. Instead, it is a long, diverse, complicated intellectual tradition. The British historian of Islam H.A.R. Gibb put it best. It is, he says, essentially "a discussion on the duties of Muslims."[3]

The *sharia* has always been a systematic but an *uncodified* law. It is systematic because it represents a coherent system of doctrines and institutions based on widely accepted religious beliefs.[4] It is uncodified because it has never been collected and written down in one authoritative volume or in a set of volumes. Islamic scholars did write a number of legal manuals during the eighth and ninth centuries, but this process is held to have been completed by the end of the ninth century. Today, none of their works can be said to constitute the *sharia* in its entirety. Criminal law is perhaps an instructive example here.

There are very few general concepts of Islamic criminal law. Classical law books do not contain separate chapters dealing with such concepts or with comprehensive rules. The concepts and rules that are in fact specified are either mentioned in chapters devoted to specific crimes or must be ferreted out indirectly, i.e., by deduction. Often, general principles of criminal responsibility for given crimes must be deduced from the legal defenses or pleas allowed by the law.[5]

As the modern scholar Knut S. Vikør explains, "The *Sharia* is best understood as a *shared opinion* of the [Islamic] community, based on a literature that is extensive, but not necessarily coherent or authorized by any single body."[6] This can make it quite difficult for outsiders to say exactly what the *sharia* really is. Devout Muslims believe that a great deal about the *sharia* lies beyond the boundaries of legitimate dispute.

They believe, for example, that Islam teaches that the primary duty of human beings is to submit totally to the will of God. The *sharia* shows the faithful how this submission should be put into practice in daily life. By following the dictates of Islamic law, believers hope to find favor with God, both here on earth and in the heavenly life to come. In this process, the role of the religious scholars (*ulama*) is crucial, since it is they who study Islamic law most carefully and have the authority to interpret it and apply it to resolve the legal problems of everyday life.

In 2005, this is how the Muslim Brotherhood — an Egyptian organization described by its opponents as fundamentalist and by its supporters as a political party and religious and social movement with its own welfare organization — explained its objectives. In a pamphlet titled "Initiative," the Brotherhood claimed that it is working to

> establish God's law [the *sharia*] as we believe it to be the real effective way out of all sufferings and problems.... The mission could be achieved by building the Muslim individual, Muslim family, Muslim government and the Muslim state that leads Islamic countries, gathers all Muslims, regains Islamic glory, gives lost Muslim land [e.g., Palestine] back to its owners and carries the flag of the call to God, thus making the world happy via the teachings and right of Islam.[7]

Islamic law has another important function as well. As the scholar W. Montgomery Watt once put it, careful observance of this law is the hallmark of "the community that saves." Islam, like Judaism and some types of Christianity, is therefore the religion of a charismatic, self-asserted "chosen community." Members prove their partnership in this community of the saved by observing at least a locally defined minimum of this law, e.g., not eating pork.

Islamic regulations are becoming increasingly important in Western countries. For example, when European or North American courts may have to decide whether Islamic marriages or business contracts are valid. Moreover, as the New York–based Council on Foreign Relations reports, "Islamic banking and finance is a rapidly expanding industry that seeks to harmonize modern business practices with traditional religious norms."[8] (Islamic banking is discussed here in Chapter VIII.) According to a January 2006 report issued jointly by the Islamic Financial Services Board in Kuala Lumpur, Malaysia, and the Islamic Development Bank of Saudi Arabia, worldwide assets of the Islamic finance industry, including banking assets, funds under management and insurance, were then running between US$70 billion and US$1 trillion.[9]

To keep the text as uncluttered as possible, very few diacritical marks have been used here when transliterating words from Arabic or other Islamic languages into English. The transliteration for "Islamic law," for example, should technically be written *shari'a*, the apostrophe standing for the Arabic letter *'ayn*. In the interests of simplicity and uniformity, however, we shall consistently spell it as simply *sharia*.

Arabic words can legitimately be spelled in English in several ways. For example, the holy scripture of Islam can be spelled "Quran," "Qur'an" or "Koran." Any variations in the Arabic translations used in this book come about because of citations from different authors.

There are many English translations of the Quran. Unless otherwise noted, the translation used here is N.J. Dawood's *The Koran*, first published by Penguin in 1956 and revised frequently thereafter. It is an accurate and at the same time readable translation of this holy book.

To avoid digressions on the frequently changing political geography of the Islamic world, the names of countries as they exist today have in most cases been used here, e.g., Iran rather than Persia.

Because this book is an introductory text, we have relied more heavily on secondary than on primary sources. For example, some of the quotations, examples and conclusions used here are drawn from co-author Janin's earlier work on Islam, *The Pursuit of Learning in the Islamic World, 610–2003* (Jefferson, NC: McFarland, 2005). Many primary sources, however, are quoted verbatim in certain chapters and in the appendices.

Some Difficulties in Writing on the Sharia

Like the holy laws of other religions, the *sharia* can be difficult, convoluted, subtle and frustratingly complex. Consider, for example, two hypothetical cases cited in *al-Minhaj*, a medieval manual of Islamic law written by the Syrian scholar Muhyi al-Din al-Nawawi, who died in 1277. This book was widely used as a textbook for students and as a reference book for scholars and judges. This is what we can learn from it:

> If a husband calls one of his wives and another answers and he says to her, "You are repudiated" [meaning "I divorce you"], believing himself to be speaking to the wife he called, it is the wife that answers that is repudiated....
> When a woman has a date in her mouth and her husband repudiates her on the condition she swallows it, and then changes his mind and makes it depend on her spitting it out, and then changes his mind again and makes the repudiation depend upon her taking the date in the hollow of her hand, and the woman on hearing these words quickly swallows half the date and spits out the other half, the condition is not considered to be fulfilled.[10]

In our presentation here, we will try to avoid the perils of casuistry, i.e., resolving questions of conscience, duty or conduct by interpreting ethical principles or religious doctrines. The reason is that casuistry can easily be car-

ried to extremes: early Muslim jurists, for example, gave careful consideration to such hypothetical questions as "When a man is turned into stone by
the devil, at what precise moment does his estate open?"[11]

"Jurist" is a common term in Islamic law. It means a person, especially
a judge, or *qadi*, who has a thorough knowledge of the law. It must not be
confused with the Western concept of "juror," i.e., a member of a jury. Juries
and therefore jurors were never part of classical Islamic law. *Qadi* courts were
presided over by a sole judge, the *qadi* himself, who made legal judgments
based on his own authority. There were no judicial tribunals, no assembly of
judges, and no juries: the *qadi* was on his own.[12] As the British scholar J.N.D.
Anderson put it, until the middle of the nineteenth century,

> the *qadis'* courts were still the basic courts, the courts of all residual jurisdiction,
> throughout most of the Muslim world, and the Shari'a was the only written law,
> the law *par excellence*, the law to which reference and lip-service, at least, were
> invariably made.[13]

In this book, we will try, as non–Muslim writers, to describe Islamic law
in objective terms that are clear and easily accessible to non–Muslim readers.
Many scholarly controversies over the subtleties of Islamic law have therefore
been passed over in silence or are mentioned only briefly here. Readers who
want more detailed information on Islamic law will find good sources in the
bibliography.

Endnotes are used here extensively, both for attribution and to elaborate on points which, while interesting and relevant, are not discussed in the
text itself in order to preserve its flow.

One of the problems that Westerners encounter when writing about
Islamic law is the shortage of documentary sources with legal cases from the
centuries before good records began to be kept., e.g., before the Ottomans
occupied Constantinople in 1453 and made it their capital.[14] It is only in the
Ottoman archives that modern scholars can find a wealth of judicial records
going back to the sixteenth century.[15] Early Western legal history abounds in
documented law cases; early Islamic law does not. This is a shame because
such cases always involve real people with real problems. Such cases can cast
a dramatic personal light on legal issues which, if considered only at a theoretical level, can be deadly dull.

This shortage of early Islamic cases is part of a broader problem. In general, fewer early historic documents have survived from the Islamic world, as
compared to the Western world, for three reasons. The first was the weakness
of state institutions. Official papers were often considered to be an official's
personal property; he could take them with him when he left office. The second was the deliberate destruction of archives by successor states that wanted
to have a free hand in redistributing government assets. The third reason was

general negligence in more modern times. The only way to get around this relative shortage of early cases is to look carefully at the most important Islamic jurists themselves and at their work. This is precisely what we have tried to do here.

There was often a sizeable gap between the general principles and idealizations of the *sharia*, on the one hand, and its practical applications in daily life, on the other. As in most other legal systems, these applications could be decisively influenced by such behind-the-scenes factors as social pressures from family, friends and neighbors; political patronage; or outright bribery. Studying the written law alone can therefore be misleading. Indeed, when analyzing, in another work, the *sharia* in practice in Lebanon today, co-author Kahlmeyer found that he had to mention this fact on nearly every other page.

Islam and the West

Notwithstanding the great outpouring of books and articles which have appeared in the wake of the 11 September 2001 terrorist attacks on New York and Washington, D.C., the Islamic world is still not understood in the West today. The *sharia* is, beyond any question, one of the most important concepts of Islam, but most non–Muslims know almost nothing about it. This is indeed unfortunate because during the rest of this century — and probably well beyond it — the Islamic world seems likely to play an increasingly important role on the world stage.

There are many Muslims now and there will be even more in the future. The Muslim population of the world is currently estimated at as much as 1.5 billion people, i.e., about 20 percent of the world's total population. There are now about 192 independent countries on the globe. In 60 of these countries, Muslims constitute at least 20 percent of the population. Regardless of whether one thinks of the Islamic world as a potential friend or as a potential enemy of the West, learning more about Islam and its legal system would seem to be a sensible idea.

It would of course be too much to claim that a possible clash of civilizations between the Islamic world and the West can be averted if Westerners simply make the effort to learn more about Islam. We can hope, however, that making such an effort may help to defuse, in some small way, the intense humiliation at the hands of the West long felt by some Muslim men and women.

The burning rage that such humiliation can inspire was best expressed by Osama bin Laden in his 1996 "Declaration of War Against the Americans Occupying the Land of the Two Holy Places." (The two holy places are the mosques of Mecca and Medina in Saudi Arabia.) Bin Laden wrote: "Death is better than life in humiliation!"[16] Perhaps if we in the West can learn to think about the *sharia* with a little more knowledge, patience and good will, the chances for our peaceful coexistence with Islam may improve.

Transliteration and Other Editorial Matters

A large number of Arabic words and phrases are used in this book. This, however, should not pose any intellectual challenge for the reader. Whenever an Arabic term is used for the first time (and as often as necessary thereafter), it will be accompanied by its English equivalent. Some terms are also defined in the glossary.

A Note on Calendar Dates

With the exception of the dual entries in the Selected Chronology, all the dates given in this book correspond to the Gregorian (Western) solar calendar. The Selected Chronology gives some dates according to both the Gregorian and the Islamic calendars. A few words about this latter calendar may be in order here.

The Islamic calendar, also called the Muslim calendar, is used to date events in many predominantly Muslim countries. (In such countries, Gregorian dates are also used for "modern" purposes, e.g., for airline schedules.) It is a lunar calendar based on a year of 12 months, each month beginning approximately at the time of the sighting of the new moon, in a year of about 354 days. Because this lunar year is about 11 days shorter than the solar year, a given event, e.g., a Muslim holy day such as the beginning on end of Ramadan, usually falls 11 days earlier each successive solar year.

Islamic years are commonly called Hijra years because Muhammad's emigration from Mecca to Medina (known in Arabic as the Hijra), which took place in the Gregorian year 622, is used as the starting point for the Islamic calendar. Each Islamic year is therefore designed either as H (Hijra) or as AH (anno Hijra). An example: AH 1427 corresponds, approximately, to the calendar year 2007.

To convert from an Islamic year to a Gregorian year, multiply the Islamic year number by 0.97 and then add 622 to get the Gregorian year number. This formula shows that AH 1 (the year of the emigration) is roughly equivalent to the Gregorian year 622.

1

Fundamentals of Islam

Islam can be best understood under four intertwined headings:

- the physical and social environment that conditioned its appearance and growth
- the prophet Muhammad himself
- the doctrines, sources and manifestations of classical Islamic law
- the institutional structure of the Muslim world.

The Physical and Social Environment

To appreciate the meteoric rise of Islam, one must first understand the exceptionally harsh physical and cultural desert environment in which it took place. These pitiless surroundings were arguably responsible for the austere nature of the "pure" Islam being advocated by Islamic fundamentalists today. What is beyond dispute is that as Joseph Schacht, one of the greatest pioneers of Western studies of Islamic law, put it, this environment did indeed encourage an extremely conservative view of life. Schacht writes:

> The Arabs were, and are, bound by tradition and precedent. Whatever was customary was right and proper; whatever the forefathers had done deserved to be imitated. This was the golden rule of the Arabs whose existence on a narrow margin in an unpropitious environment *did not leave them much room for experiments and innovations* which might upset the precarious balance of their lives.[1]

By the fifth century, the Quraysh, formerly a nomadic tribe, had settled down in Mecca, on the western edge of the Arabian Peninsula. These tribesmen became traders and gradually transformed their desert hamlet into a

9

small but relatively prosperous trading city. It lay at the intersection of important trade routes and had enough water to support large herds of camels. By about the year 500, Mecca had grown into a regional trading center which sent out two great camel caravans each year: one, in the winter, to Yemen; the other, in summer, through northwest Arabia to Palestine and Syria.

Temperatures in Mecca remain high during the year; in summer, they can reach 113 degree F. (45 degrees C.). The best single description in English of traditional nomadic life in the searing heat of the Hijaz (the northern half of the west coast of Saudi Arabia) comes from Charles Montague Doughty, a British explorer with a unique, highly idiosyncratic writing style. He was one of the greatest nineteenth-century Western adventurers and in the 1870s spent two years wandering through Saudi Arabia with the camel-mounted *bedouin* (nomads). Listen now to what Doughty has to say about "Summer Days in the Wilderness":

> The sun, entering as a tyrant upon the waste landscape, darts upon us a torment of fiery beams, not to be remitted till the far-off evening.... Grave is that giddy heat upon the crown of the head; the ears tingle with a flickering shrillness, a subtle crepitation it seems, in the glassiness of this sun-stricken nature; the hot sand-blink is in the eyes, and there is little refreshment to find in the tents' shelter; the worsted booths [i.e., the tents, which were made of heavy, loosely-woven cloth] leak to this fiery rain of sunny light. Mountains looming like dry bones through the thin air, stand far around about us.... This silent air burning about us, we endure breathless until the assr [evening]: when the dazing Arabs in the tents revive after their heavy hours ... and the morrow will be as this day, days deadly drowned in the sun of the summer wilderness.[2]

Given this stark, forbidding, arid landscape, perhaps it is not surprising that the Muslim concept of paradise revolves around dreams of a lush well-watered garden. The Quran mentions gardens nearly 100 times and, indeed, "Garden" is the word that many translators choose to convey the idea of paradise. Moreover, green is the symbolic color of Islam: believers say that Muhammad wore a green turban and that green was his favorite color. Green is therefore a predominant color in Muslim banners and flags today. Not surprisingly, green is also the color of clothing said to be worn in paradise. We learn from the Quran:

> As for those who have faith and do good works, We shall not deny them their reward. They shall dwell in the gardens of Eden, where rivers will roll at their feet. Reclining there upon soft couches, they shall be decked with bracelets of gold, and arrayed in garments of fine green silk and rich brocade: blissful their reward and happy their resting-place! [*sura* 18:30].

The Prophet Muhammad

Muslims consider Muhammad (c. 570–632), whose full name was Abu al-Qasim Muhammad ibn Abd Allah ibn Abd al-Muttalib ibn Hashim, to have been the last and the greatest of the prophets. Conservative Muslims always add the phrase "peace be upon him" (often abbreviated in Muslim writings as "p.b.u.h.") after his name to express the reverence they feel toward him. They believe that Muhammad's teachings consummate, complement and elucidate the insights of earlier prophets, e.g., those figuring in the Old and New Testaments, whose messages are held to have been lost or distorted over the years. The Quran commands all Muslims to obey Muhammad's teachings and to emulate his life:

> SAY: "Obey God and obey the Messenger [Muhammad]." But if you disregard his commands, then he is responsible only for what he has been charged with, and you are responsible for what you have been charged with. If you obey him, you will do right. The Messenger has no other duty than to convey the message clearly [*sura* 24:54].[3]

Muhammad himself is never treated as a divinity. Indeed, it would be quite impossible for Muslims to regard him as such. The Quran, which Muslims believe was verbally transmitted to Muhammad by the Angel Gabriel and which remains the ultimate authority on all religious and legal matters affecting Islam, tells the faithful that God is all-powerful and *unique*, having no partner and no equal. Muslims therefore do not worship Muhammad, but they do reverence him as God's prophet, messenger and apostle. He is held to exemplify the Islamic ideal of human life.

As is the case with other religious leaders, biographical facts about Muhammad's life are inextricably mixed with pious legends. What is clear is that Muhammad was born in about 570 in Mecca, a regional trading center in the Arabian Peninsula. When he grew up, he became a trader and led camel caravans to Syria and Iraq. In about 595, at the age of 25 he married Khadija bint Khuwaylid, a distant relative and a rich businesswoman who was 15 years his senior. Theirs was a happy marriage: in fact, Muhammad did not take any other wife until after Khadija died in 619.

Muhammad had a contemplative streak and would sometimes spend the night alone in a cave in the mountains near Mecca, praying and meditating. His first biographer, Ibn Ishaq (d. 767), tells us that when Muhammad was making his way up the hills toward his hermitage, he would often hear the words "Peace be on thee, O Messenger of God," spoken very clearly. But when he turned and looked for the speaker, no one was in sight.[4]

In about 610, when Muhammad was 40 years old and was meditating alone in the cave, Muslims believe that a miraculous event occurred. This event changed his life forever. Widespread belief in it would also change the course of history and would have profound consequences for non-believers as well. These consequences are likely to become more pronounced during the twenty-first century.

What happened was that, according to al-Bukhari, a Muslim compiler of *hadith* who died in 870, "an Angel in the form of a man" appeared before Muhammad.[5] This spirit was none other than the archangel Gabriel, a messenger from God. Gabriel ordered Muhammad: "Recite!" Muhammad replied: "I am not a reciter." (Another translation of his reply is: "I am not able to read." Some Muslims prefer this version because it stresses that Muhammad was illiterate. If so, the Quran is even more remarkable.) Hearing Muhammad's reply, the angel gave him such a bone-crushing embrace that it "reached the limit of his endurance" and then released him. Again the angel ordered: "Recite!" Muhammad replied again: "I am not a reciter." After a third embrace and a third release, the angel instructed Muhammad:

> Recite in the name of thy Lord who created-
> created man from clots of blood.
> Recite! Your Lord is the Most Bountiful One, who by
> the pen taught man what he did not know.

This dramatic statement would later constitute the opening verses of chapter (*sura*) 96 of the Quran.

In the moments after his encounter with Gabriel, Muhammad was so afraid that he was possessed by demons or was losing his mind that he fled from the cave and started to run home. When he was halfway down the mountain, however, he heard a voice above him proclaiming: "O Muhammad, thou art the Messenger of God, and I am Gabriel." Muhammad then turned his eyes upward and saw Gabriel, who was now filling the whole sky. Gabriel repeated what he had just said. Legend has it that Muhammad stood still, gazing at the angel,

> then he turned away from him, but whichever way he looked the Angel was always there, astride the horizon, whether it was to the north, to the south, to the east or to the west. Finally the Angel turned away, and the Prophet descended the slope and went to his house. "Cover me! Cover me!," he said to Khadija as with still quaking heart he laid himself on his couch.[6]

Later, Muhammad began to tell others about this shattering religious experience. His preaching was inspired by additional messages from Gabriel. One of the earliest was a clear directive to spread this newly revealed word of God:

> By the light of day, and by the dark of night, your Lord has not forsaken you [Muhammad], nor does He abhor you. The life to come holds a richer prize for you than this present life. You shall be gratified with what your Lord will give you. Did He not find you an orphan and give you shelter? Did He not find you in error and guide you? Did He not find you poor and enrich you? Therefore do not wrong the orphan, nor chide away the beggar. But proclaim the goodness of your Lord [*sura* 93].

Muhammad would continue to receive these messages until the end of his life. In 620, he had another important mystical experience, in which he made a miraculous Night Journey (*isra*) from Mecca to Jerusalem (to the spot where, for this reason, the Dome of the Rock stands today) and thence to heaven. Some Muslims today think this was a physical journey; others believe that it was a vision or a dream experienced by Muhammad.

Muhammad won some converts to his new religion but his monotheist teachings so annoyed the polytheist Meccans that they planned to kill him. For this reason, in 622 he led his followers to the city of Yathrib (later known as Medina), about 200 miles north of Mecca. This emigration (*hijra*) marks the start of the Islamic era and is the first year of the Muslim calendar today.

The final decade of Muhammad's life — from the emigration of 622 until his death in 632 — was highlighted by legal and diplomatic maneuvering and by small-scale but frequent military clashes. One important development was a charter now known as the "Constitution of Medina." Muslim fundamentalists today like to claim that this was the world's first constitution and proves the Islamic world invented this concept. Secular historians, however, do not agree with these assertions.

This detailed (47-point) document was written in 622 and embodies two agreements. The first agreement welds together nine tribes of the Arabian Peninsula and so creates the first Muslim community (*umma*). The Constitution of Medina states:

In the name of God, the Compassionate, the Merciful.

1. This is a document from Muhammad the Prophet [governing the relations] between the believers and Muslims of Quraysh [Muhammad's tribe] and Yathrib [Medina], and those who followed them and joined them and labored with them.
2. They are one community [*umma*] to the exclusion of all [other] men.[7]

The second agreement regulates the nascent Islamic community's relations with the Jews of Medina. These relations are outlined in seven points, e.g., "To the Jew who follows us belong help and equality. He shall not be wronged nor shall his enemies be aided."[8] Taken as a whole, the Constitution of Medina shows a highly skilled legal mind at work. This is not surprising because, among his many other leadership activities, Muhammad was also an arbitration judge in Mecca and Medina.[9]

During this decade, Muhammad and his followers were completely victorious. During "the year of embassies" (631), most of the tribes of Arabia converted to Islam. Since Muslims were instructed not to fight other Muslims, this marked the beginning of the end of tribal warfare in Muhammad's era.

Although by the time of his death Muhammad had unified most of Arabia and had readied its tribesmen for expansion into Syria and Iraq, he had never designated a successor. The subsequent dispute over who should lead the Muslim community is still with us today in the form of the Sunni-Shiite (or Shia — these terms will be used interchangeably here) schism. This will be discussed below in the section on the structure of the Islamic world.

Doctrines, Sources and Manifestations of Classical Islamic Law

In Arabic, *islam* means "to surrender." Juristically, Islam connotes a person's submission to, resignation to, and acceptance of the will of God (Allah).[10] A Muslim is one who so surrenders himself or herself. This surrender is considered essential because God is seen as the sole creator, preserver and restorer of the universe. This is how the Quran defines Him:

GOD: there is no god but Him, the Living, the Eternal One. Neither slumber nor sleep overtakes Him. To Him belongs all that the heavens and the earth contain. Who can intercede with Him except by His permission? He knows what is before and behind men. They can grasp only that part of His knowledge which he wills. His throne is as vast as the heavens and the earth, and the preservation of both does not weary Him. He is the Exalted, the Immense One [*sura* 2:255].

The Quran admonishes the faithful:

Praise be to God, Creator of the heavens and the earth! He sends forth the angels as His messengers, with two, three or four pair of wings. He multiplies His creatures according to His will. God has power over all things. The blessings God bestows on men none can withhold; and what He withholds none can bestow, apart from Him. He is the Mighty, the Wise One. You people! Bear in mind God's goodness to you. Is there any other creator who provides for you from heaven and earth? There is no god but Him. How can you turn away? [*sura* 35:1–2].

Islam is an all-embracing faith. In theory, there can be no difference in a "pure" Islamic state between the temporal sphere of life, i.e., the state, and the religious sphere of life, i.e., the church. In practice, however, there have long been such differences in all Islamic countries. Another way of making this same point is to note that in the classical Islamic world-view there could be, in theory at least, no gap between politics and law. Traditional, the ruler was also the highest judge. Politics and law are thus supposed to walk hand-in-hand. The law is seen as God's command: it therefore comes first. The state is merely the tool through which the divine law is put into practice in the world.[11]

To borrow a concept from Christianity, Islam is a "broad church." In other words, it has ample room for a variety of practices. A fundamental reason is that ever since the death of Muhammad the Islamic world has had no central authority — no papacy — to set standards for believers. Another reason is that seventh century Islam was less demanding and more inclusive. It did not regulate all the aspects of life that Muslims later decided to regulate.

As mentioned earlier, Islam teaches that God is all-powerful and unique, i.e., there is only one God. He brought the cosmos into being with a single word of command: "Be." The proof of His infinite mercy, the Muslims believe, is his continual willingness to teach man how to follow "the straight path," i.e., the Muslim way of life as laid out in the Quran and his continual responsiveness to human needs. One familiar Islamic invocation is "In the Name of God, the Compassionate, the Merciful." Pious Muslims say this today before reading the Quran, before eating, and before beginning the discussion of any subject. One of our Muslim friends, for example, who is working for a non-governmental organization, always begins a lecture about Middle East corruption with this phrase.

If we have to choose one citation from the Quran that sums up most succinctly what Islam expects from its followers, we can contemplate these words:

> Those who submit to God and accept the true Faith; who are devout, sincere, patient, humble, charitable, and chaste; who fast and are ever mindful of God — on these, both men and women, God will bestow forgiveness and a rich recompense. It is not for true believers — men or women — to order their own affairs if God and His apostle [Muhammad] decree otherwise. He that disobeys God and His apostle strays far indeed [*sura* 33:35–36].

In less abstract and more practical terms, Muslims are exhorted to adhere to the famous "Five Pillars of Islam" (*al-arkan al-khamsa*) in their daily lives. These pillars are the profession of faith (*shahada*); five obligatory prayers (*salat*) a day; annual alms (*zakat*); fasting during the lunar month of Ramadan (*sawm*); and making the pilgrimage to Mecca (*hajj*), if one can afford it. Each year, more than two million pilgrims make the *hajj* during Ramadan and many more make what is called the "small pilgrimage" (*umrah*) at other times of the year.

The sources of classical Muslim jurisprudence itself are referred to collectively as the *usul al-fiqh*, i.e., the "roots" or principles of Islamic jurisprudence. These crystallized early in the tenth century. They became what the definitive *Encyclopaedia of Islam* calls "a powerful and flexible intellectual tool, adapted to various social needs, aesthetic and theological as well as strictly legal."[12] Mastery of *fiqh* (Islamic jurisprudence) became the chief aim of Islamic education as soon as theological colleges (*madrasas*) appeared in the eleventh century. Indeed, *fiqh* retained its central position in Islamic education and thought until the decline of the *sharia* as a whole during the nineteenth and twentieth centuries.

In the final form it reached during the tenth century, classical Islamic law was based on four main and highly revered sources. These are: a holy book (the Quran); the social and legal traditions (the *sunna*) of the Muslim community; scholarly consensus (*ijma*); and legal reasoning by analogy (*qiyas*).

The Quran

The Quran (the best translation of this Arabic word is "Recitation") is regarded by Muslims as the verbatim word, or speech, of God, as transmitted to human beings, through Muhammad, by the angel Gabriel. Muslims say that Muhammad himself was illiterate but that his literate followers wrote down some of his utterances, which were usually delivered when he was in a state of trance or ecstasy, on whatever writing material they had at hand. This is traditionally said to have been "pieces of paper, stones, palm-leaves, shoulder-blades, ribs, and bits of leather."[13] After his death in 632, an authoritative recension (version) of the Quran was eventually produced during the reign of Uthman, the third caliph (r. 644–656). The English word "caliph" comes from the Arabic *khalifa* and means a deputy or a successor.

For the early Muslims, this vulgate (i.e., the commonly accepted text or reading) had a crucially important *legal* as well as religious significance. As the *textus receptus* (the authoritative text), it became the framework within which legal disputes had to be analyzed and resolved. To make this possible, analogies were stretched to and perhaps even beyond the breaking point.

For example, the Quran prohibits consumption of alcohol but it does not define what the penalty should be for breaking this law.[14] Searching hard for an analogy, the second caliph, Omar I (r. 634–644) took note of the Quranic penalty for a false accusation of committing adultery: "Those that defame honourable women and cannot produce four witnesses shall be given eighty lashes." (*sura* 24:4). He decided that the same number of lashes should able be given to those who drank alcohol. The relationship, if any, between intoxication and bearing false witness may elude us today but Omar I was clearly looking for a way to bring drinking more firmly within the scope of the Quran.

We should note that flogging was a common penalty under traditional Islamic law. Only very conservative Muslim states still use it today. Usually it is administered by a leather whip but if the culprit is suffering from a serious or incurable illness, the lashing can be administered very lightly, e.g., by means of a braided length of cloth, a shoe, or even with a bundle of 50 or

100 twigs. In this latter case, only one or two blows are needed to administer a punishment of 100 lashes.[15]

The Quran, which is roughly the same length as the New Testament, is considered by Muslim and by Western scholars alike to be the finest work of Classical Arabic rhymed prose. Except for the opening verses and a few passages where Muhammad or Gabriel is the speaker, the speaker is God Himself. He uses either the *pluralis majestatis* ("We"), the first person singular ("I") or the third person singular ("He"). Together with the Torah and the Bible, the Quran can confidently claim to be one of the most influential books of all time. Indeed, it seems quite likely that during the twenty-first century the Quran will be *more important*— in terms of the impact it may have on the world — than either of the other holy books.

The Quran is not an easy book for non–Muslim readers to master. Many Muslims believe that only when the Quran is recited aloud in Arabic can the eloquence, denseness, complexity and allusiveness of its classical language be fully appreciated. Moreover, conservative Muslims often hold that because the Quran is the literal world of God, no human translation can hope to convey adequately its great beauty, power and literary perfection. From an orthodox point of view, any translation of the Quran into another language can only be a paraphrase, not a genuine translation. For this reason, many translations are usually entitled something along the lines of "The Meaning of the Holy Quran."

The Quran has 114 *suras*, each of which bears a traditional name which refers to a creature, object or event mentioned in the text, e.g., *sura* 2, the longest *sura*, is entitled "The Cow." The *suras* are not arranged in chronological order. Instead, with the exception of the very short opening prayer, the *fatiha*, which is described below, they are generally grouped in order of their length, with the longest chapters coming first in the Quran and the shortest at the end. To understand the longer and more complicated *suras* in the early pages of the Quran, however, a considerable amount of background knowledge is essential. The reader must understand not only the major events of Islam's earliest years but also the minor incidents that occurred just before the revelation of a given verse.

Despite these difficulties, the non–Muslim reader can still find much literary excellence in the Quran. To take but one of many examples, the *fatiha* ("opening") is the short prayer that begins the Quran. It starts with a traditional invocation (the *bismillah*: "In the Name of God, the Compassionate, the Merciful") and then continues in these measured and stately phrases:

> Praise be to God, Lord of the Universe,
> The Compassionate, the Merciful,
> Sovereign of the Day of Judgment!

You alone we worship, and to You alone
we turn for help.
Guide us to the straight path,
The path of those whom You have favored,
Not of those who have incurred Your Wrath,
Nor of these who have gone astray.

The Quran is the fundamental wellspring of Islamic culture but it does not contain many specific rules of law. The exact number of legal verses in the Quran depends on who is doing the counting. The traditional estimate is that about 500 verses have some degree of legal content. Later Muslim sources, however, have put this figure considerably lower. The modern scholar Mohammed Hashim Kamali, for example, concluded that less than 3 percent of the text of the Quran deals with legal matters.[16]

He found that there are 350 legal verses in the Quran but that they cover a sizeable range of issues — legal and non-legal. About 140 of these verses relate to dogma and to devotional matters, e.g., ritual prayer, legal alms and other charitable acts, fasting, and pilgrimage. Another 70 are devoted to marriage, divorce, paternity, child custody, inheritance, and bequests. A further 70 verses deal with commercial transactions, e.g., sales, leases, loans, usury, and mortgages. Of the remainder, 30 verses address crimes and penalties; another 30 speak of justice, equality, evidence, citizens' rights and duties, and consultation in government affairs; and 10 verses focus on economic matters. Kamali ends by noting that other Islamic scholars do not necessarily agree with all of his estimates.

At the lower end of the scale, the British scholar N.J. Coulson concluded that

> For the first Muslim community established under the leadership of the Prophet at Medina in 622, the Qur'anic revelations laid down basic standards of conduct. But the Qur'an is in no sense a comprehensive legal code. No more than 80 verses deal with strictly legal matters; while these verses cover a wide range of topics and introduce many novel rules, their general effect is simply to modify the existing Arabian customary law in certain important particulars.[17]

Finally, in the index to his own translation of the Quran, N.J. Dawood lists only 49 legal verses: 19 under "law," 24 under "diet regulations," and 6 under "inheritance."[18] On balance, what is clear is that the Quran itself does not contain enough legislative verses to permit its followers to govern even a small state successfully. As we shall see, the Ottomans overcame this problem by devising a parallel and extensive system of administrative laws (*kanun*), which were ostensibly designed to augment the *sharia*.

Regardless of how many specific legal verses there are, what is more important for our purposes here are the *legal principles* put forward by the

Quran. Norms for business transactions, for example, were presented in ethical rather than in legal terms. For example, traders are urged, in ethical terms, to deal fairly with each other and with their customers, to bear true witness, and not to seek or accept usurious interest.[19] No details are given on precise modes of behavior or the proper rate of interest, if any.

This means in practice that to develop informed opinions on the many legal matters which are not directly covered by the Quran, Muslim jurists must draw on the ethical and moral principles which form the core of the Islamic message. Such thinkers range from rationalist reformers who want to modernize Islam to violence-prone fundamentalists who want to return it to a mythical archaic state of purity. All jurists, however, must face the severe limitations of Quranic exegesis.

Exegesis (*tafsir*) is a learned explanation or critical interpretation of a text, often of the Quran itself. A Swedish scholar, Helmer Ringgren, has given a good summary of the orthodox position on the inherent nature of the Quran. Traditionalists, he said, take the view that *the essence of the Quran* is always "left untouched by criticism; as the infallible word of God it cannot have been influenced by the circumstances under which it was revealed, it can contain no mistakes, and it cannot be superseded by any new discovery."[20]

Just as Christian fundamentalists oppose exegesis when it whittles away at the literal truths of the Bible, so too do Muslim fundamentalists oppose exegesis when it threatens the veracity of the Quran itself. Rationalist Muslim reformers, however, have long made two points. They argue that to adapt Islam to modern conditions it must first be interpreted in light of modern knowledge. Second, they hold that such new interpretations will not in fact threaten the *core* of traditional Islamic faith. In their view, the text of the Quran has eternal validity but it is the duty of each generation to use reason to discover the meaning of a given verse in the changing conditions of contemporary life. This struggle over Quranic exegesis has been going on at least since the nineteenth century and shows no sign of abating now.

Social and Legal Traditions (Sunna and Hadith)

Sunna literally means "a well-trodden path." It is the whole body of customary social and legal traditions and obligations of the Muslim community, based authoritatively on the life, teachings and practices of Muhammad. By expansion, the concept of *sunna* refers to Islamic traditions in their entirety, that is to say, examples taken from the prophet's life, coupled with the work of the Muslim jurists who spent centuries spelling out the legal principles and implications of these examples.

The prophet's words and deeds were recorded in a large number of verbally documented traditional reports known collectively as *hadith* (literally "Report"). Here is a lightly edited example of a *hadith*. Sourced to Aisha, Muhammad's favorite wife, in whose arms he died, it was collected by the great scholar al-Bukhari:

> Al-Harith bin Hisham asked Allah's Apostle [i.e. Muhammad] "O Allah's Apostle! How is the Divine Inspiration revealed to you." Allah's Apostle replied, "Sometimes it is revealed like the ringing of a bell; this form of Inspiration is the hardest of all and then this state passes after I have grasped what is inspired. Sometimes the Angel [Gabriel] comes in the form of a man and talks to me and I grasp whatever he says." Aisha added: "Verily I saw the Prophet being divinely inspired on a very cold day and noticed the sweat dropping from his forehead."[21]

For Sunni Islam, there are numerous *hadith* collections. Among the most reliable are held to be those by al-Bukhari (d. 870), who listed 7,275 *hadith*, and by Muslim b. al-Hajjaj (d. 875), who listed 9,200 of them. (In Arabic, the abbreviation "b." when inserted between two names stands for "ibn" or "bin" and means "the son of.") Shia Islam has four canonical collections of its own.

Scholarly Consensus (*Ijma*)

Ijma is the consensus of the Islamic community on religious and legal matters. This consensus was articulated by the carefully trained Muslim scholars who were held to be the only legitimate spokesmen of the community for this purpose. No contemporary jurist would have considered the opinions of the "man in the street" when deliberating a legal case.

Consensus plays a vital role in Islamic thought: as a well-known *hadith* sourced to Muhammad states, "My people [the Islamic community, *umma*] will never agree upon an error." To achieve consensus, then, is to confer legitimacy on scholarly decisions. The great jurist Muhammad al-Shafi'i (767–820), who is revered as the founder of the Shafi'i of law, used *ijma* to determine which *hadith* were authentic and which were not. (Many *hadith* were, in effect backdated and spuriously sourced to Muhammad to gain legitimacy for their proponents. By the ninth century, about 500,000 *hadith* were in circulation. When scholars of that era weeded out the forgeries, they were left with a corpus of only about 4,000 to 5,000 legitimate *hadith*.[22])

Although *ijma* has usually served as a brake on religious innovation, it also has an inherent flexibility. Muslim scholars were allowed, within circumscribed and well-understood limits, to hold differing opinions. This was seen as an essential part of the process of reaching a consensus. (Heretical opinions, e.g., doubts about whether God exits or whether Muhammad is the Messenger of God, could not, of course, be entertained.) Despite this flexibility, *ijma* in the classical system of thought ultimately became ossified. As the British scholar N.J. Coulson explained

> Once formed the *ijma* was infallible; to contradict it was heresy, and the possibility of its repeal by a similar *ijma* of a later generation, though admitted in theory, was thus highly unlikely in practice. Further discussion was precluded not only on those points which were the subject of a consensus, but also on those matters where the jurists had agreed to differ; for if the *ijma* covered two variant opinions, to adduce a third opinion was to contradict it ... *Ijma* had thus set the final seal upon the process of increasing rigidity of the law.[23]

Legal Reasoning by Analogy (Qiyas)

Qiyas means strict analogical deductions drawn from the Quran, the *sunna*, and *ijma*. These deductions give Sunni legal scholars a way to apply traditional religious law to contemporary issues and therefore reach decisions on them. *Qiyas* ranges from the simple to the complex.[24] Shiite law, on the other hand, does not in general recognize *qiyas* as a legitimate source of the law. The sixth Shiite imam, Ja'far al-Sidiq (699–765), considered reasoning by analogy to be pure conjecture and therefore rejected it.

At an elementary level, for example, the Quran prohibits wine (often made from grapes) because it can cause intoxication. The Quran tells the faithful:

> Wine and games of chance, idols and divining arrows, are abominations devised by Satan. Avoid them, so that you may prosper. Satan seeks to stir up enmity and hatred among you by means of wine and gambling, and to keep you from the remembrance of God and from your prayers. Will you not abstain from them? [*sura* 5:90–92].

By analogy, if wine made from grapes is forbidden, wine made from dates must therefore be forbidden as well: it too can cause intoxication. By the same token, a ban on narcotics can be based on the Quranic injunction against wine-drinking.

Here is a more subtle case from Iraq. A man bought a married female slave. (Although the Quran accepted the institution of slavery, a practice that predated Islam, it set limits on a master's power over his slaves.) The law provided that if purchased goods contained a defect, the buyer had the option of canceling the sale within three days and getting the purchase price back from the seller. In this case, the buyer claimed that he was entitled to exercise this option. The female slave, he argued, contained a defect — she was married. This meant that he was not allowed to have sexual intercourse with her. Since having intercourse was considered part of exercising full rights over a female slave, his inability to do was, by analogy, an impediment similar to a medical defect making her unfit for sexual relations. He won the case.

LEGAL THEORY

Traditional Islamic legal theory deserves our attention at this point. For devout Muslims, all acts are normative, i.e., all of them are, to varying degrees, good or bad. For this reason, they must be placed into one of five legal categories: the obligatory (*wajib*), the recommended (*mandub*), the permissible or the indifferent (*mubah*), the prohibited (*haram*), or the repugnant (*makruh*). A word of explanation may be useful here.[25]

- Obligatory actions are those where performance earns a spiritual reward and where failure to perform merits spiritual punishment. Prayer is perhaps the best example.
- Recommended actions entail a reward but their omission does not bring punishment. Such acts are designed to encourage piety.
- Permissible actions are those whose commission or omission is of equal weight.
- Prohibited actions bring only punishment.
- Repugnant acts are rewarded when they are omitted but are not punished when committed.

Islamic law attaches great importance to legal language. When a jurist is looking for ways to resolve a new legal problem, he must first decide which holy or scholarly text is most relevant. This he does through linguistic analysis and interpretation. This process is too complicated to be discussed in much detail here but, in general, it involves deciding what given words mean in a legal context.

It is important to determine, for example, whether a word is being used in a real or in a metaphorical sense. When the Quran tells us in *sura* 19:4 that Zechariah's head "glows silver with age," we understand intuitively that the reference here is to gray hair, not to a silver cranium. Other cases, however, may not be so simple.

It is also important for the jurist to know whether the meaning of a given word is clear or whether it is ambiguous. Ambiguity is evident in *sura* 17:33, which provides that "If a man is slain unjustly, his heir shall be entitled to satisfaction." Here, "satisfaction" is not defined: does it mean the right to take vengeance on the killer, to accept a compensatory payment, to forgive the offense, or to do something else? A similar ambiguity can been seen in *sura* 5:1: "Believers, be true to your obligations. It is lawful for you to eat the flesh of all beasts *other than which is hereby announced to you.*" The first part of the second sentence is clear enough but the italicized part does not offer any such announcement.

Such difficulties are resolved in Islamic legal thought by making a conceptual division between words that are so ambiguous that they cannot be clarified by any means, and words that are either clear to begin with or can be clarified by further study. The forever-ambiguous words are not held to be significant in a legal sense and thus cannot be the source of rulings. The can-be-clarified words are further subdivided into those in which the language itself is so clear that their meaning is certain, and words that can be clarified by their linguistic overtones.

Linguistic complexity does not stop here. Jurists must distinguish between equivocal words or phrases that are general and those that are more focused and particularized. *Sura* 2:238 is an example of a general statement: "Attend regularly to your prayers, including the middle [midday] prayer...." On the other hand, *sura* 5:3 ("You are forbidden carrion...") was particularized by a Prophetic *hadith* permitting the faithful to eat dead fish. The Quran also particularizes the word "slave." A man who divorces his wife and then changes his mind "shall free a slave" before having sex with his wife again (*sura* 58:3). The penalty for accidentally killing another Muslim, however, is freeing a *Muslim* slave (*sura* 4:92).

Jurists must also master both the imperative form of religious commands and the prohibitive form. The majority of Islamic thinkers have held that the imperative form conveys a clear obligation to perform a certain act, e.g., "Attend to your prayers, render the alms levy, and kneel with those who kneel" (*sura* 43). The prohibitive form requires the faithful *not* to perform a certain act, e.g., "Do not knowingly set up other gods besides God" (*sura* 2:22). More details on these and other subtleties of Islamic legal thought can be found in Wael B. Hallaq's thorough and readable *History of Islamic Legal Theories* (2004).

LEARNING THE LAW

The traditional process of learning Islamic law did not involve mastering only a specific body of factual material. Instead, the true goal of studying Islamic law (a term which should be broadly understand here to connote a complex body of linguistic, philosophical and theological scholarship) was to absorb a sequence of texts, commentaries on specific practices, and commentaries on these commentaries. The modern scholar Timothy Mitchell has aptly summarized this carefully scripted process. He described it along the following lines.[26]

A student always began the process of learning with the study of the Quran. There was one very important reason for this choice. As the very word of God, the Quran was the original, fundamental text of the law — that is to say, it was the only text which did not reflect any earlier scholarly sources. The Quran was thus unique. It was the highest theological peak and the first one that an aspiring student had to begin to climb.

Next in importance were the sayings and actions attributed to Muhammad (*hadith*). These explained and extended the doctrines of the Quran. Then came the major commentaries on the Quran and other related assignments, e.g., the art of reciting it aloud and the study of different readings. After that were biographies of the transmitters of *hadith*; principles of theology; principles of legal interpretation; the divergent interpretations championed by the different schools of law; and, finally, the study of Islamic mysticism. All these subjects could be and were studied during the course of a typical day. After dawn prayers, the Quran was studied. *Hadith*, Quranic interpretation, and other subjects came later in the day. Mysticism was studied after evening prayers.

The Structure of the Islamic World

Sunnis and Shiites constitute the two major branches of Islam. Sunnis form the vast majority (about 90 percent) of the Muslims in the world today. Their name is an abbreviation of an Arabic phrase which means the "People of Tradition and Community." It reflects the particular importance they attach to the *sunna*, the set of traditional social and legal traditions of the Muslim community. They revere the first four "rightly guided" caliphs, who were the Companions and immediate successors of the prophet, as the legitimate leaders of Islam.

"Rightly guided" means that these men are held to have governed in accordance with the principles established by Muhammad. These four caliphs were Abu Bakr (r. 632–634), Umar ibn al-Khattab (r. 634–644), Uthman ibn Affan (r. 644–656), and Ali ibn Abi Talib (r. 656–661). Because they were Muhammad's closest friends and allies, it was assumed that they were thus the most suitable persons to follow him.

Unlike their Shiite brethren, Sunni imams (religious leaders of the community) do not usually wield a great deal of political or religious power. For the Sunnis, an imam is simply the leader of a religious community, e.g., any devout Muslim who runs a mosque. Shiite learning today retains some of the philosophical, reflective and even mystical elements of medieval Islam, whereas Sunni thought imposes textual and legalistic limitations on such speculation.[27] In broader terms, however, Shiites share most of the major doctrinal beliefs of the Sunnis — with one very important exception.

As stated earlier, Muhammad died without designating a successor. Shiites — their name comes from the Arabic phrase *shi'at Ali* (the party or faction of Ali) — claim that Muhammad wanted his only male blood relative, Ali ibn Abi Talib, to be his successor. They therefore revere Ali as the First Imam (leader of the community) of the Islamic community. All later Shiite imams are the direct male descendants of Ali and his wife Fatimah, Muhammad's daughter. There have been four very famous Shiite imams, in whose names various schools or sects were founded.

From the Western point of view, the most interesting of these is the twelfth and last imam, Muhammad al-Mahdi al-Hujjah. Today the dominant and orthodox Shiite sect is the Ja'fari school of thought, or "the Twelvers," as they are called. They believe in 12 imams. This school was named after the sixth Shiite imam, Ja'far al-Sadiq, who wrote a legal treatise. Shiite law is thus known as Ja'fari law. Shiites consider the Twelfth Imam, also referred to as the "Hidden Imam," to have been divinely inspired. He vanished from human sight in 878 and they are still patiently awaiting his return. God is thought to have hidden him from view, a doctrine known as *ghaybah*, or occultation. The Twelvers confidently expect that this imam will eventually reappear and will be their *mahdi* (literally the "divinely guided one" or "messiah"), that is, the restorer of the political power and religious purity of Islam, who will fill the world with justice and equity.

The Shiite imamate, i.e., the office held by an imam, is believed to be infallible and was strictly hereditary. That said, successors did require designation by the previous imam. Not all imams were eldest sons, but all of them were expressly designated by their fathers. Shiite Muslims now live chiefly in Iran, Iraq, Bahrain, Yemen, Lebanon, India and Pakistan.

Historically, the Sunni majority has generally treated Shiites as second-class citizens: Iraq before the fall of Saddam Hussein is an excellent case in point here. The Sunni-Shiite split originated in the first civil war of Islam in 661 and shows no sign of abating in the foreseeable future. Until the 1978–1979 revolution in Iran, however, few Westerners paid much attention to the Shiites, probably because they were only a minority without any political power.

Since then, however, the dynamism of Shiite Islam, which lies in its self-proclaimed role as champion of the downtrodden, has made it an important force in the world today.[28] Shiites are already playing a key role in the Middle East. Thanks to Iran's nuclear ambitions, they are likely to play an even greater role in coming years. It is therefore worthwhile to understand their interpretation of the *sharia*.

There are significant Sunni-Shiite differences in the prayer ritual, in inheritance laws, in marriage ceremonies, and in the use of "independent reasoning" (*ijtihad*) to resolve legal and doctrinal problems. Modern scholars have disagreed about the importance of these differences. Joseph Schacht held that, except for the law of inheritance, other Shiite legal doctrines "do not differ from the doctrines of the Sunni schools of law more widely than these last differ from one another."[29] N.J. Coulson, on the other hand, stressed that "Shiite law in its final form possesses certain distinctive characteristics which stand in sharp contrast to the principles recognized by the Sunnite systems as a whole."[30]

Ironically, both scholars were right. If we look at these differences from an emotional and physical distance, say, as non–Muslims living in non–Muslim countries, they seem of only marginal importance. To this extent, Schacht was correct. But if we look more closely, we can see that the protagonists themselves — the Shiites and Sunnis on the ground, as it were — believe that these differences are very important. To understand why, let us trace Coulson's line of thought. He tells us that there are four significant differences between Sunnis and Shiites[31]:

- Shiite jurisprudence is totally dominated by the doctrine of the Imamate. Legal sovereignty is vested in the person of the Imam who speaks infallibly, nearly with the authority of God Himself. The Sunni concept of consensus (*ijma*), which is based on recognition of the possibility of several equally valid interpretations of the *sharia*, finds little room in Shiite law.
- Classical Sunni law recognized only two kinds of permissible sexual intercourse: the dominion that a man had over his slave-girl, and a valid contract of marriage. Shiite law, on the other hand, recognized a third, unique form of sexual relationship, known as *mut'a*. This was a marriage contract for a fixed period.
- Sunnis and Shiites both agree that a husband may unilaterally repudiate his wife at will (*talaq*, i.e., divorce by repudiation). Three repudiations (the triple *talaq*) cause an irrevocable divorce. Shiite law, however, puts much stricter limits on the husband's exercise of this power.
- The Sunni law of inheritance is broadly based. It recognizes three separate groups of legal heirs as being entitled to succeed on intestacy. Shiite law, in contrast, is narrowly based on a single entitlement. Females and cognate relatives (those descended from a common ancestor) have a more privileged position under Shiite law than under Sunni law.

In addition to Sunnis and Shiites, the two major branches of Islam, we should also mention the Kharijites, because they, too, are important in Islamic history. The term "Kharijite" literally means "those who go out," i.e., those who in the early days of Islam decided to withdraw from the political-religious process. This sect did so because its members were equally opposed to the rival caliphal claims of Muawiyah (the governor of Syria) and those of Ali (Muhammad's son-in-law).

The Kharijites rejected not only these two caliphal candidates but also all other Muslims who did not accept their own point of view. They argued that the will of God could be realized only through the free choice of the entire Muslim community, not through heredity. As they famously put it, anyone — even a black slave — who was pious and morally pure could be elected leader of their community. They launched fierce campaigns of harassment and terror to make their point.

Such actions and opinions kept them on a collision course with both the Sunnis and the Shiites, who favored their own hereditary rulers. Noted for their puritanism and fanaticism, the Kharijites were eventually defeated militarily. They are survived today by the more moderate sub-sect of the Ibadis. Now numbering about 500,000 people, most of the Ibadis live in Oman but there are Ibadi communities in North Africa and in Zanzibar as well.

2

Traditional Sharia *Law: Obligations to God and to Fellow Human Beings*

Sharia comes from the root *shara'a*, which has various derivatives. What is quite remarkable is that the term *sharia* itself makes only one major appearance in the Quran. This is the verse used as the epigraph for the book you now have in your hands: "And now We have set you on the right path [*sharia*]..." (*sura* 45:18). Here it designates a way or path, divinely appointed.

It also makes three other lesser appearances in the Quran, shown below in italics. It is used once as the cognate *shir'a* (a cognate is a word related by derivation), in parallel to *minhadj*, meaning way or path: "To each we have appointed a *law* and assigned a *path*" (*sura* 5:48). It is also used twice as the verb *shar'a*: "He has *laid down* for you as religion that which he appointed also for Noah" (*sura* 42:13)" and "Or do they have companions who have *laid down* for them as religion that which God did not permit? (*sura* 7:163).[1]

Moreover, in the *hadith*, *sharia* occurs only once, in the singular, in a *hadith* collected by the early jurist Ibn Hanbal (who will be discussed later) in his great work, the *Musnad*. He recorded it thus: "The [Islamic] community shall remain on the *sharia* [path or way] as long as there does not occur in it three things..." The *sharia* is mentioned not more than a dozen times in the remainder of this long treatise.

Such paucity of usage in the Quran and the *Musnad* suggests to some modern scholars that this word did not originate with the Muslims themselves. More likely, it had already become common in Arabic-speaking Jewish and Christian communities. For example, an early tenth century translation of the Old Testament into Arabic uses *sharia* to translate the Hebrew word *torah*, meaning a single rule or a set of rules, while a tenth century Christian tract directed against the Jews uses *sharia* to refer to a system of laws brought by a prophet.[2]

Muslim scholars of the late eighth and early ninth centuries drafted a collection of texts that are the earliest large-scale and systematic expressions of Islamic law.[3] As we have seen, the *sharia* has never been distilled into a single book. Each legal school has had a version of its own; the differences between them fall within the wide margins of Islamic orthodoxy. But the *sharia* is not amorphous. It is classically divided into two broad categories. Between them, they embrace almost all aspects of human life.

The first category deals with ritual acts of worship (*ibadat*). This is, as it were, a vertical category, stretching from human beings to God. To borrow a term from Western philosophy, it is essentially "natural law," i.e., the laws of nature, or the divine laws, which are held to govern the workings of the universe. (One of the clearest statements of natural law is Thomas Jefferson's definition of unalienable rights in the American *Declaration of Independence*: "We hold these truths to be self-evident, that all men are created equal, that they are endowed by their Creator with certain unalienable Rights, that among these are Life, Liberty and the pursuit of Happiness.")

Ibadat acts of worship include purification, praying, giving to charity, fasting, and making the pilgrimage to Mecca. In principle, these acts are not subject to major changes because in their present form they are held to express God's will as perfectly as possible. It is up to the individual to follow the prescribed patterns of worship, knowing full well that, whether he follows them conscientiously or not, he will not be judged in this world but by God Himself after death. There are some small differences between the legal schools in how these ritual acts should be performed. Islamic jurists have often included chapters on *ibadat* in their works.

The second category of the *sharia* comes closer to constituting "positive law," i.e., man-made law, as we know it in the West today. This category is called *mu'amalat* and it governs the horizontal relations between human beings themselves.[4] These relations can and indeed, according to Islamic jurists, should change over time to reflect new social realities. Any modifications of *mu'amalat*, however, must be worked out strictly in accordance with the principles of the Quran, *hadith*, and local legal traditions. Thus, unlike Western positive law, *mu'amalat* is firmly grounded in religious principles that are relatively impervious to change.

Some examples of *mu'amalat* are commercial transactions, including Islamic banking (an undertaking of growing importance in the world today); land ownership; religious endowments; family law, i.e., marriage, divorce, inheritance, caring for children, and, broadly speaking, the role of women in

Islam; food and drink, e.g., ritual slaughtering; hunting; penal law and its divinely specified penalties for adultery, false accusation of adultery, theft, wine drinking, and highway robbery; war and peace; and, finally, judicial processes, e.g., procedures, witnesses, and evidence.[5]

The *sharia* no longer holds undisputed sway over the Muslim world. There are enormous variations in how this holy law is interpreted and applied today. Turkey, for example, formally abolished the *sharia* in 1926; Albania did so two years later. Most countries of the Middle East and North Africa now have a dual system of secular courts and religious (*sharia*) courts. Saudi Arabia and Iran, however, still use *sharia* courts for all aspects of jurisprudence. The *sharia* is also used extensively in the Sudan and northern Nigeria.

Islamic fundamentalists are rebelling against modernity, which they correctly fear will undermine the orthodox foundations of conservative belief. They have long wanted the *sharia* to become the only system of law in the Muslim world — and, ultimately, the only system of law in all countries of the world. As the modern scholar Wael B. Hallaq explains,

> One of the fundamental features of the so-called modern Islamic resurgence is the call to restore the *Sharia*, the religious law of Islam. During the past two and a half decades, this call has grown ever more forceful, generating religious movements, a vast amount of literature, and affecting world politics. There is no doubt that Islamic law today is a significant cornerstone in the reaffirmation of Islamic identity, not only as a matter of positive law but also, and more importantly, as the foundation of a cultural uniqueness. Indeed, for many of today's Muslims, to live by Islamic law is not merely a legal issue, but one that is distinctly psychological.[6]

For all these reasons, it is instructive for us to trace the development of the *sharia* over the centuries. In an introductory survey like this, we cannot hope to examine thoroughly all the important legal thinkers of Islam.[7] A more modest approach commends itself. First, in this chapter we will look at some of the provisions of traditional *sharia* law. In the next chapter, we will discuss, selectively and briefly, some of the most important legal scholars who were active between the earliest days of the *sharia* and the legal reforms proposed by the fourteenth century Granada jurist Abu Ishaq. The thinking of later Islamic jurists and activists on the relationship between the *sharia* and *jihad* will be examined in a separate chapter. Case studies will be used as often as possible.

What must be kept uppermost in mind in this general survey is that the *sharia* differs from the Western legal systems of today in four critically important ways:

- It is traditionally seen by Islamic conservatives as the unchanging expression of God's will, not as a structure of man-made law that can easily be modified at will to fit new social and political conditions. Although incremental changes are possible and have in fact occurred over the years, the divine revelation that constitutes the essence of Islamic law is thought by the faithful to have come to a final end with the death of Muhammad in 632.

- Its scope is much broader than Western law. Like Judaic law and canonical Christian law, it is as much concerned with *ethical standards* as well as with purely legal matters. The *sharia*, in short, is both a system of morality and a system of law.

- The *sharia* is largely a jurists' law. That is to say, it arose from, and was spelled out by means of, private scholarly studies of Islamic jurisprudence. It was not drafted, dictated or approved by any centralized national authority or by Islamic society as a whole. At some risk of exaggeration, it can be said that Islamic society did not give birth to the law: it was the *sharia* itself which gave birth to Islamic society.

- As a modern expert on Islam, Christopher Melchert, explains, Islamic law has been, above all, *concerned with private duties*. This is because of the social milieu in which it evolved: it was developed by private jurists sitting in mosques. Sometimes these scholars were patronized by rulers, but usually they were their own masters. They reinforced a social and intellectual sphere of Islamic life that was well insulated from political direction. Dynasties might come and go, but society — and, we might add the *sharia* itself — would go on forever.[8]

In short, the *sharia* has never been a carbon copy of the statute law, so familiar to the West, which has evolved from royal edicts or from national legal traditions. The fact that the *sharia* is a jurists' law is also responsible for one of its greatest weaknesses. Roman law had its jurists too, but of necessity they focused on the practical needs of their commercial clients. *Sharia* law, however, has lacked this pragmatic touchstone. As a result, there has often been a sizeable gap between its religiously based prescriptions and the practical legal needs of everyday life.

It is now thought by some Western scholars that in its primordial stages Islamic law was essentially based on a living legal tradition that had gradually arisen in the major towns — in Kufa, Basra, Damascus, Mecca and Medina. This tradition evolved both from customary legal practices and from the work of contemporary Islamic scholars. Thus in its earliest stages Islamic law was not directly, or even necessarily, based only on the legal verses of the Quran or on *hadith*.[9]

Muhammad himself had been more interested in founding a new religion and creating an Islamic community than in developing a comprehensive legal system. Nevertheless, by about 626, he had decided that the nascent Islamic community (the *umma*) deserved and, indeed, needed a law of its own.[10] Accordingly, the Quran states in a *sura* sourced to that time:

> And to you We have revealed the Book [the Quran] with the truth. It confirms the Scriptures [the Torah and the Bible] which came before it and stands as a guardian over them. Therefore give judgement among men according to God's revelations, and do not yield to their whims or swerve from the truth made known to you [*sura* 5:48].

This *sura* is held to mark the beginning of what has been called "substantive legislation" in the Quran, that is, the revelation of Islamic laws that address a range of issues, not ritual matters alone.[11] Muhammad's chief objective here was to weld the *umma* into a cohesive whole by gradually replacing disparate tribal norms with divine revelations that applied uniformly to all believers.

The Sharia *in Action*

Traditional *sharia* courts usually heard private complaints, that is, they dealt only with private disputes between individuals. Public complaints, e.g., breaches of the peace, immoral behavior or offenses against the ruler, were normally handled by the police or by government officials. Thus *sharia* litigation was usually set in motion when one private citizen raised a complaint against another citizen, asserting that this person had caused him harm, e.g., by failing to fulfill a contract or failing to repay a loan.[12]

The plaintiff would state his case and would then be required to offer proof, unless the defendant immediately confessed to the charge. Proof usually consisted of the oral testimony of two Muslim males. Oral testimony from women was accepted (two women were equivalent to one man) and the testimony of a non–Muslim was allowed, if at all, only when a non–Muslim was a party to the litigation. Professional witnesses, whose probity and learning was beyond dispute, were available to help lubricate the wheels of justice.

Documents could be submitted too, but written evidence was considered to be much inferior to oral testimony — on the grounds that documents could easily be forged. The importance of memorization and orality in traditional Islamic legal thought can be traced back to the Quran itself.[13] As we have seen, this holy book is held to have been transmitted from God to man by *recitation*— that is, by the angel Gabriel's recitation of verses to Muhammad, who memorized them and in turn recited them to his fellow tribesmen. Memorization and oral skills were so important in early Islam that the Hanbali jurist and traditionalist Ishaq b. Rahwayh (d. 853), a member of the Hanbali school of law and a staunch traditionalist, could boast, "I know 70,000 *hadiths* by heart, and I can discuss 100,000." He added "I have never heard anything that I did not learn by heart, and I have never learned anything by heart and forgotten it."[14]

If neither party in a legal case could furnish sufficient proof, the plaintiff could insist that the defendant swear a formal oath. In such an intensely religious society, oaths carried a great deal of weight: lying under oath might easily jeopardize one's spiritual salvation. For this reason, in some cases the accused, if guilty, would refuse to take an oath, thus legally admitting his guilt.

In complex cases where innocence and guilt could not be judged easily, professional mediators or distinguished local citizens might be called in to help resolve the dispute. In seventeenth century Cairo, the central court, known as *Al-bab al-'ali* (literally "the high gate") was located in a government palace. The chief justice of this central court was always a member of the Hanafi school because the Hanafi doctrine was the school favored by the Ottomans.

His deputies, however, might represent the other schools. Court functionaries included the professional witnesses, who also served as notaries and scribes. Their role was especially important because they had to affirm, orally and in court, that the signatures on documents submitted to the court were indeed those of the litigants. These men were also officers of the court and could be sent out by the judge to determine the probity of the participants and to question witnesses to the events that had led to the suit. The central court in Cairo had no fewer than 19 legal functionaries.

Nearly all the cases coming before this central court involved civil and family matters rather than criminal offenses. The decision of the court was binding and most litigants complied with its findings. If the losing party — say, a debtor or defaulter — refused to do so, the plaintiff could ask that the guilty person be jailed until he paid up. Court orders for detention or, in criminal cases, for corporal punishment, were carried out by the police.

In a masterful and groundbreaking study of the city of Aleppo (Syria) in the eighteenth century, the modern scholar Abraham Marcus used contemporary legal records to reach this conclusion: Aleppo at that time "was generally a society that believed in the rule of law, invested in efforts to enforce it, and achieved a good measure of success in upholding its legal norms."[15] Nevertheless, as in most developed societies today there was still a great deal of legal wrangling involving matters of civil law.

For example, co-owners of property argued about their respective rights and obligations. Heirs argued about the distribution of estates. Couples argued about marriages, divorce payments, and child support. Businessmen argued about the prospects of their joint ventures. Lenders and borrowers argued about repayment schedules. Such disagreements were taken for granted and did not detract from the general perception of Aleppo's citizens that adequate laws existed and that the courts functioned relatively well.

Remarkably, there were not many criminal offenses in Aleppo at this time: some assaults and murders, some money and goods stolen from homes or shops, some thefts of donkeys, mules, and horses left unattended in public places. Although not all criminal offenses received legal attention, the crime rate was low. Marcus found that

> only a dozen or so complaints reached the *sharia* court every month.... On the whole, serious crimes against life and property appear to have been less numerous than violations of public morals, such as drinking, gambling, the production of wine, and illicit sexual relations. Usually discreet and victimless, many of the moral offenses never reached official attention or found their way into the records.[16]

In civil and criminal matters, as well as in their personal behavior, the citizens of Aleppo were subject to the *sharia*, usually as interpreted by the Hanafi school. The complexities of *sharia* law were unraveled by a large body of manuals, commentaries, legal opinions, and classical legal texts. Collectively, these documents tried to provide answers to the innumerable and often difficult questions raised by lawyers and students of the law.

Aleppo citizens were also subject both to government laws and to local customary laws. The Ottoman government had made the *sharia* the supreme law of its empire but had carefully reserved for itself the right to regulate life on all matters where the *sharia* was silent or inadequate. Government laws and regulations dealt with taxes, official appointments, administrative matters, privileges for high-ranking individuals, and criminal matters. Customary laws had to be obeyed as well. Where long usage had hallowed "established custom," the courts enforced it as law. For example, when some Aleppo bakers began to sell a new kind of bread in 1786, their competitors successfully sued them — on the grounds that the bakers' guild customarily produced only four kinds of bread. The judge who heard the case supported the traditionalists: he held that "The old custom must stand undisturbed."[17]

The judicial process in Aleppo that dealt with *sharia* matters seems to have worked relatively well. At minimum, it worked very quickly: a legal dispute that arose in the morning might come before a judge for decision by the end of that same day. Non-Muslims, i.e., Jews and Christians, seem to have been treated fairly. In 1757, for example, Jews proved in court that Ibrahim Effendi ibn Ibshir Agha, the official in charge of collecting a tax on cheese, was imposing an overly heavy tax on them. The *qadi* (judge) told the defendant that he could not change tax rates without official permission.[18]

Not long thereafter (in 1788), Christians asked the court to void new dress restrictions that had been imposed on them by an interim governor, who had ignored a standing order from the central government in Istanbul approving the current dress code. The *qadi* ruled in favor of the plaintiffs and the interim governor had to back down.[19]

There were no juries under *sharia* law but a significant number of witnesses or observers were invariably present at a trial. One or two of them were officers of the court, but most were friends, neighbors and associates of the parties. In Aleppo, there were usually six or seven witnesses or observers in attendance but in cases which attracted a great deal of public interest there could be as many as 40 or 50 of them. They were not trained lawyers but they knew enough about *sharia* proceedings so that any variations from the usual form would be noticed quickly. By their very presence, they helped assure that the legal process ran according to traditional form.

Nevertheless, as in most legal systems there was plenty of room for dishonesty and corruption. Evidence could be fabricated and witnesses could be bribed. *Qadis* — and their wives — could be swayed by gifts. A prosperous and well-connected litigant who felt he had been cheated could appeal his case to Istanbul. In 1773, this is just what the heirs of a rich merchant, Bakri Chalabi Tabla Zadeh, did when the local *qadi* illegally seized part of his estate. The *qadi* was forced to return what he had taken.[20]

A poor litigant could not afford this recourse but, on balance, the legal system seems to have worked reasonably well in eighteenth-century Aleppo. This is how Marcus summarizes the state of play:

> Although venality and abuses tainted the image of the *sharia* court, its level of dishonesty was probably within the bounds of ordinary and acceptable judicial practice. In the milieu in which it was set the court performed fairly well and served the cause of justice. Its protective services were not lost on the thousands of people who over the years recovered their rights with the judges' help. In court, countless women were able to obtain dowers and child support payments from reluctant ex-husbands, creditors recovered overdue debts, and victims of cheating and harm won compensation. The *sharia* court appeared especially fair and just in comparison with the judicial practices of the governors.[21]

Ritual Acts of Worship vs. Relations Between Human Beings

We have already noted that the classic division of the *sharia* is between ritual acts of worship (*ibadat*), on the one hand, and relations between human beings themselves (*mu'amalat*), on the other. The former are believed to reflect God's express will and are not appropriate candidates for man-made changes.

Because these ritual acts spring from deeply held religious convictions rather than from scholarly opinions about the changing legal needs of the Muslim community, we shall not discuss them any further here.

However, the broad second category of the *sharia*, namely, relations between human beings themselves, is well suited for our analytical purposes. Frequently using the present tense for convenience, we can profitably examine, albeit only very briefly, three areas of this law. These are[22]:

- Those areas where the impact of the *sharia* is greatest: family law, inheritance and succession, the religious endowment known as *waqf* (the plural is *awqaf* but the singular will be used in this book), and judicial procedures.
- Those where the impact is considerable but not dominant: laws of transactions (contracts and obligations).
- Those where the impact is weakest: penal law, taxation, constitutional law, and the law of war.

Areas of Greatest Impact

Family Law

The Islamic world has traditionally considered "personal status" law (a legal phrase often shortened to "family law") as being part-and-parcel of religion. As such, it has long been governed by the *sharia*.

"Personal status" law (*ahwal sakhsiyya*) is, in fact, a relatively recent legal term. It is not mentioned at all in the classic texts of Islamic jurisprudence because it is an idea copied and adapted from European legal systems. Early jurists conceptually divided the *sharia* into only two categories — one referring to theological beliefs, the other to human actions. The term "personal status" was first used by Muhammad Qadri Pasha, then Egypt's Minister of Justice, in 1893 as the title of his book, *Sharia Provisions on Personal Status*. It contained 646 articles covering marriage, divorce, gift, interdiction, wills and inheritance. His conclusions were based mainly but not entirely on Hanafi doctrine. Although this book was never proclaimed as the official legal code of Egypt, it remains a manual for *sharia* courts in Egypt and is the basis of the personal status laws that are still valid in other Arab countries today.[23]

A modern definition of personal status is provided by a Tunisian Presidential Decree of 1957, which reads as follows:

> Personal status shall include disputes over the status of the persons and their legal capacity, marriage, property dispositions between spouses, mutual rights and duties of the spouses, divorce, repudiation and judicial separation, parentage, acknowledgement or disavowal of paternity, family and descendants' relationships, maintenance duties among relatives and others, rectification of

parentage, adoption, tutelage, guardianship, interdiction, attainment of majority, gifts, inheritance, wills and other acts taking effect subsequent to death, the absent person and the declaration of a missing person to be dead [sic].[24]

Family law is vital to Islam. The family is the only group based on consanguinity or affinity which Islam recognizes.[25] A few words about marriage and divorce may therefore be useful here. It should be stressed, however, that such a brief summary cannot hope to do justice to the great depth and complexities of Islamic law on these topics.

The traditional Islamic family is patriarchal. Marriage is a civil contract, not a religious sacrament, between two individuals. The prospective husband makes a contract with the legal guardian of the bride, i.e., her nearest male relative (usually her father), and agrees to give a nuptial gift (dower) to the bride herself. Here is a lightly edited but otherwise typical marriage contract drawn up in Nablus in 1725 for the offspring of two prosperous Palestinian families:

> The groom, the youth of right conduct, Salih al-Din, son of the merchant Umar Ya'ish. The bride, the pride of guarded women, the *sayyida* [this is the feminine form of an honorific indicating descent from Muhammad; the masculine form is *sayyid*] Khadija, daughter of the pride of the nobles, the *sayyid* Hashim al-Hanbali, the virgin, in her majority, whose dower is 100 *dhahab bunduqi* [Venetian sequins], a kaftan [an ankle-length cotton or silk garment with long sleeves], a silk cloth, a run, a belt, 20 *ratls* [a unit of weight] of cotton, 10 dresses, and a black female slave to serve her. She receives now 60 *dhahab bunduqi*, the above-mentioned items, and the slave by her acknowledgment of her agent for the contract, and the rest is deferred until one of them dies.
>
> Her brother, *sayyid* Hasan, son of the *sayyid* Hashim, is her agent.... And the agent of the groom is the merchant Muhi-al Din Ya'ish.[26]

Two trustworthy adult Muslim men, or one Muslim man and two Muslim women, must witness and sign this marriage contract. For both cultural and financial reasons, in conservative circles the bride is expected to be a virgin.

A *fatwa* is an authoritative legal opinion issued by a *mufti*, i.e., a highly qualified scholar of Islamic law and theology. Often provided in response to a petitioner's question on a religious issue, it can be used privately or in court. (*Fatwa*s can have a strong political component too. Both the British and the French, for example, managed to get *fatwa*s confirming that they were the legal rulers of their colonies and that rebellion against their administration was not allowed.[27])

Here is a lightly edited traditional *fatwa* issued by Shaykh Khayr al-Din al-Ramli (1585–1671), who lived and worked in the Palestinian town of Ramla. He was a member of the Shafi'i school of law and his finely crafted *fatwa*s became models for later generations of jurists. He wrote:

QUESTION: Two men were married to two virgins and each consummated the marriage. Then one claimed after consummation that he had found his bride already deflowered, and he sent her back to her family. Then he abducted her sister by making a night raid on her [the sister's] husband's house in the village... Now he wants to annul the marriage, but his wife claims that it was indeed he who deflowered her. Can he annul the marriage? If he accuses her of *zina* [illicit sexual intercourse, which is a capital crime under the *sharia*] and she is found [somehow] to have been previously deflowered, should she be sentenced for *zina*, and then killed, or suffer *hadd* punishment [severe punishments prescribed by the Quran for "offenses against God"; the plural of *hadd* is *hudud* and is sometimes used in its place] or *ta'zir* [corrective discretionary punishment imposed by a jurist], or is her testimony to be accepted?

ANSWER: The man's claim that "I found her deflowered" is of no consequence, because even if he really had found her deflowered he must still pay the entire *mahr* [dower] as legal opinion stipulates, and he does not have the option of annulling the marriage. And in any case, being deflowered does not necessarily mean that illicit intercourse has taken place, for virginity can be lost by jumping, or through menstruation, or with age, and so forth. The wife is guilty of nothing, and the one who did to her what has been mentioned above disobeys God, may He be exalted. The testimony of the woman is valid, such is the situation, and the dower in its entirety is required.... He [the husband] must bring his wife's sister back to the place from which he abducted her, and he should be imprisoned until he does so.[28]

Under Islamic law, a man may be married to up to four wives at the same time, provided that he has the means to support them and that he treats them all equally. Today, this Quranic provision is in fact interpreted by many Islamic jurists as *forbidding* polygamy — on the grounds that a husband can never treat two or more wives with equal fairness.

The husband may use a very limited amount of physical force to compel a disobedient wife to behave and may stop supporting her financially as part of this process. Excessive physical force is not permitted, as witness this verbatim *fatwa* issued by Khayr al-Din al-Ramli:

QUESTION: There is an evil man who harms his wife, hits her without right and rebukes her without cause. He swore many times to divorce her until she proved that a thrice divorce [a final and irrevocable divorce] had taken effect.

ANSWER: He is forbidden to do that, and he is rebuked and enjoined from her. If she has proved that a thrice divorce has taken place, it is permissible for her to kill him, according to many of the *ulama* [religious scholars] if he is not prevented except by killing. [In other words, she can kill him if murder is the only way to stop him from having intercourse with her].[29]

The wife's position is inherently much weaker than the man's under the *sharia* but she may legitimately refuse, both for herself and for her children, to accompany her husband on his travels. On a positive note, she has the right to the nuptial gift and to maintenance. She does not have to pay for any part of the matrimonial home. Barring divorce or the husband's death, she has a life-long right to maintenance. This consists of food, clothing, medical treatment, and lodging, i.e., either a separate room that can be locked or a separate house. A prosperous husband is also required to provide a servant for his wife's household if this was what she was used to when she was growing up. A mother has the right to care for her sons until they are seven or nine years old and to care for her daughters until they reach puberty.

Divorce procedures vary under Islamic law. A judge may divorce a couple if a man mistreats his wife, or in case of his long absence away from home and his possible death. A divorce can also be arranged by mutual consent or in a case of severe economic hardship. In this *fatwa*, Khayr al-Din al-Ramli showed true sympathy for a wife's plight:

> QUESTION: There is a poor man who married a virgin in her legal majority, but he did not pay her the stipulated *mahr* [dower], nor did he provide *nafaqa* [financial support], nor did he clothe her. This caused her great harm. Must he follow one of God's two commands: "Either you maintain her well or you release her with kindness?" And if the judge annuls the marriage, is it on account of the severe harm being done to her?
> ANSWER: Yes, the husband should do one of the two things, according to God's command: "maintain her well or release her with kindness...." You cannot sustain [indefinitely] such needs through borrowing, and it appears that she does not have anyone to lend her money, and the husband has no actual wealth. They [the *sharia* and Hanafi legal thinkers] refer that the qadi [judge] appoint a Shafi'i *na'ib* [assistant judge] to separate them. Many of our [Hanafi] legal thinkers chose this path in cases of extreme necessity, and it pleases the *faqih* [*sharia* jurist] because it spares him an awkward situation and saves the woman from harm. And God knows best.[30]

In traditional Islam, only the husband has the right to end a marriage unilaterally. (Today there are also several other ways to divorce or demand divorce under Islamic regulations.) Traditional divorce is "divorce by repudiation" (*talaq*), i.e., the husband repudiates the wife by saying, three times, "I divorce you." If he says it only once, he may revoke his pronouncement at any time during the following mandatory three-menstruation waiting period (*idda*). If he says it three times, however, this constitutes a final and irrevocable end to the marriage. If a divorced wife is pregnant, she cannot remarry until after her delivery. If she is not pregnant, she must wait until three menstruations have occurred.

INHERITANCE AND SUCCESSION

The Islamic law of inheritance defines the fixed shares, specified in the Quran, that take precedence over the succession of the next of kin. In general, an individual may will only one-third of his net estate; the remaining two-thirds of the estate automatically passes to his legal heirs under the mandatory Islamic rules of inheritance. Sunnis and Shiites differ appreciably over inheritance procedures: under Shiite law, women can in certain circumstances inherit the same share as a man. What is most important for us to note is that Islamic inheritance and succession issues can quickly become exceedingly complex. Their potential complexity is reflected in this description by Schacht:

> Half-brothers and half-sisters on the mother's side [of the deceased], if there are two or more of them, receive one-third [of the estate], the males and females dividing it in equal portions; one half-brother or half-sister on the mother's side receives one-sixth. One-sixth is also the share of the father (or, if there is no father, the nearest male or female ascendant in the male line), provided there are children or son's children, of the son's daughter (or son's daughters who divide it in equal portions), provided there is one daughter, and of the half-sister (or half-sisters) on the father's side, provided there is one full sister (and no daughter or son's daughter)....[31]

Schacht then goes on to list even further possible complexities, which need not detain us here.

WAQF FOUNDATIONS

Waqf foundations, i.e., religious endowments, are a uniquely Islamic institution and an important subject in Islamic countries. We cannot go into them here in any depth but in essence the founder of a *waqf* surrenders his ownership of land or some other real property and legally gives it to God. The income or usufruct of such a property is then dedicated, forever, to a pious or charitable cause. This arrangement is not, however, purely as selfless at it may seem: long running financial agreements may legitimately be made in favor of the founder's own relatives.

JUDICIAL PROCEDURES

Under *sharia* law, the *qadi* is a judge appointed by the ruling political authority. He presides alone, not as part of a multi-judge team. He is not all-powerful but is legally competent in a number of important areas, e.g., public welfare in general, where he functions as "the guardian of those who have no other guardian."[32] The *qadi* is assisted by a number of officers of the court. He may also seek the help of a *mufti* on especially difficult cases. The *qadi*'s clerk plays an essential role in court proceedings, e.g., by committing the *qadi*'s judgments to writing. The *qadi* himself and all the officers of the court must be adult Muslim men of good moral character and well schooled in the *sharia*.

Islamic laws of procedure direct the *qadi* to behave honorably. For example, he must treat all parties equally and must not try to put words into their mouths. When a claimant brings a legal action against a defendant, the *qadi* first asks the defendant about this allegation. If the defendant concedes that the claim is indeed correct, all that remains for the *qadi* to do is to pass judgment. If the defendant denies the claim, however, the *qadi* then orders him to produce evidence, i.e., witnesses, or to take an oath relating to the facts of the case.

Such witnesses — two male, adult Muslims of unblemished character were preferred, but one man and two women were also acceptable — would give their oral testimony about the case. The witnesses could testify only to what they themselves had seen (except in such issues as family relationships and death) and their stories had to tally. If, for example, two witnesses claimed that Ahmed killed Hassan on a given day in Mecca, but two other witnesses said the murder actually took place in Medina, both testimonies would be rejected by the *qadi*.[33]

Written evidence and circumstantial evidence generally were not admissible: as mentioned earlier, the witnesses' oral testimony was supremely important. If the testimony of the witnesses was entirely persuasive, the *qadi* could pass judgment at that point. If it was not, the defendant could be asked to swear an oath. Swearing an oath was a very serious matter: properly sworn, such an oath would win the case for him. If the defendant refused to take the oath, however, judgment would automatically be handed down in favor of the plaintiff.

Traditional Islamic legal procedures, especially those concerning evidence, were not necessarily designed to ferret out the truth, but rather to make sure that certain formal rules of procedure were brought to bear on the case at hand. As examples, let us consider two cases from Egypt.

The first case comes from a report written in 1879–1880. A gang of thieves, arrested in Cairo in 1812, had been brought before the chief judge there. Lightly edited, this is what the report tells us:

> [The thieves] confessed to having committed many crimes, yet the *qadi* could not sentence them to the fixed punishment for theft [retaliatory amputation of the hand] since, in their confessions, they used not the words "we have stolen," but the words "we have taken." Under the *Shari'a*, this constitutes uncertainty, which precludes the application of such a punishment. The *qadi* then wrote a report to [the governor of Cairo] and entrusted the matter to him for further disposal. The latter, after some reflection, sentenced them to retaliatory amputation of their right hands on the strength of his authority to impose *siyasa* punishments [penalties designed to uphold law and order].[34]

Under Ottoman law, both the *qadi* and the governor acted correctly here. If a *qadi* could not, under the provisions of the *sharia*, reach a decision in a criminal case, he was required to forward the case to his supervisor. The governor, for his part, had the power to order the appropriate punishment if abiding by the strict rules of the *sharia* would otherwise let the guilty go free.[35]

The second case involves a homicide case brought before a judge in Tanta, Egypt, in 1860. A legal compilation of criminal cases, produced in Cairo in 1884, describes this case as follows:

The plaintiffs, the heirs of the deceased, sued the *qadi* of Burullus, claiming that "during a fight in his courtroom, he had struck the deceased with a thin palm branch twice, once on his head and once his face, that he had then chased the deceased from the courtroom and kicked him in the belly, that this had caused his belly and breast to bloat and that he had stayed in bed until he died eight days later as a result of this assault."

The defendant replied that he had indeed struck the deceased for having been insolent during court proceedings, but only very lightly and only on his turban. The plaintiffs then produced three witnesses. The first testified that the *qadi* had merely struck the deceased with a palm branch. The second witness reported that the *qadi* had kicked the deceased once in the belly *with his left foot* and then twice in the belly *with his right foot*. The third witness said that the *qadi* had kicked the deceased twice in the belly *with his left foot*. This was the judge's verdict:

> After consultation with the Grand Mufti, the judge who heard this case decided that the testimony of the first witness was irrelevant as he had not seen the fatal blows and kicks and that the testimonies of the second and third witnesses were contradictory and could not serve as a basis for a sentence against the defendant.

Accordingly, the homicide case was dismissed for lack of evidence.[36]

Other things being equal, when the testimonies of reliable witnesses conflicted they could all be judged as being partially true, even though this might seem to be impossible from a strictly logical point of view. For purposes of illustration, let us imagine a hypothetical case involving the disputed ownership of a house.

Mansur claims that he has bought the house. Husayn says that the house was donated to him. Ibrahim asserts that he inherited the house from his father. Musa states that he received the house as a gift from a charity. Rather than forcing the *qadi* to decide between such mutually contradictory claims, the *sharia* permits him (assuming that all the correct formal procedures have been observed in this case) to rule that *all the claims are partially true*. From a legal point of view, then, the house is held to be common property owned by all four claimants.[37]

Areas of Considerable Impact

TRANSACTIONS: CONTRACTS AND OBLIGATIONS

Traditionally, puberty was the legal crossover point from child to grownup for both males and females. With it came the legal capacity to conduct transactions, provided that the person did not lack "prudent judgment," e.g., due to mental deficiency or being financially irresponsible. In such cases, the person's affairs were managed by a guardian. In most Islamic societies today, the legal coming of age is 18, not puberty.

The *sharia* outlines the principles underlying four kinds of commercial transactions:

- Selling or transferring the ownership of property or the property itself.
- Hiring or transferring the usufruct (the right to use a property).
- Giving away property.
- Loaning or giving away the usufruct of a property.

These principles come into play in specific commercial actions, e.g., pledges, deposits, guarantees, assignments, land tenancy, partnership, agency (the capacity, condition or state of acting or of exerting power), and *waqf* foundations. To these principles we should also add the Quranic prohibition on *riba*—literally "increase," i.e. interest and usury or, more broadly, any unjustified increase of capital for which no compensation has been given. Islam's "*riba* rules" will be discussed later. Here we shall note that Quran quite clearly prohibits usury, as the following citation from the early Medinan period shows:

> Those that live on usury shall rise up before God like men whom Satan has
> demented by his touch; for they claim that trading is no different from usury.
> But God has permitted trading and made usury unlawful. He that has received
> an admonition from his Lord and mended his ways may keep his previous gains;
> God will be his judge. Those that turn back shall be the inmates of the Fire,
> wherein they shall abide forever. God has laid his curse on usury and blessed
> almsgiving with increase... Believers, have fear of God and waive what is still due
> you from usury, if your faith be true; or war shall be declared against you by
> God and His apostle. If you repent, you may retain your principal, suffering no
> loss and causing loss to none [*sura* 2:275–280].

The Islamic definition of usury extends to the prohibition of any form of interest on a loan or investment. The Quran also prohibits gambling. The bottom line for devout Muslims is that the *sharia* does not permit any transaction in which the material benefits to each party cannot be precisely known in advance. It is, moreover, a general precept of Islamic law that unjustified enrichment, which is defined as "receiving a monetary advantage without giving a counter value," is forbidden. Should a man receive such a windfall, he is required to donate it to charity.[38]

Areas of Weakest Impact

PENAL LAW

In general, rulers and their officials took over the administration of criminal justice at an early point in Islamic history. There seem to have been three reasons for this.[39] The *sharia* mandates fixed penalties for only a small number of crimes. Many crimes are not addressed at all. Finally, rules of evidence are so rigorous that many offenses go unpunished. Nevertheless, the *sharia* is not silent on penal law and, indeed, has had an impact on it. The Quran, for examples, calls for fierce measures against transgressors:

> Those that make war against God and His apostle [Muhammad] and spread disorder in the land shall be slain or crucified or have their hands and feet cut off on alternate sides, or be banished from the land. They shall be held up to shame in this world and sternly punished in the hereafter ... [*sura* 5:33].
>
> As for the man or woman who is guilty of theft, cut off their hands to punish them for their crimes. That is the punishment enjoined by God [*sura* 5:38].

To use an expression from the British sport of cricket, the *sharia* has had a long innings. For example, in modified form it remained the basis of criminal law in Bengal and other Muslim parts of British India until as late as 1862.[40] As we shall see, the *sharia* is still in use in Saudi Arabia today.

Islamic law has a special section — the right or claim of Allah (*haqq Allah*) — in contrast to the private claims made by human beings (*haqq adami*). Since *hadd* offenses are considered to be offenses against God Himself, when they occur no pardon or amicable settlement is, in theory, possible.[41] Islam sets fixed punishments for crimes that are considered especially serious because they are held to offend God Himself and to undermine the integrity of the Muslim community as a whole. These crimes are illegal sexual relations, i.e., those conducted outside a legal context, such as a marriage contract; unproven allegations of unchastity; theft; wine-drinking; armed robbery; and apostasy.[42] Thus the law of *hadd* was designed to protect four central values of Islamic society: law and order, private property, sex, and personal honor.[43]

The classical *hadd* penalties are severe. For apostasy and for highway robbery with homicide, the sentence is death, either by crucifixion or by beheading with a sword. For theft and highway robbery without homicide, it is retaliatory amputation of the hand and or the foot. For extramarital sex, it is death by lapidation (stoning) if the offender is married and 100 lashes if he or she is not married. For an unproven accusation of unchastity and for consuming alcohol, it is 80 lashes. Local regulations govern the amount of force that can be used in administering these lashes. In many Islamic countries today, this penalty is forbidden or not enforced.

In practice, the application of some *hadd* penalties has traditionally been limited by the extraordinarily strict rules of evidence applied to such cases. The *sharia* seeks to establish the truth of the most dramatic *hadd* claims by demanding a very high degree of certainty. Most striking, perhaps, is the rule that fornication (*zina*) can be proved only by the testimony four upright male Muslims, *who have personally witnessed the sexual act taking place*. Otherwise, a voluntary confession is necessary.

The great caution exhibited by the *sharia* when dealing with cases involving illegal sexual relations reportedly dates from a Prophetic *hadith*. The basic version of this *hadith* tells us that a man named Ma'iz confessed four times to Muhammad that he had had illegal sex. Rather simply condemning Ma'iz to be stoned to death, Muhammad patiently questioned him and suggested various legal defenses he could use to save his life. It is worth quoting this *hadith* at some length here. Lightly edited, it runs as follows:

> When Ma'iz came to [Muhammad] to confess that he [had] committed *zina* and repeated his confession, the Prophet asked whether he was insane or whether he had drunk wine, and ordered someone to smell his breath. Thereupon he questioned him about *zina*, saying, "Have you perhaps just kissed her or touched her?" In another version, "Did you lie down with her?" He said, "Yes." Then [the Prophet] asked, "Did your body touch hers?" He answered, "Yes." Then he asked, "Did you have intercourse with her?" He said, "Yes." Then he asked, "Did that thing of yours enter that thing of hers?" He answered, "Yes." He asked, "Like the *kohl* stick [a stick used to apply the eyelid-darkening cosmetic *kohl*] disappears into the *kohl* container and the bucket into the well?" He said, "Yes." Then he asked, "Do you know what *zina* means?" He said, "Yes, I did with her unlawfully what a man does with his wife lawfully." Then the Prophet asked, "What do you intend with these words?" He answered, "That you purify me." Then [Muhammad] ordered him to be stoned.[44]

There are at least two explanations for the somewhat surprising reluctance of Muslim jurists to implement the most serious *hadd* penalties. Some of these jurists have argued that since God is omnipotent and merciful, he does not need to have his all claims satisfied, no matter how legitimate these claims may be. Other Islamic scholars have held instead that the severe *hadd* penalties are essentially meant as rhetorical threats to encourage socially approved behavior.[45]

When non-*hadd* crimes are committed, the *sharia* leaves it up to the ruler or to the courts to determine the appropriate punishments. Traditionally, the penalty for homicide and assault was corrective discretionary punishment (*ta'zir*). This often meant retaliation, i.e., the assailant deserving the same injury that he had inflicted on his victim. This kind of offense was regarded not as a crime against the state but as a civil injury. As a result, the victim or his family could take the case to court and demand blood money or some other form of private compensation, rather than insisting on retaliation *per se*.

Setting the bar of proof so high for fornication and other offenses must have protected the innocent but it also rendered the *sharia* quite unusable in certain fields. Chief among these was criminal law, where *de facto* jurisdiction was usually handed over to the police. The man who exercised it was known as the "official in charge of crimes." Police courts could employ a range of coercive measures, e.g., imprisoning suspects and using force to extort confessions. They could also determine appropriate punishments. Such wide powers gave the police much greater flexibility in administering criminal justice, but they also made the whole process somewhat arbitrary and potentially unfair.[46]

TAXATION

The *sharia* imposes only modest taxes on the faithful and in its classical form regarded all other taxes, e.g., "market dues," as illegal. Nevertheless, other taxes were of course imposed — for example, the taxes (*jizya*) that Christians and Jews had to pay in order to receive protection from their Muslim rulers. The Syrian scholar Muhyi al-Din al-Nawawi (d. 1277) left this guidance on how the poll tax should be collected:

> An infidel who has to pay his poll tax should be treated by the tax collector with disdain; the collector remaining seated and the infidel standing before him, the head bent and the body bowed. The infidel should personally place the money in the balance, while the collector holds him by the beard and strikes him upon both cheeks. These practices, however, according to some jurists, are merely commendable, but not obligatory, as some think.[47]

CONSTITUTIONAL LAW

The ideal state, as imagined by Islamic law, has never existed. If it had existed, it would never have needed a constitution: the *sharia* itself would have provided enough guidance. In practical terms, even non-ideal Islamic states did not rely on constitutions. Historically, there were no constitutions in the pre-modern Islamic world. This meant that there was no need for constitutional law. Today, however, most Islamic countries do have constitutions. These are mixtures of *sharia* law, customary law, and Western legal concepts.

LAW OF WAR

Traditional Islamic legal thought defined war as a justified struggle against infidel nations who were hostile to Islam. In theory, such a just war was designed solely to protect and expand the territory ruled by Islam. During domestic rebellions on Islamic soil, the goal of war was to reintegrate the rebels as quickly and as painlessly as possible into the Muslim body politic. Classic legal scholars saw the world as consisting of only two major competing systems.

The first was known as *Dar al-Islam*, the "House of Islam," also termed *Dar al-Salam*, the "House of Peace." This "House" was the Islamic world itself. The second system was called *Dar-al-Harb*, the "House of War," i.e., the non–Muslim or the not-yet–Muslim world. It was the duty of Islamic rulers to work to incorporate *Dar-al-Harb* into *Dar-al-Islam*— through peaceful means if possible but by military means if necessary.

This bipolar concept had the virtue of simplicity but it left no room for treatises on the law of war, so Islamic jurists did not write them. Moreover, jurists differed on the possibility and duration of any lasting peace between these two competing "Houses." Some Quranic verses do suggest that peaceful coexistence with nonbelievers is possible and even desirable. *Sura* 2:193, for example, tells the faithful "...if they [the nonbelievers] desist [from fighting], fight none except the evil-doers," while *sura* 8:61 advises, "If they incline to peace, make peace with them, and put your trust in God." These verses, however, were declared to have been abrogated (replaced) by later, more belligerent ones.[48] The Islamic concept of abrogation (*naskh*) will be discussed later.

There is a close relationship between the *sharia* and *jihad. Jihad* is often mistranslated into English simply as "holy war" but its literal meaning is more along the lines of "to exert effort, i.e., to struggle or to fight, towards a specific objective." Thus "holy struggle" is a more accurate term than "holy war." However, *jihad* is a sufficiently complicated subject so that it is best to discuss it at some length later, in the chapter on the *sharia* and *jihad*. This will permit us to quote, verbatim, some of the interesting and important texts on which this Islamic theory of war is based.

3

The Sharia *and Its Jurists: From the Beginnings to al-Shatibi's Legal Reforms*

Muhammad died in 632. According to the Sunnis, he did not designate a successor. (The Shiites, however, believe that he designated Ali ibn Talib.) The first caliph was Abu Bakr, whose reign was marked by the "wars of apostasy." These arose because some of the nomadic tribes that had fought on Muhammad's side decided that their commitment to the *umma* (the Islamic community) had expired with his death. They tried to reassert their independence, but Abu Bakr kept them in line by using the carrot of plunder expected from future raids against neighboring countries and the stick of military force. His short two-year reign (632–634) did not result, however, in any new legal developments.

Now began the great and ultimately world-shaking expansion of Islam. The second caliph, Umar ibn al-Khattab, successfully invaded what is today Iraq, Syria and Egypt. Jerusalem surrendered peaceably to the Muslims in 638; it would become the third holiest city of the Islamic world, after Mecca and Medina. Despite all the booty collected during these campaigns, however, Umar understood very clearly that the supply of plunder was not infinite and that he would need something else to keep his free-spirited nomadic warriors in the ranks.

He found the solution: building mosques in all the garrisons where his troops lived and, indeed, in every civilian town heavily populated by Muslims.[1] The mosques provided Friday prayers, sermons and teachers of the Quran — all excellent vehicles for conveying to the restless, unlettered *bedouin* the gist of the Quranic message and the supreme importance of the community, the *umma*.

Umar also posted *qadis* (judges) in the garrison towns. Islamic law was still in its infancy, so these early *qadis* were only magistrates, i.e., senior government officials, not formally trained judges. An organized judiciary slowly came into being only after the Umayyad dynasty seized power in 661. Some the earliest judicial rulings were either arbitrary or were based only on a rough-and-ready sense of justice — certainly not on the provisions of the Quran as they would later be spelled out in careful legal detail.[2]

For example, a *qadi* named Ka'b was assigned to Basra, Iraq and had to adjudicate a dispute over land. One man had bought land from another on the understanding that it was fertile and could be cultivated. The land turned out to be rocky and sterile; understandably, the buyer soon wanted his money back. This *qadi*'s creative solution was to ask the buyer whether he would still want his money back if he had found gold on the land. When the buyer said "no," Ka'b ruled that he was not entitled to any repayment. (Under later Islamic law, as we have already seen, the buyer would be entitled to get his money back if the object he bought, in this case the land, proved to be defective.)

In another relevant case, the *qadi* Hisham presided over a trial in which some men were charged in 684 with fraudulently selling grain that they had claimed was pure wheat. In fact, their "wheat" was heavily adulterated with barley, an inferior grain. Hisham found the men guilty and, applying an ancient Middle Eastern punishment that pre-dated Islam, ordered that half of their beards and all the hair on their heads to be shaved off in punishment. (Under later Islamic law, the men would have had to pay damages equal to the reduced value of the adulterated wheat.)

Later judges dealt with many aspects of family law (marriage, divorce and inheritance) and with a range of other issues, for example, administering religious endowments, managing the property of orphans, and resolving civil disputes. One of the earliest steps in systematizing Islamic law was the search for useable precedents. This took the form of an increasing reliance on "Prophetic *sunna*," i.e., the social and legal traditions sourced to Muhammad himself or to his reliable Companions.

A good example here is the issue traditionally known as "surplus of property." What should a good Muslim do when he had an income exceeding his personal needs? Pre-Islamic Arabs used to give their surplus to charity or use it for other social purposes. Umar, however, recalled that the prophet was said to have devoted his own surplus to buying military equipment for his troops. The caliph therefore endorsed this practice as a Prophetic *sunna*.[3]

Another issue was how to interpret the Quran and the *sunna* so that they could be brought to bear on the legal disputes at hand. Increasing reliance was placed on "juristic speculation" (i.e., personal opinion, or *ra'y*) based on a thorough knowledge of Islamic precedent (*ilm*). These two concepts were closely associated with, and sometimes overlapped, with "independent reasoning" (*ijtihad*), which also had to be drawn from the Quran and the *sunna*. Such independent reasoning would become the foundation stone on which past and present reformers of Islam have based their proposals.

We shall learn more about *ijtihad* later on. But because many non–Muslims have difficulty with this important and (to Western eyes) highly controversial concept, it is a good idea to pause here and see what a scholarly and dispassionate source has to say about it. The following account, taken from the *Encyclopaedia of Islam*, has been lightly edited:

> During the first two and half centuries of Islam [i.e., until about the middle of the ninth century CE], there was never any question of denying to any scholar or specialist in the sacred Law the right to find his own solutions of legal problems. It was only after the formative period of Islamic law had come to an end that the question of who was qualified to exercise *ijtihad* was raised. From about the middle of the [ninth century] the idea began to gain ground that only the great scholars of the past, and not the epigones [followers or disciples], had the right to *ijtihad*. By about [the year 900], the point had been reached when the scholars of all schools felt that all the essential questions had been thoroughly discussed and finally settled, and a consensus gradually established itself to the effect that from that time onwards no one might been deemed to have the necessary qualifications for independent reasoning in law, and that all future activity would have to be confined to the explanation, application, and, at the most, interpretation of the doctrine as it had been laid down once and for all. This "closing of the door of *ijtihad*," as it was called, amounted to the demand for *taqlid*, the unquestioning acceptance of the doctrines of established [Sunni] schools and authorities.[4]

Four doctrinal Sunni schools (*madhabs*— the Arabic plural is *madhahib* but for convenience the singular is used here in English plural form) arose from the teachings of famous jurists — or from later teachings that were backdated and attributed to them. Named in honor of their leading figures, these four schools were the Hanafi, the Maliki, the Shafi'i, and the Hanbali. There is also one major Shiite school — the Ja'fari. Hanafi law came to predominate in the Middle East and India; Maliki law in North, West, and Central Africa; Shafi'i law in East Africa, southern Arabia, and Southeast Asia; Hanbali law in Saudi Arabia, after the rise of Wahhabism (discussed below) in the eighteenth century; and Ja'fari law in Iran.

Although the Hanbali school had fewer adherents than its rivals, it was the upholder *par excellence* of Sunni orthodoxy and today is still the strictest of the four legal schools of Sunni Islam. As a result, it has wielded an influence greater than its numbers would suggest.[5] The growth of these schools marks the real beginnings of Islamic jurisprudence. The goal of the schools was to make contemporary legal practice reflect the ideals laid down in the Quran and *hadith*. Each school emphasized different legal issues or put forward its own interpretations.

Legal discussions in these schools did not produce what could be described as the cold, impersonal statute law of the West. Instead, they generated a warmer, more people-friendly body of rules, which were leavened and spiced by the ethical, moral, and theological concepts of Islam.[6] Despite its commitment to continuity, Islamic law has always had a surprising amount of flexibility and open-endedness.[7] Working at the same time in the same city and using the same primary sources, different jurists produced different works. These reflected their special interests, so as a practical matter the law depended very much on personal and local factors. Thus the findings of Muslim jurists could differ, often significantly, both on matters of substance and detail. As the modern scholar Haim Gerber tells us.

> [The jurist] is supposed to apply the law handed down to him by the Islamic tradition of many generations, and he has a number of important methodological ways to extract this law from the books. But the principles are not iron rules; in fact, they are quite elastic and subtle, and they include the principle of taking into account the changing circumstances and habits of his time and place. While it is evident that the principle of personal discretion was not supposed to be theorized into the [legal] model, it can be amply shown that it was unavoidable, exactly as it is in any modern Western legal system.[8]

Sharia law is pluralistic. The opinions of the various schools could vary, but they usually carried equal doctrinal weight. Muslims often explain the equal authority of the various legal schools by quoting a *hadith* attributed to Muhammad: "Difference of opinion among my community is a sign of the bounty of Allah." Today, the four Sunni schools are said to agree on most of their legal conclusions. In the remaining cases, their differences are usually due to methodological variances in interpreting the primary textual evidence. Indeed, different viewpoints can exist even within the same school of thought.[9]

Nevertheless, there can still be substantive differences between the schools. Let us take three examples of conflicting interpretations — the first on usurpation, i.e., seizing and holding, by force or without right, something belonging to another person; the second on usury (*riba*); and the third on family relationships.

The Hanafi school technically defined usurpation as "the unlawful *removal of property* from its original place, where it had been possessed by the owner."[10] The Hanbalis, on the other hand, held that it was only the *seizure* of property — and not its physical removal — which constituted usurpation. This Hanbali doctrine therefore suggested that taking possession of another person's rug merely by sitting on it could be considered usurpation, even if the rug was not actually taken away. The Hanafis, however, would not have considered this usurpation.

This difference may seem trivial now but it did have important legal consequences. In the hypothetical case mentioned above, the Hanbalis would have argued that the usurper was also liable to the original owner for any increase in the value of the usurped object or any proceeds from the use of that object. The Hanafis, however, would have rejected this claim. From their point of view, neither the growth nor the proceeds existed when the object was usurped: therefore, it followed that the usurper could not be held liable on these grounds.

Let us now turn to the second example. A Prophetic *hadith* explains the Quranic prohibitions of usury. The Quran condemns usury in some eight verses. The most dramatic of these tells the faithful:

> Those that live on usury shall rise up before God like men whom Satan has demented by his touch; for they claim that trading is no different from usury. But God has permitted trading and made usury unlawful. He that has received an admonition from his Lord and mended his ways may keep his previous gains; God will be his judge. Those that turn back shall be the inmates of the Fire, wherein they shall abide forever. God has laid his curse on usury and blessed almsgiving with increase. God bears no love for the impious and the sinful [*sura* 2:275–276].

When certain items — gold, silver, wheat, barley, dates, and raisins — are bartered against each other, usury is said to exist if the amounts offered are not equal or if there is a delay in delivery on one side.[11] By analogy, these "*riba* rules," as they are called, were also applied to other commodities. Different schools, however, took different positions on this issue.

Shafi'i and Hanbali law held that these rules applied to the barter of all foodstuffs. Maliki law said they applied only to foodstuffs that can be stored or preserved. Hanafi law, on the other hand, said the *riba* rules applied to all commodities normally exchanged by weight or measure. We may therefore assume that local merchants and traders had to know which system of law was in force in their own area.

There is an interesting historical footnote here. For traditional Islam, whenever a contradiction arose between the idealized prescriptions of the *sharia* and the practical demands of everyday life, the usual solution was to uphold, in theory at least, the purity of the *sharia* while at the same time permitting legal concessions to economic realities. Because charging some amount of interest was a commercial necessity, the manipulation of *riba* is a good case in point here.

Although the Quran clearly prohibits interest, loans with interest could in fact be arranged through an elaborate system of legal stratagems known as "devices" (*hiyal*, literally "legal tricks"), which would be upheld by a *sharia* court.[12] In a "double sale," for instance, Abdullah, the lender, would buy a camel from Faisal, the borrower, for an agreed price of X *dirham*s (silver coins), payable immediately in cash. Faisal would then contract to re-purchase this same camel from Abdullah for a price of X+i *dirham*s (i being the interest), payable at some future specified date. The Hanafi school was the most favorably inclined to the use of such legal stratagems.[13]

The third example of significant differences between the legal schools concerns a case known, for reasons that are now unclear, as the "House of the Elephants." This case was heard by *sharia* judges in Egypt over a period of more than 100 years. In its final stages, it hinged on the question of whether the children of the settlor's daughter were "descendants" within the meaning of the law. Hanafi law said that they were; Maliki law said that they were not. As a result, a Maliki judge dismissed the plaintiffs' claims in 835. Ten years later, however, the Hanafi successor of this judge ruled in favor of the plaintiffs. A later Maliki judge reversed this decision in 859. The plaintiffs then appealed to the caliph, who on the advice of Hanafi jurists assembled to review the case, ordered that a final verdict be entered in favor of the plaintiffs.[14]

A Silk Trader Turned Jurist: Abu Hanifah (699–767)

Abu Hanifah was a renowned jurist and theologian who was born in Kufa, an intellectual center of Iraq.[15] His systematization of legal learning gave birth to the Hanafi school, one of the four canonical institutions of Sunni Islamic law. This school began in Iraq but was soon flourishing in western Iran and Transoxania, i.e., the lands across the Oxus River, now known as the Amu Darya. The Hanafi school, which allows more room than other schools for independent reasoning (*ijtihad*), still has many followers today in India, Pakistan, Turkey and Central Asia, as well as in Arab lands.

The Hanafi school won much of its original popularity by adopting a Murjiite teaching that held out a clear tax advantage for newly converted Muslims. The Murjiites, an Islamic sect, believed that full membership in the *umma* (the Muslim community) depended only on the formal profession of faith (*shahada*) and not on actually discharging the religious obligations of Islam, e.g., paying annual alms (*zakat*). Consequently, new converts to Islam, who were trying to avoid paying the heavy tax imposed on them by the ruling Umayyad dynasty, were quickly attracted to the Hanafi school and its laws.[16]

After a successful career in the silk trade, Abu Hanifah first studied theology but then turned to law. For some 18 years, he was a student of the famous Iraqi jurist Hammad; when Hammad died in 738, Abu Hanifah took his place. This pattern of students emulating their teachers would become a familiar one in Islamic jurisprudence. Founders of a school did not create their own doctrines by themselves. They stood on the shoulders of those who had gone before and were intellectually (and probably emotionally) closely tied to their predecessors. As one contemporary Muslim writer put it, later doctrines clung to the reputation of a revered predecessor "as ivy entwines the powerful trunk of the oak."[17]

Abu Hanifah also traveled extensively and profited from contacts within the intellectual circles of his region. His school would grow up in Baghdad, the greatest city of the Abbasid dynasty. He did not write any books on law but dictated his opinions to his disciples, who recorded them. Thanks to his intelligence, scholarly background and worldly experience, he was inspired to undertake a formidable task — developing a uniform code for Islamic law.

Over the years, this law had become extremely complex and contradictory. Earlier efforts to put Muslim doctrines into practice had resulted in a confusing corpus of diverse legal doctrines. Abu Hanifah's greatest achievement was to strike a new balance between specific legal problems, on the one hand, and broad legal doctrines, on the other.

Before he tackled this problem, legal doctrines were usually developed only after jurists had come across specific problems that required new solutions. Abu Hanifah established the groundwork for solving new problems that seemed likely to arise in the future. He did this by looking for the *legal principles* inherent in a case at hand. Once these principles were understood, he reasoned, they could then be applied to future cases as well.

This novel approach greatly enlarged the scope of Islamic law but it also led conservative rivals to criticize Abu Hanifah for being too free in his personal legal reasoning (*ra'y*). Nevertheless, his fame is solidly based. One of his scholarly contemporaries, for example, offered this assessment:

> All men of *fiqh* [literally "understanding," i.e., formal juristic thinking — the discipline whereby scholars explore and describe the *sharia*] are Abu Hanifah's children.... I would not have acquired anything of knowledge had it not been for my teacher. All men of knowledge are children of the *ulama* [religious scholars or, more broadly, the Islamic leadership], who were the disciples of Kufa, and they were the disciples of Abu Hanifah.[18]

His fame continues today. A modern scholar, Zafar Ishaq Ansari, has written: "His legal acumen and juristic strictness were such that Abu Hanifah reached the highest level of legal thought achieved up to his time."[19] While joining in the general praise for Abu Hanifah, the German Arabist Joseph

Schacht pointed out what may have been his only failing. Since Abu Hanifah was not a judge, he was not restricted by the practical realities of dispensing justice on a daily basis. Schacht concluded that while Abu Hanifah was "a theoretical systematizer who achieved considerable progress in technical legal thought," his legal reasoning was "often somewhat ruthless and unbalanced, with little regard for practice."[20]

Fame had its price. Abu Hanifah opposed both the ruling Umayyad and Abbasid dynasties, favoring what would later become a Shiite point of view. He consistently refused to become a judge (*qadi*) because such an official post would have made him part of these dynasties, which he considered to be impious. Although he was persecuted by both of them, he adamantly refused to compromise his principles. Late in life, he was jailed in Baghdad because he refused to agree that an aspiring political candidate was indeed the rightful caliph. He also rejected this man's proposed bribe — to make Abu Hanifah the senior judge of the land. Because of his refusal to give in, Abu Hanifah is said to have been poisoned. He died in prison at the age of 70 and was buried there. A dome was built over his tomb in 1066; the Baghdad quarter around it is still named in his honor.

Bridging the Gap Between Authorities: Malik ibn Anas (c. 715–795)

Not much personal information survives about Malik ibn Anas himself, who was known as the Imam of Medina. His major book, entitled *Al-Muwatta* (*The Beaten Path*), is the oldest surviving compendium on Islamic law. It is a full account of the customary laws and religious practices of Medina, where Malik lived and worked and where he believed the memory of the prophet's life was most accurately preserved. In cases where neither the traditional reports of Muhammad's life nor local consensus (*ijma*) offered solutions, Malik relied on legal reasoning by analogy (*qiyas*) instead. This approach, he felt, best provided a smooth or beaten path to the truth — hence the title of his book. The consensus of local legal opinion was so important to him that, in cases of conflict, he held that it should even take precedence over *hadith*.

Malik was one of the first to try to bridge the gaps between three disparate sources of authority: local doctrines, local scholars, and the reported teachings of the prophet. To see how he approached this task, let us consider two problems — one involving contracts, and the other slaves.

Concerning contracts, the prophet was alleged to have said: "Each of the parties to a contract of sale has the option against the other party as long as they have not separated."[21] Traditionally, what this meant in practice was that all parties to a contract that had been formally offered and formally accepted still retained the right to reject this agreement as long as the process of negotiations was continuing. Malik, however, felt otherwise. "Here in Medina," he said, "we have no such known limit and no established practice for this." His position was that a contract was both complete and binding as soon as mutual agreement had been reached — even though a Prophetic *hadith* held otherwise.

A more complicated case involves the sale of slaves.[22] Malik fires his opening salvo by quoting a statement attributed to Caliph Umar: "If a slave who has property is sold, the property of the slave belongs to the seller unless the buyer stipulates that it shall belong to him." Malik goes on to show that Medinan doctrine, i.e., the dominant line of thought in Medina, was that a slave owns his own property. For this reason, both the slave himself and his property can legally be sold at the same time, i.e., in a single transaction and for a single price.

This point of view was important because of a rival doctrine then current in Kufa. Kufan doctrine held that a slave was legally incapable of ownership. Thus the slave and his property were considered as two separate items, both of which belonged to the master of the slave. The problem here was that Islamic law provided that in the case of composite sales, i.e., when two or more separate items are sold at the same time, the price of each must be determined individually and must be clearly known to both buyer and seller. Failing this, under a strict interpretation of the *riba* (usury) rules mentioned earlier, any proposed transaction would be void because it violated the doctrine of "uncertainty" (*gharar*). The Islamic jurist Ibn Mazm, who died in 1064 and who will be discussed later, defined such uncertainty as existing when "the buyer does not know what he bought, or the seller does not know what he sold."

For Malik, on the other hand, the slave and his property constituted a single unit that could legally be transferred simultaneously at one price, provided that buyer and seller so agreed. It was important, however, that both acknowledged that this transaction would take place under the Medinan and not the Kufan doctrine.

Malik also pioneered a literary tradition that was to become a lasting feature of Islamic law.[23] His *Muwatta* is divided into several "books," i.e., chapters, which are based on major branches of the law (marriage, contracts, penal law, etc.). The contents of a given book, however, are not logically organized but consist instead of a disparate collection of individual topics and individual rules. This confusing format arose because Islamic law was recorded as it evolved, bit by bit, during the Umayyad dynasty: it did not flow from the top down, i.e., from generally accepted legal principles. This eighth-century methodology became so embedded in Islamic law that it would continue to be used by jurists until modern times.

Malik became famous for his legal knowledge and did not shy away from the political arena. During a Shiite revolt against the local ruler, Caliph al-Mansur, Malik stated publicly that, during such a rebellion, loyalty to the caliph was not a religious imperative because it had been given only under duress, i.e., to avoid punishment. The caliph was infuriated. When he was finally restored to power after the uprising, he had Malik flogged for this subversive utterance. Ironically, however, the beating only increased Malik's personal prestige. Probably because of this, he was later restored to official favor under a new central government: Caliph al-Rashid visited him during the pilgrimage (*hajj*) of 795.

The Maliki school developed in the Arabian peninsula and then spread to the Persian Gulf, Egypt, the Sudan, and North Africa. It held extremely conservative views on the status of women. Moreover, unlike other legal schools, it intolerantly rejected the Shiite points of view. It also refused any deviation from the path of orthodoxy and continually stressed the legal importance of consensus (*ijma*).[24]

Determining the Proper Basis for Legal Rulings: Muhammad al-Shaybani (d. 804)

This eminent Hanafi jurist wrote the first major Islamic treatise on the law of nations and is often called the Hugo Grotius of Islam.[25] (In 1625, Grotius, a Dutch jurist, published a definitive work, *Of laws of war and peace*, in which he presented his theory of just war.) Al-Shaybani was also the first legal scholar to hold that no legal ruling can be valid unless it is solidly based on a binding text of the Quran or on a Prophetic *hadith*. He stressed the importance of scholarly consensus, going so far as to declare that "Whatever the Muslims [i.e., Muslim jurists] see as good is good in the eyes of God, and whatever they see as bad is bad in the eyes of God."[26] The reports left by Muhammad's Companions still had some value for al-Shaybani but they were clearly relegated to a secondary position.[27]

Although a vast body of work was piously attributed to al-Shaybani, its legal substance is less important than the underlying lesson to be drawn from it. In al-Shaybani's day, the concept of a book written by a single author did not exist. Instead, a disciple of a revered jurist would collect and eventually commit to writing the teachings of his master, adding his own comments. This compilation would then be passed down from one disciple to another, each of whom added his own thoughts, until at last a final version came into being and was attributed solely to the revered jurist himself.[28]

Western scholars once held that because so much work had been attributed to him, al-Shaybani must have played a decisive role in developing the doctrines of the Hanafi school. If so, it thus appeared that he was instrumental in advancing Islamic legal thought as a whole. It is now believed, however, that for the reasons given above he could not possibly have done so by himself. Confirming this judgment, Hanafi biographers do not accord him their highest legal honors.

The "Renewer of Islam": Muhammad ibn Idris al-Shafi'i (767–820)

Al-Shafi'i, an outstanding jurist, was the eponym (one after whom something is named) rather than the founder of the Shafi'i school of law. He was the first Islamic scholar to lay down a clear system of legal reasoning. A modern translator, Majid Khadduri, tells us that "The impress of his systematic method, which has never been superseded in Islam, has remained permanent."[29] His influence was so great that he was considered by his followers to have been the "renewer of Islam" (*mujaddid*) for his era. (A *hadith* says that God sends to the world one such renewer at the beginning of each century.) Al-Shafi'i's successors had little choice but to follow his commanding lead.[30]

During Islam's second century, i.e., during al-Shafi'i's era, legal theory was dominated by two concepts that were frequently in conflict with each other. The first was the common religious practices of the Islamic community. The second was the authority of the traditions (*hadith*) associated with Muhammad himself. Al-Shafi'i came down firmly on the side of the traditions. He held that they were a source of the divine will and complemented the Quran. It followed, then, that they could not be negated by any objective criticism of their contents. Unless a tradition could somehow be shown inauthentic, it was binding on the faithful.[31]

Little hard information about al-Shafi'i's early life has survived. Legend has it that as a young man he was both a good student and an excellent archer, able to hit the bulls-eye in nine out of 10 shots — or sometimes even with every shot. One day a tribal elder, who was watching him shoot, told him that he was a better scholar than an archer. Al-Shafi'i thereafter gave up archery and devoted himself entirely to study.

As he grew older, he became a cautious, ascetic man. When asked a question about Islam, it was his custom never to answer immediately. On being asked why he would not speak, he would reply: "Not until I know which is better: to keep silent or to speak."[32] On one occasion, his pupils bought a slave girl to spend the night with him. She waited in vain throughout the night for al-Shafi'i to come to her bed but he continued his studies, alone, in another part of the house. In the morning, she complained to the slave dealer that it had sold her to a "crazy man." When al-Shafi'i heard this, he replied: "Crazy is he who knows the value of knowledge, and who then squanders it, or hesitates so that it passes him by."[33]

Al-Shafi'i's school flourished in Egypt (his monumental tomb in Cairo became a center of popular piety) but by the tenth century it was also well established in Syria, Saudi Arabia, Iraq, East Africa and Southeast Asia. Al-Shafi'i himself did not invent bold concepts but rather synthesized into a coherent whole many ideas that were already current in learned circles. His conclusions are contained in his major work, *al-Risala* ("the epistle") or, to use its formal title, the *Treatise on the Foundations of Islamic Jurisprudence*, which he wrote in Cairo during the five years before his death. It is called the "epistle" because al-Shafi'i is said to have sent it to a leading traditionalist in Basra, who had asked him to write a long treatise on the authoritative sources of the *sharia*.[34]

The *Risala* soon became a required textbook for students of Islamic law and a favorite subject for commentaries written by later jurists. (For a good sample of his thought, see Appendix 1: Al-Shafi'i's Views on Legal Knowledge.) *Al-Risala* is important in historical terms as well: it contains the first general account of the methodology of relating law to revealed texts.[35] His book is based on one fundamental postulate: that for every act performed by a believer, a statute (*hukm*) exists somewhere in the divine law.[36] Even if this statute is not readily apparent, it can, by definition, always be discovered by careful research. It will either exist explicitly in the Quran or *sunna*, or it can be unearthed through analogical reasoning (*qiyas*).

Al-Shafi'i's insistence on such legal proof has traditionally led Muslim scholars to acknowledge him as the father of Islamic jurisprudence. The British scholar N.J. Coulson supported this evaluation, judging that

> the grandeur of the role he assumed and the force of intellect he brought to bear upon its implementation mark him out as the colossus of Islamic legal history. His supreme purpose was the unification of the law, his method of neutralising the forces of disintegration the exposition of a firm theory of the sources from which the law must be derived.[37]

Al-Shafi'i mastered the full range of Islamic jurisprudence by studying in the Arabian Peninsula (Mecca and Medina), Iraq, Syria, Yemen, and Egypt. These experiences gave him the background necessary to address one of the essential legal and theological questions of his time: what is the proper relationship between the *sunna* and the Quran itself?

His answer, put forward in the *Risala*, is that since the *sunna* reflects the actual implementation of the prophet's teachings as expressed in the Quran, the *sunna* has a holy quality too. Thus, al-Shafi'i insists, Islamic law must be based on *both* the Quran and the *sunna*. Subsequently, the expression "the Quran and the *sunna*" came into scholarly use to define these two sources of doctrinal authority for Sunni Islam.

Al-Shafi'i also affirmed that there are four major "roots" or principles (*usul al-fiqh*) of Islamic law. As mentioned earlier, these are the Quran; social and legal traditions (*sunna*); scholarly consensus (*ijma*); and legal reasoning by analogy (*qiyas*). The Quran is the most important of the "roots" of Islamic law because it is the word of God Himself. However, its repeated commandment that the faithful must "obey God and his Prophet" proved to al-Shafi'i that the *sunna*, which reflected the life of Muhammad, was the second-most important source of law.

Al-Shafi'i argued that traditionalist scholars were wrong when they claimed that since Muhammad was only human, any of his rulings that conflicted with the Quran could safely be ignored. Instead, al-Shafi'i insisted that the Quranic injunctions to "obey God and his Prophet" and to follow "the Book [the Quran] and the Wisdom [i.e., recognizing and accepting the mercy of God]" could only mean that all of Muhammad's actions and all of his legal decisions were themselves divinely inspired. Indeed, they thus represented what could be called the "living-out-in-practice" of the teachings of the Quran. They must therefore be obeyed. Al-Shafi'i accordingly concluded that Islamic law must be based on *both* the Quran and the *sunna*.

There was, however, a hidden problem lurking within this succinct formulation. As already mentioned, a large number of later and spurious *hadith* had been backdated and ascribed to the prophet himself. This process resulted in frequent, serious conflicts between some of these *hadith* and the text of the Quran itself. How could such conflicts be overcome?

Al-Shafi'i resolved this problem by drawing on the doctrine of abrogation (*naskh*), which is based on two rules: the Quran can be abrogated only by the Quran, and the *sunna* can be abrogated only by the *sunna*.[38] The Quran can be abrogated by the Quran if, for example, the verse in question is thought to be *later than* an earlier version and thus can be said to supersede it. The Quran cannot be abrogated by the *sunna* because, by al-Shafi'i's definition, the task of the *sunna* is to *interpret* the Quran, not to contradict it.

The *sunna*, for its part, cannot be abrogated by the Quran because, if it could be, its own role as the interpreter of the Quran would therefore be nullified. In upholding the importance of the *sunna*, al-Shafi'i was actually making a point in his long running battle with earlier scholars. They had claimed that the validity of *hadith* (part of the *sunna*) depended entirely on their *not contradicting* the Quran.

To see how, under al-Shafi'i's concept of the principles of Islamic law, apparent contradictions can be resolved by abrogation, let us take the issue of bequests. This problem involves three conflicting texts.[39] The first is a verse from the Quran ordering that bequests should be made in favor of close relatives. The second are Quranic verses on the law of succession (the *fara'id* verses on "duty" or "obligation") that give specific portions of an estate to relatives. The third is a Prophetic *hadith* that states: "No bequest in favor of an heir."

Now, the Quranic verse on bequests does not abrogate *hadith* prohibiting bequests to an heir, and vice versa: as stated above, the Quran can be abrogated only by the Quran, and the *sunna* can be abrogated only by the *sunna*. It is therefore up to *hadith* to explain the *fara'id* verses of the Quran. *Hadith* can in fact do this under the following interpretation: whatever balance is worked out between the competing claims of various relatives must not be jeopardized by an additional bequest to any one of them. In effect, then, the *fara'id* verses abrogate the first Quranic verse commanding bequests, at least as it applies to relatives entitled to portions of the estate.

Scholarly consensus (*ijma*) was important in al-Shafi'i's campaign to make Islamic law more uniform. He rejected the idea that the consensus of local scholars in a given community, e.g., those in Medina, could ever apply to the Muslim community as a whole. He argued instead that the only valid consensus was that of *all* Muslim lawyers and laymen — in other words, the community of Muslims as a whole. Al-Shafi'i identified four kinds of consensus, ranging from the most to the least reliable. The best, in his view, was the unanimous or partial consensus of the Companions of the prophet. Next, in descending order, was the respective consensus of the second, third, and subsequent generations.[40]

Al-Shafi'i's fourth and final source of Islamic law is legal reasoning by analogy (*qiyas*). Such reasoning must be based on the Quran, on the *sunna*, or on consensus. It is, in short, completely dependent on these sources and cannot be used to reach any conclusion that contradicts them. Here again, al-Shafi'i wanted to make Muslim practices more uniform. He rejected other forms of reasoning, i.e., personal legal reasoning or juristic preference, because they inevitably led to a plethora of conflicting doctrines. This is how Al-Shafi'i summarized his own legal theory:

> On points on which there exists an explicit decision of God or a sunna of the Prophet or a consensus of the Muslims, no disagreement is allowed; on other points scholars must exert their own judgment (ijtihad) in search of an indication in one of these three sources.... If a problem is capable of two solutions,

either opinion may be held as result of systematic reasoning (qiyas); but this occurs only rarely.[41]

Personal Courage and Legal Orthodoxy: Ahmad ibn Hanbal (780–855)

The Hanbali school is named after Ahmad ibn Hanbal, a famous Sunni jurist and collector of *hadith*. This school emerged in Baghdad as an orthodox reaction against what its adherents denounced as the speculative innovations and excesses of the other schools. The Hanbali school soon spread to northern Iraq, Syria and Iran. Although it was much smaller than the other schools, the Hanbali school was very influential and made a strong impact on Islamic law though its eloquent insistence on upholding traditionalist patterns of thought. Two of Ibn Hanbal's most important later followers were Ibn Taymiyya (1263–1328) and Muhammad ibn Abd al-Wahhab (1703–1792). These men are among the founding fathers of Islamic fundamentalism; both will be discussed later.

Known as the "Imam of Baghdad," Ibn Hanbal himself was so careful that he is alleged never to have eaten watermelons, which grew well in the hot sun and alluvial soils of Iraq, because he did not have any Prophetic teachings on this particular food.[42] He has been praised in modern times as "one of the most vigorous personalities of Islam, which he has profoundly influenced both in its historical development and in its modern revival."[43] He is remembered in the Muslim world today not only for his great learning but also for his personal courage and for his staunch religious orthodoxy.

The seeds of Ibn Hanbal's conflict with the government were planted in 825, when the ruling caliph, al-Ma'mun, endorsed Mutazili teachings. This movement and line of thought urged Muslims to adopt the rationalist approaches of the Greek philosophers (which were then available in Arabic translations) in order to combat the spread of Manichaeism, a dualistic religion originating in Iran. Mutazali doctrine held, among other radical doctrines, that the Quran was a "created" work, i.e., that it was not, as traditionalists had always believed, the uncreated eternal word of God.

In 833, al-Ma'mun required that all his subjects abandon their traditional views and adhere instead to Mutazili teachings. He set himself up as the sole steward of true belief, explaining to the governor of Iraq,

That which God has laid upon the imams of the Muslims, their Khalifs [leaders], is to be zealous in the maintenance of the religion of God ... in the inheritance of prophecy which he has granted them to inherit ... to act justly, also in those interests of his subjects over which God by his grace and bounty has appointed him to have rule.[44]

To make sure his wish was carried out, al-Ma'mun assigned this task to his chief of police, who set up an inquisition that would continue for about 20 years. Ibn Hanbal, however, refused to abandon his orthodox views and insisted that, contrary to the Mutazili party line, the Quran was in fact "uncreated." The government had him chained, flogged repeatedly, and jailed for two years. But even so, Ibn Hanbal would not give in, nor would he take refuge in the Shiite doctrine of dissimulation (*taqiyah*), which permits a Muslim who is under great duress to pretend to agree with a false doctrine — while secretly maintaining his real beliefs. This remains an important doctrine for Shiites. If need be, they can invoke it when they are being persecuted, e.g., in Saudi Arabia today.

Later caliphs continued to persecute Ibn Hanbal. It is said that on one occasion he was beaten by 150 floggers, each of whom struck him twice. He survived this ordeal but carried to his grave the scars of the wounds thus inflicted on him. Despite his sufferings, he reiterated that he would never change his conservative beliefs unless presented with truly authoritative reasons (that is to say, those drawn from the Quran or from the *sunna*) why he should do so. These reasons the caliphs could not, of course, supply.

When the inquisition finally ended in 848, the traditionalists, exemplified by Ibn Hanbal, emerged victorious; the rationalists were defeated. Nevertheless, the respective positions staked out by these two sides were so extreme that in the end they did not attract the silent majority of rank and file Muslims. These men tacitly opted for a centrist midpoint and were later called "the middle of the roaders." It was from this compromise position that mainstream Sunni doctrine began to emerge.[45]

Pious legend assures us that Ibn Hanbal memorized "a million *hadith*." From these and other traditional sources, he wrote the *Musnad* (*Traditions of the Prophet Muhammad*), a collection of some 29,000 *hadith*.[46] From these he chose the most reliable, i.e., those whose "chain of transmission" (*isnad*) was unbroken and could be traced all the way back to Muhammad himself.

To mix a modern metaphor, an *isnad* is an exclusively oral transmission that can be thought of as a *verbal* paper trail. It usually took this literary form: "I was told by A, who received this report from B, on the authority of C, who learned it from D, who was told by E [one of Muhammad's Companions], that the Prophet said..." An early Muslim scholar, al-Mubarak, explained the overriding importance of *isnad* by drawing a striking parallel: "One who studies his religion without an *isnad* is like the one who attempts to ascend a roof without a ladder."[47]

Ironically, despite its conservative bent, Hanbali law endorsed the concept of individual freedom in arranging contracts.[48] This freedom, the Hanbalis argued, applied to marriage and to the rights of women as well. The reason for their apparent liberalism on this point was that, unlike other schools of thought, the Hanbalis considered the traditional Islamic texts to be the only valid sources of law. They thus attached overriding importance to the Quranic injunction, "Muslims must abide by their stipulations." For them, any agreement entered into voluntarily by a husband and his wife as part of their marriage contract was therefore valid and enforceable, provided that it did not contain any provisions expressly prohibited by Muslim law or clearly contrary to the institution of Islamic marriage.

What this meant in practice was that since these undertakings were not expressly forbidden or contrary to the institution of marriage, a man was free to have more than one wife and a woman was free to engage in social or professional activities on her own. This Hanbali doctrine had such a great appeal for Muslim reformers in the nineteenth and twentieth centuries that it was adopted, in varying degrees, by many Arab countries.

Ibn Hanbal himself worked strictly within the framework of Islamic traditions but broke so much new ground that he is regarded as one of the few men authorized, by virtue of their encyclopedic knowledge, to use independent reasoning (*ijtihad*). Writing in Cairo in 1931, Ibn al-Djawzi, a Muslim scholar, tells us that "certain positions adopted by Ibn Hanbal are supported by him on traditions with such consummate skill as few have equalled, and certain of his decisions bear witness to a juridical subtlety without parallel."[49]

Choices for the Enemy and the Role of Women in Battle: Muslim ibn al-Hajjaj (c. 817–875)

Muslim ibn al-Hajjaj, traditionally referred to simply as "Muslim," was an Islamic scholar who assembled a canonical work containing 300,000 *hadith* that he had personally collected in Arabia, Egypt, Syria and Iraq. Known as *al-Sahih* (literally the "healthy, i.e., the true or genuine version), this book was an encyclopedic guide to all aspects of Sunni life. Although Western scholars regard many of Muslim's *hadith* on legal topics to be later forgeries, these *hadith* are nevertheless extremely important for the study of Islam. Muslims today still consider *hadith* to be second only to the Quran as a source of information about their faith. They cannot be neglected if one wants to reach a full understanding of Islam today.

The following *hadith*, which has been lightly edited, records the instructions Muhammad gave to his military commanders in the field. He would tell them:

> Fight in the name of Allah and in the way of Allah. Fight against those who disbelieve in Allah. Make a holy war: do not embezzle the spoils; do not break your

pledge; and do not mutilate the [dead] bodies; do not kill the children. When you meet your enemies who are polytheists, invite them to three courses of action. If they respond to any one of them, you also accept it and withhold yourself from doing them any harm. Invite them to [accept] Islam; if they respond to you, accept it from them and desist from fighting against them.... If they refuse to accept Islam, demand from them the *jizya* [taxes that Christians and Jews had to pay in order to receive protection from their Muslim rulers]. If they agree to pay, accept it from them and hold off your hands. If they refuse to pay the tax, seek Allah's help and fight them.[50]

Perhaps surprisingly, *jihad* appealed to women as well as to their men folk. Another of Muslim's *hadith* tells us that one day a soldier saw a woman, Umm Sulaim, pull out a dagger. He brought her before Muhammad, who asked her, "Why are you holding this dagger?" She replied, "I took it up so that I may tear open the belly of a polytheist who comes near me." Muhammad began to smile at her words and told her there was no reason for her to carry a knife. "Umm Sulaim," he said, "God is sufficient [i.e., He is sufficiently powerful to cope with the polytheists] and He will be kind to us."

This same *hadith* also reports that during one battle, when the sun was so hot that Muslim soldiers were dropping their swords because of faintness, Umm Sulaim and Aisha (Muhammad's favorite wife), at the risk of their own lives, brought water up to the front lines. One soldier remembered that

Both of them had tucked up their garments, so I could see the ankles on their feet. They were carrying water-skins on their backs and would pour water into the mouths of the people. They would then go back [to the well] and fill them again and would return to pour water into the mouths of the soldiers. [On this day], Abu Talha's sword dropped down from his hands twice or thrice because of drowsiness.

An Inflexible Jurist of Islamic Spain: Ibn Hazm (994–1064)

Ibn Hazm was a leading exponent of the Zahiri school of law, a small group of jurists who based their interpretations on a strictly literal (*zahir*) reading of the Quran and *hadith*. He is said to have produced 400 treatises (some 80,000 pages of writing) on a broad range of subjects. Indeed, one of his most remembered works is *The Dove's Neck-Ring* (*Tawq al-Hamama*), a treatise on the art of love.

On the legal front, Ibn Hazm rebelled against the "hidden" or esoteric means that Ismaili scholars purported to find in the Quran and *hadith*. (The Ismailis, headed by the Aga Khan, are a branch and a community of Shiite Islam.) He called instead for a simple piety based on the literal reading of these texts. His line of thought was based on the simple argument that God had revealed the Quran in clear Arabic and that He had used language that conveyed precisely what He wished to say. Not surprisingly, Ibn Hazm therefore rejected other jurist's advocacy of, in his view, meddling with the divine will by using reasoning by analogy (*qiyas*) and having recourse to personal opinion (*ra'y*). He also limited the basis of consensus (*ijma*) to that based on the agreement of the Companions of the prophet, arguing that the agreement of later scholars on a legal question was not by itself a legitimate basis of Islamic law.[51]

Flexibility was never the hallmark of Ibn Hazm's legal thought. He interpreted the teachings of Muslim scriptures so literally that he soon reached the point of absurdity. There is one *hadith*, for example, which states: "Let no one urinate in still, non-running water and then use it to bathe in." From this *hadith*, the modern scholar G.F. Haddad tells us that Ibn Hazm drew the following formal conclusions:

- This interdiction about bathing applies *exclusively to the person who urinated*. It therefore follows that anyone else is free to bathe in that water.
- The *hadith* is applicable only if a person urinates *directly into the water*. If the urine has reached the ground indirectly — for example, by running off the ground or by being poured out of a container — then the water can still be used for bathing.
- This *hadith* applies *only to urination*. Therefore, water that has been used to clean oneself after defecation can still be used for bathing.[52]

"To Promote What Is Right and to Prevent What Is Wrong": Abu Hamid al-Ghazali (1058–1111)

Abu Hamid al-Ghazali's early training was as a jurist but he was also an intellectual, an original thinker, an advocate of Aristotelian logic, a Sufi, and a member of the Asharite school of theology. (Sufism is the mysticism of Islam. The Asharites advocated a synthesis of rationalism and traditionalism.) The Hanbali school of law never forgave al-Ghazali for introducing rationalistic philosophy into Sunnite theology but he was still revered in his own time as an outstanding legal and religious authority.

His great four-volume work, *The Revival of the Religious Sciences (Ihya ulum al-din)*, was written in the last decade of the eleventh century. Consisting of 40 "books," i.e., chapters, it describes the prescriptions of the *sharia* in detail and shows how important it is for Muslims to abide by them in order to achieve salvation.[53] This book was so highly acclaimed by al-Ghazali's contemporaries that they accorded him the honorifics of "Proof of Islam" (*Hujjat al-Islam*) and the "renewer of Islam" (*mujaddid*) of his age.

The *Revival* soon became one of the most frequently cited texts after the Quran and *hadith*. Its greatest achievement was to bring orthodox Sunni theology and Sufi mysticism into a useful, comprehensive guide to every aspect of Muslim life. Another book by al-Ghazali was very influential as well. Entitled *The Incoherence* [or *Inconsistency*] *of the Philosophers*, this argued that Islamic philosophers contracted themselves — and were even heretical — because they not did not abide by the Quran.

Al-Ghazali held that God could not be known by reason alone. He was convinced that only Sufi doctrines and Sufi practices, combined with independent reasoning (*ijtihad*), could keep Islam alive and well. He feared, however, that, if left unchecked and used alone, *ijtihad* would jeopardize traditional Islamic beliefs. It is even claimed that al-Ghazali single-handedly "closed the gate of independent reasoning" and thus cut off the only legitimate wellspring of creative Islamic thought. Was this indeed the case?

The scholarly jury is still out on this point. In the past, many Muslim and Western scholars believed that, by the twelfth century at least, if not even earlier, Sunni jurists had agreed that "the gate of *ijtihad* was closed." At minimum, this meant that no new schools of legal thought could henceforth arise in Sunni Islam. At maximum, it meant that no original thought was now permitted on major doctrinal issues: Sunni scholars were supposed to rely entirely on the past decisions of eminent legal authorities. On the other hand, senior Shiite leaders, e.g., the ayatollahs of Iran who belonged to the Ja'fari school of law, were permitted to interpret the holy texts themselves. Thus for the Shiites the gate of *ijtihad* was never closed.

There is still a vigorous scholarly debate about whether al-Ghazali himself "closed the gate," whether he was simply carrying out a long established policy begun by earlier thinkers, or whether the gate was never closed entirely and is thus still open today. According to James Piscatori, a modern specialist in Islamic thought, the current academic view is something of a halfway house that runs along these lines:

> The door in Sunni jurisprudence was never tightly shut and it was always open to some extent; and the door in Shi'i jurisprudence — supposedly wide open — did not preclude following precedent (*taqlid*).[54]

By the time al-Ghazali wrote his *Revival*, he had lived in Baghdad, Damascus, and Jerusalem.[55] In his wide-ranging travels he had learned the importance of moderation and balance, which he felt were the central features of the "straight path" (*sirat al-mustaqim*) of the Muslim way of life. He was also familiar with the legal and ethical problems inherent in daily life in the bazaars and homes of the big cities. This is where the *sharia* came into daily play. As Basim Musallam, a Cambridge historian of Islam, tells us,

> When we speak of a certain society as Muslim, if we do not mean that Islamic law has formed to a recognizable extent its social institutions..., we do not mean much. The sharia was an ideal system of social morality which constantly pressed to shape society. But it was more than the sum of legal regulations, for it embodied a certain general outlook or attitude, which combined the certainty that God-given truth ought to guide individual lives, with the understanding that right behavior depended primarily on the individual conscience and the need to conform.[56]

With this background in mind, it is instructive to look at *hisba* (literally "accountability"), which is the duty of every Muslim "to promote what is right and to prevent what is wrong" (*Al-amr bi al-maruf wa al-nahy an al-munkar*).[57] This policy is very much alive in Saudi Arabia today, where men, usually referred to by expatriates as the "religious police," make sure that the conservative norms of the kingdom are obeyed in public places. Legal scholars such as al-Ghazali provided the intellectual elaboration of *hisba*: official "market inspectors" (*muhtasib*, i.e., one who practices *hisba*) made sure it was implemented in practice.

The offenses they were supposed to correct included:

- Building balconies on houses or installing benches in front of shops, thereby intruding on public space
- Piling up large amounts of wood or grain in the streets, thus obstructing passage in the narrow spaces of the bazaar
- Slaughtering animals in front of butchers' shops, polluting the street with blood and offal
- Pouring out jars of water onto the street, making it muddy and slippery
- Tethering riding animals longer than necessary, fouling the street with their droppings and restricting passage
- Transporting sharp-edged loads, which could tear people's clothes, through the narrow alleys
- Ogling women outside the women's public baths (a favorite pastime of gangs of teenage boys).

Al-Ghazali endorsed *hisba* as an inherent duty of every Muslim. At the same time, however, he wanted to make sure that overly zealous citizens did not act illegally and thereby infringe on the rights of others. To this end, he drew up an eight-stage "intervention plan" designed to correct offenses with minimum damage to the individuals and social institutions involved. The market inspectors were supposed to work their way patiently through these eight steps before they resorted to violent action:[58]

- Ascertain that the offense in question is in fact a public breach of Islamic law.
- Politely explain to the offender, who might not know the law, that what he is doing, e.g., drinking wine, is illegal.
- Gently counsel a persistent offender, e.g., a confirmed alcoholic, to mend his ways.
- Harshly rebuke a repeat offender who fails to reform.
- Physically halt the prohibited action, e.g., by spilling the drinker's wine.
- Threaten to use force to uphold the law.
- Use the minimum of force — but not weapons — needed to stop the offense.
- Call for weapons and for armed assistance only as a last resort.

This final stage was to be avoided if at all possible because it could easily degenerate into street fighting. When attacked physically, an offender might well respond by calling on his own friends to arm themselves and come to his help. To avoid sectarian violence and civil war, al-Ghazali therefore held that an individual's duty to practice *hisba* did not extend to the unilateral suppression of heresy. He wrote: "The heretic believes he is right, and believes that the man of right belief is wrong; each claims that he is right, and denies that he is a heretic."[59] To keep the peace both within Muslim communities themselves and also in Muslims' dealings with peoples of other faiths, al-Ghazali concluded that only the government, acting on the wishes of the Muslim community (as expressed by its religious scholars) could deal forcibly with heresy.

On the legal front, al-Ghazali was ultimately very much of a conservative. He believed that what an Islamic state desperately needed was "an imam who is obeyed."[60] Only a strong imam, he reasoned, could maintain social and therefore religious order. Ideally, the imam should act within the limits of Islamic law and should do his best to uphold it. Without order, however, both Islam itself and the Islamic community in question would be in grave danger.

Maintaining order was fundamentally a legal process; for al-Ghazali the main job of the imam was therefore to support the legal system. Any imam was better than none: any leader was better than the anarchy and the "confusion of opinions" that would inevitably prevail during political upheavals. An unjust ruler should not be overthrown, al-Ghazali advised, if his fall would lead to civil strife. Indeed, the faithful had a clear duty to obey the ruler of the day, even though in his personal life he might be impious and in his official life oppressive. In al-Ghazali's words,

> We consider that the function of the caliphate is contractually assumed by that person of the Abbasid house [i.e., the Abbasid dynasty] who is charged with it, and that the function of government in the various lands is carried out by means of sultans, who owe allegiance to the caliphate. Government in these days is a consequence solely of military power, and whosoever he may be to whom the possessor of military power gives his allegiance, that person is the caliph.[61]

In the *Revival*, al-Ghazali also wrote about *jihad*. He focused on what can best be called internal *jihad*, that is, to use his own words, "fighting one's own desires" (*jihad al-nafs*). This meant bringing one's own ego firmly under ethical control. For example, in a section of the *Revival* entitled "Book of the training of the ego and the disciplining of manners and the healing of the heart's diseases," al-Ghazali quotes, approvingly, a contemporary religious figure, al-Razi, who gave this advice to the faithful: "Fight against your ego with the four swords of training: eat little, sleep little, speak little, and be patient when people harm you.... Then the ego will walk the path of obedience...."[62]

Contemporary biographical notices state that in the year of his death (1111), al-Ghazali was still deeply engaged in further study of Muslim traditions. The *Encyclopaedia of Islam* judges that "He undoubtedly performed a great service for Muslims of every level of education by presenting obedience to the prescriptions of the *Sharia* as a meaningful way of life."[63]

In Defense of Reason: Ibn Rushd (1126–1198)

Known in the West as Averroës (the Latin version of his name), Ibn Rushd was a Spanish Arab who was a polymath, i.e., a person of encyclopedic learning. He served as the *qadi* of Cordoba and Seville. He tried hard but ultimately unsuccessfully to meld Islam with classical Greek thought by proving that reason was a valid tool for the study of revealed religion.[64]

Refuting the conservative doctrines of al-Ghazali, he insisted that philosophy, i.e., reason, and religion do in fact share the same goal. Ibn Rushd wrote:

> The business of philosophy is nothing other than to look into creation and to ponder over it in order to be guided by the Creator — in other words, to look into the meaning of existence. For the knowledge of creation leads to the cognizance of the Creator, through the knowledge that he created. The more perfect the knowledge of creation, the more perfect becomes the knowledge of the Creator. The Law [*sharia*] encourages and exhorts us to observe creation ... the Law urges us to observe creation by means of reason and demands the knowledge thereof through reason.[65]

Ibn Rushd also cited passages from the Quran extolling the use of reason. Here are two of them:

Will [human beings] not ponder upon the kingdom of the heavens and the earth, and all that God created ... [*sura* 7:184].

Do [human beings] never reflect on the camels, and how they were created? The heaven, how it was raised on high? The mountains, how they were set down? The earth, how it was made flat? [*sura* 88:17].

Ibn Rushd is said to have written more than 20,000 pages on jurisprudence, philosophy and medicine. Eighty-seven of his treaties are still extant. He fell from political favor, however, because he repeatedly crossed swords with powerful conservative Islamic scholars. They declared that he was a heretic. The caliph, who needed the conservatives' support because he was waging a holy war against the Christians in Spain, exiled Ibn Rushd in 1195 and permitted his works on logic and metaphysics to be burned.

Nevertheless, Ibn Rushd's fame lives on. He has been hailed as one of the greatest Muslim thinkers and scientists of the twelfth century. It was through his translations of and commentaries on Aristotle's work that Aristotle's legacy was finally recovered in the West. Ibn Rushd was also a highly regarded legal scholar of the Maliki school and wrote extensively on Maliki law. His book, *The Distinguished Jurist's Primer* (*Bidayat al-Mujtahid*), for example, prepared jurists to become scholars of Islamic thought who are permitted to use independent reasoning on doctrinal issues. Such men are known as *mujtahids*.

Ibn Rushd used independent reasoning (*ijtihad*) himself. Under traditional Islamic law, there were two kinds of homicide — intentional and unintentional. The penalty for the former was retaliation or payment of blood money; for the latter, blood money plus some act of charity, e.g., freeing a slave or feeding the poor.[66]

An intentional homicide occurred in Cordoba in 1122.[67] The victim was survived not only by three young children of his own but also by a brother who had two adult sons. The murderer admitted his guilt and, at the instigation of the victim's brother and his sons, was put to death. The fact that he was drunk when he committed the murder was held to be irrelevant. This death penalty was fully in accord with classic Maliki doctrine. According the Malikis, if the children of the murder victim, who were the primary heirs, were minors, the right to demand punishment automatically passed to the adult agnates (paternal kinsmen).

Ibn Rushd, however, issued a *fatwa* stating that this case should not have been settled until the victim's children were of age. Reasoning by analogy (*qiyas*), Ibn Rushd began by citing two Quranic verses. The first was *sura* 17:33: "If a man is slain unjustly, his heir shall be entitled to satisfaction. But let him not carry his vengeance to excess, for his victim is sure to be assisted and avenged." This statement, however, is ambiguous because the "heir" is not defined. The second verse (*sura* 2:178) was ambiguous too: "He who is pardoned by his aggrieved [or murdered] brother shall be prosecuted according to usage and shall pay him a liberal fine." Here, "he" is unclear: does it refer to the agnates of the victim or to the murderer himself?

Ibn Rushd resolved this confusion by citing a Prophetic *hadith*: "The victim's kin may opt for the death penalty or may pardon the murderer and receive blood money." This indicated that only the wishes of the agnates, not those of the murderer himself, were relevant. A central question, though, remained unanswered here: who was entitled to demand the murderer's punishment or payment of blood money — the children of the victim or his brother?

Arguing in support of the children's rights, Ibn Rushd drew analogies with other area of the law that held that the children's rights should be protected until they reached majority. By a series of intricate steps in Quranic and legal logic too detailed to be recounted here, he challenged a fundamental assumption of this case — that retaliation was inherently better than compensation or forgiveness. He claimed that a consensus had been reached on the idea that a lesser punishment, not the death penalty, might actually be more appropriate here. If so, he reasoned, the children should be allowed to become adults before making their own decision: they might well have decided to pardon the murderer.

Ibn Rushd based this ruling on his responsibility as a jurist to apply his full intelligence to a case at hand, not just to follow precedent. He defended himself against critics in these words:

> [The critics] did not understand what lay behind my opinion, and they thought that the jurisconsult [a man very learned in the law] must not abandon the authoritative doctrine applicable to the case. But what they thought is incorrect, for the jurisconsult must not follow a doctrine, nor issue legal opinions according to it, unless he knows that it is sound.... The doctrine contrary to which I have issued a legal opinion runs counter to the fundamental principles of Islamic jurisprudence.... Accordingly, sound reasoning requires one to abandon the [traditional] doctrine in favor of that which is more appropriate, especially in view of the fact that the killer was intoxicated when he committed the crime.[68]

Ibn Rushd's *fatwa* was later adopted by the Maliki school and appeared in its law manuals. Moreover, together with other important *fatwas*, it was gradually assimilated into the mainstream of Islamic law. This was only one of Ibn Rushd's many achievements. Summing up his varied and stellar career, a contemporary scholar reported that:

> He excelled in the Law, heard *hadith*, mastered medicine, and embraced speculative theology and philosophy until his erudition became proverbial in the latter.

He authored works together with intellectual brilliance and diligent work night and day. He authored numerous works in jurisprudence, medicine, logic, mathematics, [and] theology.[69]

Even Sultans Are Not Above the Sharia: *Ibn Abd al-Zahir (fl. 1260–1277)*

Ibn Abd al-Zahir was the head chancery clerk of the Mamluk sultan Baybars I (1223–1277).[70] He was an eyewitness to the events of Baybars' reign and wrote, for the royal library, a hagiography (an idealizing or idolizing biography) of the sultan. This consists of about 400 pages extolling the sultan's many virtues and chronicling his numerous achievements. Ibn Abd al-Zahir successfully depicted his patron as the ideal Islamic ruler. This was no small feat because Baybars had come to power by treacherously murdering his own patron, who was Sultan Qutuz, the third Mamluk sultan.

The story of Baybars' accession is of some interest. Having just defeated a Mongol army in Palestine, Baybars expected to be rewarded with the town of Aleppo, Syria. Sultan Qutuz refused to give it to him. Soon thereafter, Baybars approached the sultan and asked him instead for the gift of a captive Mongol girl. The sultan agreed, and Baybars kissed his hand in thanks. This submissive gesture was, however, the prearranged signal for Baybar's troops to attack the sultan. Baybars stabbed the sultan in the neck with a sword and killed him, thus becoming the fourth Mamluk sultan. (Baybars himself would die in Damascus in 1277 after drinking a cup of poison intended for someone else.)[71]

In his biography, Ibn Abd al-Zahir devotes several chapters to presenting Baybars as the ideal Muslim ruler, hailing his abolition of taxes not sanctioned by the *sharia*, his restoration of the palace of justice, and his insistence on paying for the goods he ordered for use on his military campaigns. A chapter on the sultan's meritorious upholding of the *sharia* contains the following anecdote.

Before he became sultan, Baybars had ordered that a well be dug for the poor. While he was in exile, a common soldier set to work and dug the well. The soldier eventually got into an argument with the intended beneficiaries of the well over who actually owned it. Baybars, who by this time had become sultan, had the man brought before him. The soldier demanded judgment according to the *sharia*. A trial was therefore arranged in the palace of justice. Ibn Abd al-Zahir tells us that when the soldier appeared, the chief judge said to the sultan:

> "Let my lord betake himself with him to the Holy Law." So the sultan arose, ungirt his sword, and placed himself on an equality with his opponent, standing before the chief judge, who was seated.

Ibn Abd al-Zahir adds that scholars of the four law schools agreed that, under the provisions of the *sharia*, the sultan was in fact the legal owner of the well but that he must pay the soldier for his labor and for the fittings used in the well. Baybars agreed and, to assure good feelings on all sides, then gave fine robes to the official in charge of the palace of justice, to the chief judge and his servant, and to the solider himself.[72]

Regulating the Whole Range of Human Activities: Muhyi al-Din al-Nawawi (d. 1277)

We have already mentioned and quoted from *Al-Minhaj*, the legal text-book and reference book written by the Syrian scholar Muhyi al-Din al-Nawawi, who died in 1277.[73] This work, which followed the doctrines of the Shafi'i school, was translated into French and published in 1882 by the government of the Netherlands Indies (today's Indonesia) for use in Islamic courts there. *Al-Minhaj* consists of 71 chapters, each dealing with a specific subject. A partial listing of these subjects shows that this book was designed to cope with legal problems arising from the whole range of human activities.[74] They include:

- Ritual purity: forms and causes of impurity, how to remove impurity, and prohibitions to be observed while in this state.
- Bodily functions: prescribed forms of washing and bathing.
- Prayer
- Funeral ceremonies
- Annual alms (*zakat*)
- Commercial transactions: Islamic banking, sales and barter, pledges, bankruptcy, partnership, companies, land holding, rent, sharecropping, hiring, and the succession and distribution of estates.
- Marriage and divorce.
- Crime and criminal penalties.
- Poll tax (*jizya*) for non–Muslims.
- Food prohibitions.
- Hunting.
- Competitions.
- Oaths and vows.
- Administration of justice: court procedure, witnesses and evidence.
- Slaves and manumission.

Under each of these headings, *Al-Minhaj* lists the Shafi'i rules, exceptions, special cases, and related legal doctrines. An interesting point here is the great importance of the *spoken word* in early Islamic law. Although literacy was the hallmark of the educated classes, buyers and sellers nevertheless had to utter certain specific phrases in order for a contract of sale, for example, to be binding. The seller was required to say, "I sell you item X" or "I make you owner of item X." The buyer then had to reply, "I buy item X" or "I accept the ownership of item X." In case of a later dispute about this transaction, each party sought witnesses who could confirm, orally, his point of view. The last resort for buyer and seller was to swear formal oaths that they were telling the truth.[75]

The First Ayatollah: The Allama al-Hilli (1250–1325)

The Shiite scholar known as the Allama al-Hilli (this honorific means "the most learned one from Hilla," a town on the Euphrates River), was instrumental in establishing Twelver Shiite law.[76] He was the first Shiite scholar to be awarded the title of Ayatollah, meaning "God's sign," and his grave in Mashhad, Iran, is still visited by Shiite pilgrims today.

Al-Hilli provided a sturdy legal foundation for the hitherto disputed principle of reaching binding rulings based on independent reasoning (*ijtihad*). He believed that the reasoning of a duly qualified jurist was capable of providing valid judgments on religious matters. In other words, it was not essential — as Sunni jurists asserted — that rational inquiry be limited only to traditional points of view. Instead, the Twelver Shiites upheld the rationalistic principle of "reasoned argument in matters of revelation."

Al-Hilli's most important work is entitled *The Points of Departure From Which Knowledge of the Principles is Attained (Mabadi al-wusul ila ilm al-usul)*. Its most important point for our purposes here is its handling of *ijtihad*. This is defined as "the utmost exertion of the faculties to speculate on those questions of law which are subject to conjecture." But *ijtihad* is fallible: al-Hilli warns us that "sometimes it is wrong, sometimes right."

It therefore followed for al-Hilli that any legal scholar resorting to *ijtihad* must be exceptionally intelligent, exceptionally well trained, and exceptionally careful. Such a jurist must know unequivocally what is set forth as revealed law: this cannot be altered. He must also be a complete master of the Arabic language and all its subtleties. It is not absolutely necessary that he know the entire Quran by heart, but he certainly must know by heart the 500 verses that refer to laws. He must also know the appropriate *hadith* and where to find them in large collections. Finally, he must be familiar with the prevailing consensus (*ijma*) of his era, lest his own rulings conflict with it.

Given these stiff requirements, *ijtihad* is clearly not for the common man. As al-Hilli puts it, "If the vast majority [of the people] were burdened with *ijtihad* in [legal] questions, the world order would consequently be disturbed and everyone would be more concerned with discussing [juristic] problems than with his livelihood."[77] Not having the time, ability or training to judge for himself, the layman must therefore follow the teachings of a learned authority. To quote the al-Hilli again,

> If two [Islamic scholars] are of equal worth in seeking expert opinion, he should choose the one he wants; if one of the two is superior in every respect this is the one he must follow; if neither of them excels the other in a particular point it is best to keep to the word of the most knowledgeable.[78]

Yet despite their best efforts, scholars can and do err, unlike the prophet and unlike Shiite imams. Is a layman, then, still obliged to follow their possibly mistaken teachings? Under the doctrine that "every *mujtahid* is right" (as noted earlier, a *mujtahid* is a scholar of Islamic law who is permitted to use independent reasoning on doctrinal issues), the answer is yes: their teachings must be obeyed. The decisions of a given *mujtahid* are potentially fallible but, given the continued absence of the infallible Twelfth (Hidden) Imam, they must be considered valid as long as that *mujtahid* is still alive.

"A Kink in the Brain": Ibn Taymiyya (1263–1328)

Ibn Taymiyya was a member of the late Hanbali school of jurisprudence and has always been a very controversial figure. He was certain that religious truth could never be attained by logic alone: for him, the intellect always had to take second place to revelation. A staunch upholder of Sunni traditionalism, he disliked both the liberal emotionalism of the Sufis and the unorthodox practices of the Shiites. Ibn Taymiyya claimed that both the Sufi *shayks* (masters or leaders) and the Shiite *imams* were treated by their followers as gods. To him, this smacked of idolatry — i.e., elevating someone or something to the point where this person or object encroaches upon the dignity of God.

Ibn Taymiyya attracted both friends and foes in large measures. One contemporary follower described him in these glowing terms:

> Our shaykh, master, and imam between us and the Allah Almighty, master of verification, the wayfarer of the best path, the owner of the multifarious merits and overpowering proofs which all hosts agree are impossible to enumerate, the Shaykh, the Imam and faithful servant of his Lord, the doctor in the Religion, the Ocean, the light-giving Pole of spirituality, the leader of imams, the blessing of the Community, the sign-post of the people of knowledge, the inheritor of the Prophets, the last of those capable of independent legal reasoning (*ijtihad*), the most unique of the scholars of the Religion, Shaykh al-Islam [i.e., the chief *mufti* of a country].[79]

On the other hand, the greatest traveler of medieval Islam, Ibn Battuta (1304–1368), a tolerant man of moderate religious views, was much more critical. He was a *qadi* (judge) and, during his travels, presided over different *sharia* courts in the Middle East and Africa. In 1326, he was present at a mosque in Syria where Ibn Taymiyya delivered the sermon. Ibn Battuta has left us this firsthand report:

> One of the principal Hanbalite doctors at Damascus was Taqi al-Din Ibn Taymiya [sic], a man of great ability and wide learning, but with some kind of kink in his brain. The people of Damascus idolized him. He used to preach to them from the pulpit, and one day he made some statement that the other theologians disapproved of; they carried the case to the sultan and in consequence Ibn Taymiya was imprisoned for some years....
>
> Later on his mother presented herself before the sultan and interceded for him, so he was set at liberty, until he did the same thing again. I was in Damascus at the time and attended the service which he was conducting one Friday, as he was addressing and admonishing the people from the pulpit. In the midst of his discourse he said "Verily God descends [from heaven] to the sky over our own world in the same bodily fashion as I make this descent," and stepped down one step of the pulpit....
>
> [Other theologians, who strongly objected to this anthropomorphic heresy,] carried the matter to the principal amir [prince], who wrote to the sultan about the matter and at the same time drew up a legal attestation against Ibn Taymiya for various heretical pronouncements. This deed was sent on to the sultan, who gave orders that Ibn Taymiya should be imprisoned in the citadel, and there he remained until his death.[80]

Perhaps because of the "kink in his brain," Ibn Taymiyya made enemies very easily. He angered his fellow Sunni scholars by denouncing the four orthodox Sunni schools of jurisprudence as stagnant, sectarian, and overly influenced by Greek logic and by Sufi mysticism. In place of these schools and sects, he called instead for total reliance on the Quran and the *sunna* as the only sure path to the revival of Islam. In debates, he overwhelmed his opponents with a broadside of quotes and citations — many of which turned out, on closer examination, to be very dubious. A contemporary critic had this to say:

> He used to bring up in one hour from the Book [the Quran], the *sunna*, the Arabic language, and philosophical speculation, material which no one could bring up in many sessions, as if these sciences were before his very eyes and he was picking and choosing from them at will. A time came when his companions took to over-praising him and this drove him to be satisfied with himself until he became conceited before his fellow human beings. He became convinced that he was a scholar capable of independent thought (*mujtahid*). Henceforth he began to answer each and every scholar great and small, past and recent, until he went all the way back to Umar [Umar ibn al-Khattab, second of the four "rightly-guided" caliphs] and faulted him in some manner. This reached the ears

of [the local ruler] who reprimanded him. Ibn Taymiyya went to see him, apologized, and asked for forgiveness.[81]

Ibn Taymiyya's outspokenness repeatedly landed him in jail, both in his native Syria and in Egypt. Because he has played a seminal role in the growth of Islamic fundamentalism, his pattern of thought is very relevant today. He begins with the premise that the chief duty of human beings is *to serve God*— not to know Him or speculate about Him (these are the mistaken goals of theology) or to love Him (the mistaken goal of Sufism). Instead, Ibn Taymiyya sternly warns the faithful that

> The religion of Islam turns on these two principles: worshipping God and worshipping Him by what He prescribes. He is not served by Innovation [Sufi *shaykh*-worship, Shiite *imam*-worship, or even blind adherence to the masters of a given law school].... It is not permissible when guilt has been established by proof or witness to suspend the legal punishment, whether by remitting it or by substituting a fine or any other thing: the hand of the thief must be cut off, for the application of the punishments is one of the acts of religion like the *jihad* in the Way of God.[82]

In the Quran, the words "in the way of God" are often inserted after the word "fighting." Their addition emphasizes the religious approval of this kind of fighting and distinguishes it from other forms of fighting that are not permitted.[83]

Ibn Taymiyya tried hard to narrow the traditional and often large gap between the altruistic prescriptions of the divine law (*sharia*) and the local ruler's self-serving administrative policies (*siyasa*, i.e., tribunals, judgments and punishments designed to keep the peace). Most Sunnis were by then content to relegate the *sharia* to private affairs, having no power themselves to impose it on the actions of their rulers. Ibn Taymiyya, however, rowed against this current by encouraging rulers to govern strictly in accordance with the *sharia*, that is, by adopting a *sharia*-based policy for public order (*siyasa shariyyah*). Not surprisingly, he failed.

His book, *Governance*, founded on the concept of the public interest (*maslaha*), encouraged jurists to bring the high ideals of righteousness and justice into daily life. But as the Dutch scholar-administrator and expert on Islamic law Snouck Hurgronje (1857–1936) noted, this effort was largely responsible for what has been called the "fictional character" of much of Hanbali public law today. As Snouck Hurgronje put it,

> The [Hanbali] School continues to teach, with great seriousness, what functionaries there are in the theoretical Muslim state [i.e., a state governed by the *sharia*], which does not exist in reality, and what are their proper functions; it continues to describe the administration of imaginary revenues of this state, according to laws which were rarely applied, and then only in the earliest years

of Islam. It continues to trace the paths which must be followed to bring the whole world under Muslim authority ... in one word, it continues to trace the rules of the law which should prevail if the world was other than it is in reality.[84]

Nevertheless, despite their apparent shortcomings, Ibn Taymiyya's doctrines have slowly grown in popularity since the seventeenth century. They have a considerable impact on fundamentalist Muslim thought today. For example, Ibn Taymiyya's most famous *fatwa*, directed against the Mongols who had conquered most of the Muslim world, still echoes in fundamentalist circles. The Mongols had nominally converted to orthodox Islam but they still ruled themselves and the lands they conquered according to the Mongol code of Genghis Khan, not according to the *sharia*. For this reason, Ibn Taymiyya denounced them as infidels living in *jahiliyya* (the state of pagan ignorance and barbarism said to have prevailed in Arabia before the coming of Islam) and called for a *jihad* against them. He cited these Quranic verses to make his point:

> And to you We have revealed the Book with the truth. It confirms the Scriptures which came before it and stands as a guardian over them. Therefore give judgement among men according to God's revelations, and do not yield to their whims or swerve from the truth made known to you.... Pronounce judgement among them according to God's revelations and do not be led by their desires.... Is it pagan laws that they wish to be judged by? Who is a better judge than God for men whose faith is firm? [*sura* 5:48–50].

In modern times, Ibn Taymiyya's trenchant criticism of Muslim-in-name-only rulers, who follow their own laws rather than the God-given *sharia*, was first applauded by Rashid Rida (1865–1935), who will be discussed later. An influential author, editor and political activist in Egypt, he followed Ibn Taymiyya's lead by denouncing the Muslim rulers of his own day who were abandoning the *sharia* and adopting Western penal codes. Some modern scholars therefore consider the teachings of Ibn Taymiyya as "embodying the spirit of the Muslim revival." [85] Prior to his teachings, it was strictly forbidden for the orthodox faithful to question the legitimacy of any Muslim ruler. Ibn Taymiyya's books are frequently reprinted today.

Looking for a Normative Basis for the Sharia: *Abu Ishaq al-Shatibi (d. 1388)*

In philosophy, normative statements define how things should or ought to be, how to value them, which things are good or bad, and which actions right and wrong. According to the modern scholar Muhammad Khalid Masud, the fourteenth-century jurist al-Shatibi, who lived and worked in Grenada, sought a normative basis for the *sharia*. Al-Shatibi is said to be "the most frequently quoted jurist on modern debates on the *sharia*."[86] His line of thought is so convoluted, however, that only a thumbnail summary of it will be attempted here.[87]

Al-Shatibi set himself the task of reforming the method of legal reasoning that had gradually emerged in Islam since the eighth century. This venerable method had become normative and was primarily based on analogy and induction. Al-Shatibi took aim at two extreme practices of his time: the overly relaxed attitudes of legal scholars of the *sunna*, on the one hand, and the overly strict demands of mystical Sufis, on the other.[88] In his epistemology (theory of knowledge), he defined "certitude" as the most important characteristic of the sources of the *sharia*. This was an essential point for him. To orthodox believers, these traditional sources are not be merely "probable": indeed, if they are held to be anything less than 100 per cent certain, the entire legal, religious, economic and social structure of Islam teeters on the brink of logical collapse.

Undoubtedly for this reason, al-Shatibi asserted that all the fundamental premises and manifestations of legal theory — for example, the five pillars of Islam — are certain and are therefore true. Using a broad inductive approach, he argued that the *sharia* was based on the principle of human good and was designed to safeguard five basic and universal human interests: religion, life, reproduction, property, and reason.

Although neither the Quran nor the *sunna* explicitly vests these interests with certainty, al-Shatibi claimed they are indeed certain because, as the modern scholar Wael B. Hallaq puts it, "the knowledge of these universals is enshrined with certainty in the collective mind of the Muslim community as well as in the mind of Muslim individuals."[89]

Al-Shatibi ultimately rested his case on the need to have faith in the Quran. To him, it clearly reveals the great gift God has bestowed on humanity: "This day I have perfected your religion for you and completed My favour to you. I have chosen Islam to be your faith" (*sura* 5:3). Here, al-Shatibi is in effect saying that the Quran can stand alone: the *sunna*, though useful in explaining and giving details about Quranic verses, is thereby relegated to a secondary position.

Although al-Shatibi's immediate successors did not adopt his inductive approach, it would eventually become a powerful tool in the hands of modern Muslim reformers such as Muhammad Abduh and Rashid Rida. These two men were not the only modern reformers of Islam — there have been many others as well — but they made some of the most important points about the intellectual foundations of the *sharia* itself.[90] For this reason, we shall discuss them later with some care.

4

Ottoman Law in the Golden Age of the Empire: Süleyman the Magnificent

The founder of the Ottoman dynasty was only a minor warlord, Osman Bey, who lived around 1300 in northwest Anatolia, Turkey. His frontier state was too insignificant to leave a written history but by fits and starts his descendants vastly expanded their possessions until at last they captured Constantinople itself in 1453. The huge Ottoman Empire would survive until 1922, though so weakened in later centuries that it became known as "the sick man of Europe."

Both *sharia* law and positive law played a central role in governing the Ottoman Empire. Beginning in the sixteenth century, *fatwas* by Ottoman legal scholars in Syria and Egypt would also introduce significant changes into classic Hanafi law (this legal school was favored by the Ottomans) concerning property, rent, and taxation of arable lands.[1]

As mentioned earlier, better legal records were kept by the Ottoman Empire, especially after the Ottomans occupied Constantinople in 1453 and made it their capital. Unfortunately, most early Ottoman reports of legal cases are limited to bare summaries, not the more interesting verbatim statements made in court by the litigants, witnesses, and judges.[2] One of the few exceptions to this rule, and one which is accessible in English, involves the dilemma of Fatma, a pregnant peasant girl. It is discussed below.

Sultan Süleyman I ruled from 1520 to 1566. In the Islamic world, he was known as the "Lawgiver" (*Kanuni*, a term that also refers to his commitment to making sure his government worked efficiently); in the West, he was called

the "Magnificent." His reign lasted for 46 years — the longest reign of any
other Ottoman ruler before or after him. This era was the golden age of the
Ottoman Empire, which in the sixteenth century embraced about 280 disparate provinces and stretched from central Europe to southern Arabia and
from Iraq almost to Morocco.

The empire was a most impressive creation. It could field big, well-
equipped, effective armies, financing them through an efficient imperial tax
collection system.[3] It seems to have enjoyed a good deal of popular support.
Writing in 1525, the Venetian ambassador reported:

> I know of no State which is happier than this one. It is furnished with all God's
> gifts. It controls war and peace; it is rich in gold, in people, in ships, and in obe-
> dience; no State can be compared with it. May God long preserve the most just
> of Emperors.[4]

The Austrian ambassador, Ghiselain de Busbecq, noted that Süleyman
chose his officials on merit alone, not by their social standing, wealth or personal popularity. He observed that the Sultan paid no regard to such matters
and instead looked carefully into a candidate's character, administrative ability and personality. At the same time, Süleyman was never shy about proclaiming his own greatness. In a letter of 1554 to the Habsburg emperor
Ferdinand, he boasted, correctly, that he was the ruler of "Mecca, Medina and
Jerusalem" — the three holiest cities of Islam.[5] On a pillar erected during his
reign, he described himself thus:

> Slave of God, powerful with the power of God, deputy of God on earth, obeying
> the commands of the Quran and enforcing them throughout the world, master
> of all lands, the shadow of God over all nations, Sultan of Sultans in all lands of
> Persians and Arabs, the propagator of Sultanic laws, the tenth Sultan of the
> Ottoman Khans, Sultan, son of Sultan, Süleyman Khan.[6]

It was these new "Sultanic laws" that contributed to Süleyman's achievements as the "Lawgiver." A fundamental premise of Ottoman rule was that
both subjects and land belonged to the sultan. Süleyman's legal authority
ultimately rested on the *sharia*, but the *sharia* could not deal, single-handedly, with all the complexities inherent in administering a vast empire. Specific
firmans (royal edicts) were first used for this purpose and were then system-
atically gathered together into codes known as *kanun*. This was purely secular administrative law but it was treated, officially, as being merely an extension
of the *sharia*. When *kanun* laws attained their most highly developed form,
Süleyman's legal code became known as the *kanun-i-Osmani*, i.e., the
"Ottoman laws." It included previous legislation, augmented by many new
additions. A standard formula, lightly edited in the quotation used here,
ordered Ottoman judges

to enforce the provisions of the law of the Prophet and to apply the divine commands without overstepping the boundaries of the true Shari'a, to study properly the various opinions from Hanafite imams with regard to the questions that present themselves, to determine the most authoritative one, and to implement it.[7]

Kanun was often used for agrarian and criminal law (there were separate rulings for each of these two areas).[8] The general rule was that it could be used for any purpose that did not directly contradict the *sharia* itself. For example, in a *fatwa* dating from the late eighteenth or early nineteenth century, the Islamic jurist Ibn Abidin commented on a complicated legal case involving the right of women to inherit land belonging to a third party. He found that the solution to this case lay in an earlier sixteenth century *kanun*, which stated that women could inherit such land only if the deceased did not have a male offspring. In translating this *kanun* into Arabic, Ibn Abidin took pains to note that

the right of possession of sultanic land belongs to the sultan, may [God] strengthen his victory, and he has the right to assign it in a special way, and no one has a right to object to this *as long as it does not contradict the lofty Sharia.*[9]

Fatma's story gives us a good snapshot of Ottoman laws in action at the local level in the year 1541, although it consists of only three specific entries in the legal records.[10] Fatma was a young peasant girl living in the village of Hiyam, which was near the provincial capital of Aintab in southern Turkey near the Syrian border. Because she was pregnant but unmarried, she was clearly guilty of some kind of illicit sex (*zina*). But her case turned out to be unexpectedly complicated. A high-ranking local official, Mustafa Çelebi, who was the trustee of the crown lands in Aintab, brought it to court. He was responsible not only for collecting taxes but also for maintaining social order there.

In the first entry, Fatma told the court: "I am pregnant, and I am pregnant by this [man] Ahmed." Ahmed denied the charge. The next day, Fatma formally told the court, in the second entry, that she was guilty of the crime of *zina*: "During the day, at noontime, I committed *zina* with Ahmed." This confession reflects her active participation in sexual intercourse with Ahmed; otherwise, she would have claimed the traditional passive role and would have pleaded instead: "Ahmed did *zina* to me."

The third and last entry, however, tells us that the village imam appeared before the court with a much different story. He claimed that it was not Ahmed who was responsible for Fatma's pregnancy, but another villager, a man named Korkud. Moreover, continued the imam, rather than being a willing partner in lovemaking, Fatma had in fact been raped by Korkud. The imam explained to the court that Fatma had told him: "When the mother of

Korkud was giving birth, I went there to carry water. Korkud shut the court-yard door and took me inside, this Korkud raped me [lit. 'did *zina* to me by force.'] I am pregnant by Korkud."

The judge now had the difficult task of ferreting out the truth. He questioned Fatma closely about the imam's account. She finally confessed, in a statement remarkable for its naive authenticity, and told the judge:

> It's not that I didn't make such a statement, I *did*, but Zeliha, Ahmed's mother, instructed me to say that. That's why I made that statement. The truth of the matter is that I am pregnant by Ahmed. I cannot slander another; it's this world today, tomorrow the hereafter. It is Ahmed who had illicit relations with me.[11]

Another instructive example of the *sharia* under the golden age of the Ottomans comes from an elementary textbook written by Ibrahim al-Halabi, who died in 1549. It was later edited and commentaries were added by another Islamic scholar, Shaykhzade (d. 1667). The passage below, which involves a lease, shows that following the *sharia* correctly means to be aware not only of its immediate religious requirements, such as prayer, but also of its more subtle legal demands, e.g., not taking any legal action now that might have negative religious consequences later on, even if these are unforeseen.

This passage is interesting but it is complicated and needs careful reading. There are three separate voices in it — those of al-Halabi, Shaykzade, and the modern editor, Rudolph Peters. The excerpts in bold print come from al-Halabi's textbook. Those in parentheses and regular print are Shaykzade's own comments. The statements in brackets and italics are by Peters. The passage is significant in legal terms because it shows the porous conceptual membrane between Islamic law and the Islamic faith. The issue here is not whether the lease contract itself is valid and binding, but whether a Muslim who concludes such a contract is inadvertently risking his immortal soul.

The passage reads as follows:

> **It is not reprehensible to lease out a house in the countryside** (i.e., in a village) **if it will subsequently be used as a Zoroastrian temple, a church or a monk's cell, or if wine will be sold in it** ... (at least according to the Imam *[Abu Hanifa (d. 767]*, because the lease confers the right to use the house and there is no sin in that. The sin is related to the acts committed by the lessee of his own accord. That means that the relationship *[between the landlord and the sin]* is interrupted, just like in the case of the sale of the slave girl ... to a person who wants to have anal intercourse with her, or the sale of a young slave to a homosexual....) **According to his companions** *[al-Shaybani (d. 805) and Abu Yusuf (d. 798)]* **it is indeed reprehensible** (to lease a house for such a use, because it promotes sin. The three other imams are of the same opinion...). **There is agreement** *[among the imams]* **that such a lease is reprehensible in a village or a region inhabited mainly by Muslims.**[12]

Another passage from this same Ottoman handbook, which is too long to quote here, shows how jurists debated with each other and thus hammered out the rules of the *sharia*. The Hanafi school of jurisprudence held a variety of opinions on the question of whether a woman who was legally capable could legally conclude her own marriage contract. According to one opinion, she was fully entitled to do so; in case of a misalliance, her agnatic male relatives (that is, her paternal kinsmen) could petition the judge for an annulment. A second opinion was that such a misalliance is invalid *per se*. The third view was that all marriages concluded by legally capable women need the ratification of their marriage guardians.[13]

Süleyman based his whole system of government on the *sharia*, as interpreted by the Hanafi school of law.[14] The Ottomans' smallest administrative unit, roughly equivalent to a European county, was made identical to the legal district over which a local judge had authority. The local chief of police was put under the orders of that judge. An empire-wide uniform training program was set up for scholars and judges; it would become the entry point for a respected career administering the *sharia*. The Grand Mufti of Istanbul was put in charge of this hierarchy and became one of the most powerful officers of Süleyman's regime.

(A Grand Mufti is the highest official of religious law in a Sunni Muslim country. He issues legal opinions and edicts, i.e., *fatwas*, for private clients or to help judges decide difficult cases. The collected *fatwas* of a Grand Mufti can be an invaluable source of information on Islamic law in practice, as opposed to its abstract formulations. Today there are approximately 16 Grand Muftis in countries with sizeable Muslim populations.)

Awarded the honorific of Shaykh al-Islam, the Ottoman Grand Mufti made sure that the *sharia* was being implemented correctly and that lesser judges were doing their jobs well. Before the imperial government took any important significant action, he was consulted to make sure the proposed action did not violate the *sharia*.

The most powerful Grand Mufti was Ebussu'ud Effendi (in Turkish, the honorific "Effendi" denotes a man of property, authority, or education). He held this important office for nearly 30 years—from 1545 until his death in 1574. He justified Süleyman's rule on classically Islamic grounds: Süleyman must be obeyed because he was the "protector of the holy ground of the two sacred sanctuaries [Mecca and Medina]."[15] Moreover, Süleyman was also "the one who makes smooth the path for the precepts of the manifest [*sharia*]."[16]

Ebussu'ud was so influential that he was able to use the authority of the sultanate to innovate and to legislate under the protective umbrella of the *sharia*. He did not shy away from hard cases. For example, the prevailing opinion of the foremost legal scholars of his day was that if the body of a murdered person was found in a house, the owner of the house had to pay blood money to the next of kin. Ebussu'ud, however, argued that this did not seem sensible to him. Instead, he persuaded the sultan to issue a degree making the person who was actually living in the house at the time the body was discovered, i.e., the lessee, responsible for the blood money.[17]

He was certainly a prodigious worker. Pious legend has it that Ebussu'ud issued a total of 1,413 *fatwas* every single day in response to the legal and religious questions put to him by the public.[18] This cannot be so, but such an impressive figurative total does suggest that he consistently issued a large number of *fatwas*. His pragmatic interpretations of the law, which maintained the legal authority of the *sharia* and its jurists, would last until the modernizing reforms of the nineteenth century. In his own mind, however, his most important achievement was not his legal work but his great commentary on the Quran. He devoted 30 years of his life to this work and it was largely thanks to it that he was showered by Süleyman with honors and wealth.[19]

What is more important for our purposes here is that he was also instrumental in bringing the *kanun* into compliance with the *sharia*. This process involved, among other challenges, finding a workable compromise between the needs of the Islamic religious endowments (*waqf*), on the one hand, and those of the Ottoman institution of land law and land taxes, on the other. It is worth looking at these two issues in some detail.[20]

The classic donation to a *waqf* was either immovable property or real estate. Giving movable property (e.g., animals) or cash was controversial in legal terms. By Ebussu'ud time, however, donating animals to dervish lodges had become quite acceptable. (Dervishes were members of a Sufi fraternity that used whirling dances and other devotional exercises to induce an ecstatic trance state.) Giving cash, on the other hand, was decidedly questionable from a legal point of view: revenue on this capital constituted interest — which, as we have seen, was strictly forbidden by the *sharia*.

Both a fundamentalist jurist and a judge had already issued *fatwas* against cash contributions to a *waqf*. Ebussu'ud issued a *fatwa* of his own, legalizing them. In doing so, he used the customary financial stratagems (*hiyal*) and confirmed that the maximum interest that could be charged could not exceed 15 percent. This flexible, pragmatic approach was applauded by both the Ottoman authorities and the endowments themselves. It had the socially beneficial effect of enlarging the scope of the *sharia* so that it could now embrace contemporary financial practices.

Ebussu'ud was equally successful in regulating Ottoman taxes on land. He did not fundamentally change Ottoman land law to bring it into conformity with the *sharia*. Instead, he either reclassified existing practices so that they fell within the purview of the *sharia* or he simply justified them in terms of consensus (*ijma*) and necessity. He ruled that all agricultural land in the Ottoman Empire had initially been won by conquest and was thus subject to the land tax, regardless of whether it was now being cultivated by Muslims or non–Muslims. In this, he was clearly following the long-standing dictum ascribed to Abu Hanifah: "In contrast to all other commodities, the productive lands of our territories are never exempted from taxation."[21] Ebussu'ud thus solidified imperial control by preventing Ottoman lands from falling into the hands of private owners.

He also regulated inheritance procedures and redefined the Ottoman tax structure in canonical terms. He held, for example, that Ottoman subjects had to pay both the sheep-tax and customs duty. These levies were not in fact mandated by the *sharia*, but Ebussu'ud enforced them by means of a legal fiction: he ruled that men paid these taxes with the "intention" of paying their annual alms [*zakat*]."[22]

Ebussu'ud reiterated, in strong terms, the policy that since Ottoman judges were appointed by the sultan, they were required to follow the sultan's directives (as transmitted by Ebussu'ud himself) in applying the *sharia*. There were 32 of these directives, which were designed to accomplish two things. First, they required the judges to follow the policies of the Hanafi school when deciding cases. Second, they removed from the judges the authority to act on certain legal matters. Following Ebussu'ud's advice, in 1550 Süleyman ordered his judges not to hear any cases that had lain dormant for more than 15 years. This was half the period of time previously allowed by the *sharia*.[23]

By thus establishing a 15-year statute of limitations, Süleyman helped to clear the way for later and far reaching changes in Islamic law. Modern reformers, for example, have used to their advantage this long-established Ottoman principle that the ruler has the right to limit the scope of judges' powers and to give official preference to the legal opinions of a favored school.[24]

Süleyman's collection of legal texts shows his own inclination, while professing unswerving allegiance to the *sharia*, to supersede it in practice with a host of *kanuns*. These new administrative laws imposed a remarkable regularity on the far-flung Ottoman Empire. They addressed the extensive range of subjects on which the *sharia* did not provide explicit legal guidance. Examples include military fiefs, the status of non–Muslim subjects, penal law, land law, the law of war, the supervision of public morals, and trade and industry.

Süleyman was so successful on the legal front that Schacht concludes: "The legal order in the Ottoman Empire in the sixteenth century was far superior to that prevailing in Western Europe, if only because of its uniformity...."[25] By the time of Süleyman's death in 1566, the Ottoman Empire was the largest and probably the most powerful military empire in the world.[26]

5

The Sharia *Under Wahhabi Puritanism and Incursions by the West*

The Ottomans were not able to maintain their ascendancy indefinitely. They slipped into a slow but terminal decline that finally ended in the wake of World War I: the Turkish caliphate was abolished in 1924. When Sir William Eton reported to London on the state of the Turkish Empire in 1799, he gave these explanations for its past successes and its current weaknesses:

> It is undeniable that the power of the Turks was once formidable to their neighbors not by their numbers only, but by their military and civil institutions, far surpassing those of their opponents. And they all trembled at the name of the Turks, who with a confidence procured by their constant successes, held the Christians no less in contempt as warriors than they did on account of their religion. Proud and vainglorious, conquest was to them a passion, a gratification, and even a means of salvation, a sure way of immediately attaining a delicious paradise. Hence their zeal for the extension of their empire; hence their profound respect for the military profession, and their glory in being obedient and submissive to discipline.
>
> [Now, however] the Turks refuse all reforms, they are seditious and mutinous.... When their sudden fury is abated, which is at the last obstinate resistance, they are seized with a panic, and have no rallying as formerly. The cavalry is as much afraid of their own infantry as of the enemy; for in a defeat they fire at them to get their horses to escape more quickly. In short, it is a mob assembled rather than an army levied.[1]

The eventual collapse of the great Ottoman Empire is an intriguing subject but one that is too complicated for us to discuss here in any depth. Still, it is important to try to explain its fall. There seems to have been no single cause. Instead, modern scholars point to some or all of the following factors:

- Two unsuccessful Ottoman sieges of Vienna (1529 and 1683) and the loss of other important battles, e.g., the sea battle of Lepanto in 1571.
- The expansion of Russia in the direction of the Ottoman Empire, i.e., Russia sought more territory and wanted to protect Russian Orthodox Christians, whose church was in Istanbul.
- The conflicting balance of power interests of the major European states, which resulted in the Crimean War of the 1850s.
- The rise of the soldier-reformer Muhammad Ali, pasha of Egypt from 1805 to 1848, which led to Egypt's breakaway from the Ottoman Empire.
- Severe administrative and financial problems, e.g., bad governance by autocratic sultans, and inflation, resulting in the loss of value of Ottoman currency.
- A sea change in the world economic order, due to the discovery of America, the Industrial Revolution, and colonial expansion by European powers.

Sunni Puritan Reformer: Muhammad ibn Abd al-Wahhab (1703–1792)

While the Turks were declining, a charismatic but extremely conservative figure arose in the Arabian Peninsula. Muhammad ibn Abd al-Wahhab was a Sunni reformer, jurist and theologian who founded the puritanical Islamic sect often referred to as Wahhabism. Highly controversial in life, he has been highly controversial in death as well.

His fundamentalist supporters in the Islamic world now hail him as a great reformer of Islam and as a learned scholar who helped to revive the Hanbali school of jurisprudence. Anti-fundamentalist reactionaries in the West denounce him as the "father of Islamic terrorism" and point out — correctly, in our view — that his teachings are primitive, intolerant and contrary to the historical mainstream of Islamic thought. Nevertheless, despite their intellectual shortcomings, his opinions have had a decisive impact on the internal and foreign policies of Saudi Arabia — the country where the *sharia* and Wahhabism is most influential today. For this reason alone they are worth examining in some detail.

Muhammad ibn Abd al-Wahhab drew very heavily on the earlier legal and religious doctrines of Ibn Hanbal and Ibn Taymiyya. He taught that in order to revitalize Islam and restore it to its former glory, it was essential for the faithful to return to the true or genuine principles of Islam. The Wahhabis still claim to be the only ones who devotedly follow the path of the "rightly guided" (very pious) predecessors of the prophet's time. They look on other Muslims simply as infidels who need to be converted to Wahhabi beliefs.

Not much is known about Muhammad ibn Abd al-Wahhab's youth in Najd (central Arabia), except that he was the son of a judge and received a traditional Islamic education in Medina. His extreme religious conservatism was fueled by his acute concern that contemporary Islam, especially in the hands of the Shiites, had fallen away from the original purity he believed it had possessed at the time of the prophet. His religious views were already so inflexible that his father and his brother, both of whom were Islamic scholars, formally warned others against him. His brother even went so far as to write a book, entitled *Divine Thunderbolts*, opposing Muhammad ibn Abd al-Wahhab's beliefs.

Later, Muhammad ibn Abd al-Wahhab traveled widely for some years and taught in what is today Iraq, Syria, Kurdistan, Iran and India. He returned to the Najd and in 1737–1740 began to rally support for Wahhabism. This creed would become crucially important in the creation of Saudi Arabia and is still dominant there today. It is the most conservative of all Muslim sects because it refuses to accept any revisions of Quranic law whatsoever. The reason is that Ibn Abd al-Wahhab wanted to restore Islamic orthodoxy. He took a very strong stand against all innovations *(bid'a)*, e.g., Sufism, or any idolatry, e.g., invoking any prophet, saint or angel in prayer, rather than addressing God alone.

Wahhabism still asserts that all Muslims who do not adhere to its beliefs — that is to say, all mainstream Sunnis, Sufis and Shiites — are simply infidels, not real Muslims. *Tawhid* means the singularity of God, that is, His absolute "oneness" — in sharp contrast to the polytheism that devout Muslims find in other faiths. As Muhammad ibn Abd al-Wahhab put it, the only way a fellow Muslim one can avoid being labeled an infidel is "by [expressing] love to those who practice *tawhid* of Allah [i.e., those who practice *tawhid* in the puritanical format demanded by the Wahhabi monotheists], devotion to them, rendering them every kind of help, as well as by hate and hostility to infidels and *mushrikun* [polytheists]."[2]

Muhammad ibn Abd al-Wahhab himself called for a very strict interpretation of the Quran. He demanded that all Muslim states be based exclusively on the *sharia*. He expounded these austere doctrines in the best known of his 14 works, the *Book of Unity* [or *Book of Monotheism*] (*Kitab al-Tawhid*). This is not an easy work to master. Translations into English confirm this.

Here, for example, is an edited excerpt taken from chapter 36 of this book. It bears a sonorous title: "Whoever Obeys a Scholar or Ruler by Prohibiting What Allah Has Permitted or Permitting What Allah has Prohibited Has Them as Partners Besides Allah."[3]

Put more simply, what this title means is that obeying such an erring scholar or ruler is tantamount to idolatry, which in Islam is a very grave sin indeed. Muhammad ibn Abd al-Wahhab assures the faithful that anyone "who makes appeal to a prophet, king, ruler or anyone else, or asks someone, besides Allah, for help" is a polytheist and an infidel.[4] He begins this chapter by citing a *hadith* that relates an incident that occurred when Ibn Abbas, a devout Muslim, was talking about Islam with one or more of his friends. Ibn Abbas said to them:

> "Stones are about to rain down upon you from the sky: I say to you: 'Allah's Messenger [Muhammad] said...' and you reply: 'But Abu Bakr and Umar said...'"

Muhammad ibn Abd al-Wahhab then explains what this *hadith* means:

> Because obedience is a form of worship, it is not allowed to obey any one—be he man or *jinn* (a spirit)—unless it conforms with obedience to Allah and His Messenger. That is why Ibn Abbas repudiated those who, when they were informed that the Prophet had pronounced upon a matter, objected that Abu Bakr and Umar [who would become the first and second caliphs, respectively] had said something different, thus, in effect, preferring the opinions of those two pious Companions over the Revelation of Allah.[5]

Muhammad ibn Abd al-Wahhab goes on to list three important "Benefits Derived From This Narration" as well as the "Relevance of This Narration to the Subject of the Chapter and to the Subject of Tawhid [the "oneness" of God]." The three Benefits are stated to be:

- "Evidence of the virtue of Ibn Abbas and his excellent understanding of religious matters."
- "*That no opinion which contradicts the Quran and* Sunnah *is to be given heed, no matter from whom it emanated.*" [Italics added]
- "The obligation to be angry for Allah and His Messenger's sake."[6]

The "Relevance" is stated to be:

- "That the narration proves that Ibn Abbas held that it is forbidden to prefer the opinion of any of Allah's creatures over the *Sunnah* of the Messenger of Allah and this is because to do so is an act of *shirk* [idolatry] since it constitutes obedience to other than Allah."[7]

This chapter continues at much greater length but in the interests of brevity we will not cite it any further here. An important point to note, however, is that the *Book of Unity* led Muhammad ibn Abd al-Wahhab's followers to call themselves "People of Unity" or "Unitarians" (*ahl al-tawhid* or *Muwahhidun*), descriptions that stem from their belief in the absolute "oneness" of God. Opponents and non–Muslims alike, however, have traditionally referred to them as Wahhabis.

Muhammad ibn Abd al-Wahhab stressed that the only religious principles worth following were those explicitly land down in the Quran and *hadith*. According to Francis Robinson, a modern scholar, Muhammad ibn Abd al-Wahhab's teachings thus mark a fundamental shift away from "an Islam that was inclusive to one which was increasingly exclusive, and from an Islam that was otherworldly to one which was concerned to put God's guidance into practice on earth."[8]

Muhammad ibn Abd al-Wahhab's puritanical views so offended the residents of his native Arabian city of Uyayna that they expelled him in 1744. He therefore moved into the northeast Najd region. There, in the village of Dariyah, he converted the Saud tribe, which was led by the chieftain Muhammad ibn Saud (d. 1765), to his religious beliefs. In 1749, he and Muhammad ibn Saud set up a unique religious-tribal government with a new and explicit division of power: Muhammad Ibn Abd al-Wahhab would wield all the religious power, while Muhammad ibn Saud would wield all the political power.

Both men believed that a military campaign (*jihad*) to unify Arabia under their joint banner was fully justified, not only in political but also in theological terms as well. As we have seen, Ibn Taymiyya had held that some self-declared Muslims, e.g., the former Mongols, were in fact still nonbelievers at heart. Moreover, he believed that all who disagreed with him were heretics and apostates. For this reason, he insisted, Muslims could and indeed *must* wage *jihad* against them to restore Islam to its former pristine glory. This conviction led him to declare *jihad* against other Muslims, i.e., neighboring Arab tribes — an act that would otherwise have been legally impossible under the *sharia.*[9]

The Saud family, for its part, was eager to expand its limited territorial base, both in hopes of plunder and of spreading Wahhabism. The Saud-Wahhabi political-religious jihad was ultimately successful. The alliance made Riyadh its capital in 1773. Mecca was captured in 1803 and Medina two years later. Despite some later severe military setbacks along the way, under the unifying banner of Wahhabism the Saud dynasty managed to conquer nearly all of the Arabian peninsula by 1932. The final result was the oil-rich, highly conservative, *sharia*-based Kingdom of Saudi Arabia as we know it today.

Remarkably, the unique eighteenth century power-sharing agreement between the Saud royal family and the Wahhabis is still very much in force in Saudi Arabia today. It continues to provide the backbone of the religious —

and therefore the *political*—legitimacy for the royal family's continuing monopoly of political and economic power. It explains why, despite rumors of the more liberal personal inclinations of some Saudi officials and Saudi citizens, strict Wahhabism still is very much the rule there.[10] Finally, it is also the reason why in recent years the Saudis have spent so many billions of dollars to finance Wahhabi-oriented religious schools, newspapers, and proselytizing organizations around the world.

Although Wahhabi thought is often held to be very rigid, Muhammad Ibn Abd al-Wahhab himself demonstrated a certain flexibility. He usually followed the classical interpretations of Islamic inheritance law as presented in the Quran and *hadith*, but in his own rulings he was sometimes guided by the *underlying intent* of these texts than by their literal readings.[11] For example, he thought that it was essential for all parties to adhere to the Quranic values of justice and equity, regardless of what the texts specifically said.

One major case in which this issue arose involved the division of the estate of a deceased person. Muhammad Ibn Abd al-Wahhab asserted the primacy of direct descendants rather than ascendants. As he put it, "Place the son of the son as a son, and do not place the father of the father as a father."[12] In simpler terms, this meant that in a case where the son was no longer living, the grandson became the primary heir: the grandfather was not entitled to take the place of a deceased parent as an heir.

Incursions by Western Law

By the end of the seventeenth century, if not before, the Islamic world had fallen seriously behind the Western world. The basic problem here was not that Islam itself had somehow "failed" but that the West's military, political and economic power had grown so exponentially that the rest of the world was simply left in its wake. (The Islamic world was not the only one that lagged far behind: the Confucian world of China singularly failed to compete with the West too.)

Incursions by Western law were an inevitable part of the expanding Western influence in the non–Western worlds. The growing power of the West dictated that the Muslim world would have to modify greatly, or perhaps even abandon entirely, its centuries-old reliance on Islamic law. Western law was positive (manmade) law. It was almost entirely divorced from religion. It was supple and could be changed easily to fit new conditions. The *sharia*, on the other hand, was inextricably bound up with Islam itself. It was rigid. The high value it placed on strict adherence to established doctrines (*taqlid*) made significant and rapid change nearly impossible.[13]

Western Europeans (chiefly the Dutch, British and French) came to exercise enormous political, military, economic, and cultural power in many parts of the world where Muslims were numerous. Listed in chronological order, here are some of the countries or regions where this expanding Western influence was most apparent:

- *The Ottoman Empire* (after 1536, when a capitulation treaty, i.e., a legal agreement giving one country extraterritorial jurisdiction over its own nationals who are living in another country, was signed between Francis I of France and Süleyman I of Turkey. It became the model for many similar treaties, officially known as Capitulations, which were negotiated with other Western powers).
- *Indonesia* (after the Dutch East India Company was formed in 1602),
- *Bengal and, later, the rest of India* (after the British East India Company took possession of Bengal in 1765),
- *Egypt* (occupied by Napoleon in 1798),
- *Algeria* (the French conquest began in 1830; Algeria eventually became, formally, part of France itself),
- *The Persian Gulf* (the coastal areas of Yemen came under British rule in 1839; a British protectorate would eventually expand to include 23 Sultanates, Emirates, and tribal regimes),
- *Tunisia* (became a French protectorate in 1881),
- *Egypt again* (occupied by the British in 1882 because it could not repay its debts),
- *Much of Africa* (in 1884–1885 the Berlin West Africa Conference divided this continent among the European powers),
- *Sudan* (in 1898 the British captured the Dervish capital of Omdurman),
- *Libya* (conquered by the Italians in 1911),
- *Morocco* (became a French protectorate in 1912),
- *The Eastern Mediterranean region* (after the end of the Ottoman Empire following World War I, Britain and France were given protectorates or mandates in 1922 over a sweeping variety of lands. The British Mandate of Palestine, for example, was a territory in the Middle East that included what are now Israel, Jordan, and the West Bank and Gaza Strip. Turkey was the only Muslim-populated region of the Middle East to emerge from World War I as an independent state).[14]

In the interest of brevity, we will confine our discussion here to the Ottomans and to Egypt. The Ottoman Turks controlled Egypt from 1517 until 1882, except for a brief period of French rule under Napoleon Bonaparte. In the Treaty of Carlowitz (1699), which ended 16 years of hostilities between the Ottoman Empire and the Holy League (Austria, Poland, Venice and Russia), the Ottomans had been forced, for the first time in their long dealings with the West, to admit defeat.

The advance guard of the gradual incursion of Western law into the Middle East was Napoleon's invasion of Egypt in 1798. As the modern scholar Francis Robinson puts it, the Islamic world was then being

> overwhelmed by forces from the West, driven by capitalism, powered by industrial revolution, and civilized, after a fashion, by the Enlightenment. The symbolic moment when the leader's standard overtly passed to the West was Napoleon's invasion of Egypt in 1798. From this moment western armies and western capital [and, we may add, Western law] overran the lands of the Muslims. By the 1920s only Afghanistan, Iran, Turkey, central Arabia and the Yemen were free from western control.[15]

Napoleon's ill-fated assault on Egypt may have had its genesis in a memorandum of 1672 to the King of France, Louis XIV, written by the German polymath Leibnitz (1646–1716). Leibnitz argued that Egypt would be an excellent cornerstone for a French empire in the Middle East. He claimed that it would give France a dominant position along the shortest sea-and-overland route from Europe to India, thus hindering British access to and trade with that rich subcontinent.

Nothing specific came of this proposal but more than a century later, in 1769, the Duc de Choiseul advised Louis XV to replace the failing French colonial efforts in North America with the conquest of Egypt. French officials, travelers and businessmen now warmed to this idea. In 1777, a French baron was sent to Egypt to study the advantages of turning it into a French colony. He was accompanied by the naturalist Sonnini de Manincourt, who filed a separate report on his scholarly observations.[16]

At first, Napoleon was quite successful against Muslim forces. He landed near Alexandria and captured that city without difficulty. In the Battle of the Pyramids, his 25,000 man strong invading force defeated a Mamluk army of 100,000 men. Nevertheless, his foray into Egypt ended in abject failure. In 1798, in the Battle of the Nile, British Admiral Horatio Nelson destroyed Napoleon's squadron off the Nile River delta at Alexandria, thus depriving French soldiers of any way to leave Egypt. Then the people of Cairo revolted against the French, whom they saw as a foreign army of occupation, not as the liberators Napoleon claimed them to be.

With his forces under constant British and Ottoman attack, Napoleon and his personal entourage secretly slipped away by sea from Egypt in 1799, leaving his troops behind under the command of General Jean-Baptiste Kléber. After Kléber was assassinated by a Syrian, command of French forces passed to General Abdullah Jacques Menou, a French convert to Islam. In

1801, however, Menou and his troops had to surrender to an Anglo-Ottoman invasion force.[17]

For our purposes here, the most significant aspects of Napoleon's Egyptian adventure were not military but cultural and, by extension, legal as well. The French expeditionary force included not only soldiers but also some 150 scholars, artists, scientists, engineers, mathematicians and technicians. These well-trained men devoted themselves, single mindedly and successfully, to the study and exploration of Egypt. Their labors had two important long-term results.

The first result was the publication in France of a magisterial reference work, *La Description de l'Egypt* (*The Description of Egypt*). This consisted of 24 volumes of text and 12 large volumes of maps, lists and drawings. The final text and plates were not published until 1822; the atlas, not until 1828. Nevertheless, together with the discovery and later translation of the ancient trilingual inscriptions on the Rosetta Stone, this book laid the foundations for modern Egyptology. Egypt would henceforth be open to study and exploitation by the West on many different levels.

The second result was that Napoleon's scholarly teams exposed Egyptian officials and scholars, usually for the first time, to the intellectual as well as to the military, economic and social might of the West. The reverse side of this same coin was even more important: the work of the French proved how feeble the Ottoman Empire was and — by extension, how feeble the Islamic world as a whole — had become in comparison with the West. Some reform-minded Muslims would eventually conclude that the relative backwardness of the Ottoman Empire was due not merely to technical shortcomings but also — and more fundamentally — to the static quality of Islamic life.

Napoleon's invasion gave a boost to latent reformist efforts. It tacitly encouraged Muslim leaders to draw a distinction between religious matters, where the orthodox thought had to prevail, and secular matters, where they must be able to learn and to use foreign methods and technologies. In any case, the French fundamentally changed the Egyptian government and legal system by abolishing serfdom and feudalism and by guaranteeing some basic individual rights. The *sharia* itself was largely replaced by the Napoleonic Code (*Code civil des français*, i.e., the civil code of the French), which would be administered by a Westernized Egyptian elite trained in France.

In the wake of the French invasion, the Ottomans seemed willing to accept Western law on a generous scale, at least temporarily. The Tanzimat ("reforms") policy, begun in 1839, is the best case in point. Based on changes begun by Sultan Mahmud II and implemented by Sultan Abdul Mejid I, this far-reaching reform program was administered by the Grand Vizier, chief executive officer of the Ottoman state. The first reform decree, known as the

Gülhane Edict of 1839 (its full title is the "Noble Edict of the Rose Chamber"), stressed the importance of new legislation. It would result in adoption of a revised Penal Code the following year. The Gülhane Edict stated:

> In order to better administer the Sublime Empire and the Well-Protected Dominions, it is deemed necessary and important to enact some new laws. The most important provisions of these indispensable laws consist of more personal safety; of a better protection of honour, decency and property; and of fixing the taxes and specifying the way of drafting the required soldiers and the period of their service.[18]

Under the direction of Mustafa Reşid Pasha (1800–1858), one of the greatest and most brilliant Ottoman statesmen of his time, the Tanzimat program covered five major fields:

- *Legal and political administration*: New codes of law were introduced. The Ottoman Commercial Code of 1850 was based on the French Commercial Code. State courts become secular and independent: they were no longer under the sway of orthodox Islamic jurists. Under the Penal Code of 1858, which was basically a translation of the French Penal Code, the traditional severe punishments of *sharia* law (*hadd*) were all abolished, except that the death penalty was retained in cases of apostasy. The Ottomans also adopted a Code of Commercial Procedure (1861) and a Code of Maritime Commerce (1863), both of which followed French law. Between 1869 and 1876, a basic law of obligations was compiled. Although this code was derived from Islamic sources alone, i.e., Hanafi law, the important act of codifying it and thereby making it uniform owed much to European influences. Finally, the Ottomans also set up provincial representative assemblies.
- *Taxation*: In the past, local rulers had enriched themselves through the tax system. A standardized system of taxation was developed, reducing abuses in this field.
- *Military conscription*: The reforms included adoption of the Prussian system of conscription. This replaced the Ottomans' traditional *devshirme* system, i.e., recruiting promising Christian boys throughout the empire for conversion to Islam and then for an intensive education in military and administrative skills.
- *Education*: Previously, Islam had been the sole foundation for schooling. Modern secular policies were now introduced.
- *Individual rights*: The security of life, property and honor of every citizen was guaranteed within the Ottoman Empire. In return, the state demanded that all citizens remain loyal to the ruling sultan and that they support the Ottoman administration.[19]

These changes were so sweeping that they seriously impinged on the powers of the sultan. For this reason, they were not destined to last very long. The final blow fell when the vizier Midhat Pasha went so far as to propose a Turkish constitution and a parliament. This was too much for the despotic sultan Abdulhamid II, who officially ended the reform program as soon as he ascended the throne in 1876.

Thus on the legal front the long-term effect of Napoleon's invasion of Egypt was that Islamic jurists suffered a setback in their own power and social status. New courts and codes were introduced. The so-called Mixed Courts, established in 1876, had jurisdiction in all civil cases where foreign nationals or foreign interests were involved. In 1883, the National Courts began to exercise civil and criminal jurisdiction over all cases involving Egyptians themselves. Most civil and criminal matters were transferred to these new courts.

Henceforth, Islamic jurists' work in Egyptian life would be limited to matters of personal status. Only marriage and family law (broadly defined to include the law of succession, donations to a *waqf*, and the law covering gifts) would still be based on the *sharia*. In Egypt, the *sharia* courts would eventually be incorporated into the National Court system in 1956.[20] This policy continued under 40 years of British rule (1882–1922). It is still the case in Egypt today and, indeed, in many other countries that also have large Muslim populations and a long history of European influence or control.[21]

How to Deal with Incursions by the West: Jamal al-Din al-Afghani (1839–1897)

A fiery orator and political activist, al-Afghani made a deep impact on the Islamic world of his time and continues to be a source of inspiration and controversy.[22] He was one of the first to sound the alarm about the incursions of the West and the concomitant decline in Islamic power. He was also one of the first to urge Muslims to reform themselves by becoming more modern and more rational, namely, by relying on *ijtihad* (independent reasoning). *Ijtihad*, he stressed, had been recommended by Muhammad himself and by the Quran.

Teaching in Cairo, where one of his disciples was the great reformer Muhammad Abduh, who is discussed below, al-Afghani held that Islam's defeats at the hands of the West were not due to any failings in Islam itself but only due to the *corruption* of Islam. In his view, it was corrupt because it had fallen away from the "pure" Islam allegedly practiced in the golden age of the prophet and the early caliphs.

Al-Afghani argued that the Islamic world had to unite and protect itself from the relentless expansion of Britain and other Western powers. To do so, he said, Muslims had to understand Islam correctly and begin to live in accordance with Islam's earliest teachings. These teachings, he asserted, were preeminently rational. Then — and only then — would the Islamic world finally become strong enough to fend off Western incursions.

Al-Afghani's theological analysis was the exact opposite of the conventional wisdom of his day. Most Westerners and many educated Muslims believed that the endemic weaknesses of the Islamic world arose chiefly because Muslims had been unable — or, more accurately, unwilling — to master the science and technology of the West. According to this school of thought, the only solution to Islamic weaknesses was simply to put aside all irrational religious elements, i.e., Islam itself, and to adopt the rational secularism of the West.

The theological solution proposed by al-Afghani was clearly an attempt to square the circle of Western rationalism and the doctrines of Islam. He failed in this effort. The Sunni clerical establishment opposed identifying early Islam with Western rationalism. Al-Afghani also failed to win popular support for his ideas. Finally, the pro–British regime of the Khedive Tawfiq deported him from Egypt because of his anti–British activism. Nevertheless, his ideas are still with us. There is no evidence that belief in a "pure" Islam will inevitably lead to a viable, powerful state — one able to defend itself against foreign incursions — but this is a core belief of violence-prone Islamic fundamentalism today.

Legal Reformer and Grand Mufti of Egypt: Muhammad Abduh (c. 1849–1905)

Muhammad Abduh was a liberal Egyptian jurist and scholar who advocated relying on *ijtihad* to strengthen Islam.[23] He was the chief architect of the nineteenth century reform movement in Islam. His teachings, which blended traditional, modernist, and reformist thought, were influential in Egypt, the Middle East, and North Africa. Abduh's major work, *The Unity of Theology*, or *Treatise on the Oneness of God* (*Risalat al-Tawhid*), is the most important summary of his thought. Although his major reforms failed to come to fruition because of strong opposition from Islamic conservatives, his efforts to modernize Islamic legal thought and practices are still important today.

Abduh was educated in the Nile Delta in Tanta, the greatest center of religious studies in Egypt aside from al-Azhar University itself. Al-Azhar was the first and is still the most important Islamic university in the world. Islamic law and theology have been taught there ever since 975, when chief justice

Abu El-Hassan sat in the courtyard of the university and, reading from a book on jurisprudence written by his father, instructed students in the intricacies of Shiite law. (In the twelfth century, al-Azhar became and still is a Sunni university. Nasser brought it under state control in 1961 and since then one of its important tasks has been to provide religious — and thus political — legitimacy for the Egyptian government.[24])

From 1869 to 1877, Abduh studied at al-Azhar, where he earned the degree of "scholar." At the university, he met the fiery orator, political activist and writer Jamal al-Din al-Afghani (1839–1897), who had a profound influence on him. Because Egypt could not pay its debts to Britain, the British occupied Egypt in 1882. Abduh played a leadership role in the anti–British movement and echoed al-Afghani's nationalist views in numerous articles written for the Egyptian press. For his pains, the British exiled him from Egypt for six years. When he was finally allowed to return to Egypt in 1888, he reached the conclusion that political protest against colonialism was futile unless Islam could first reform itself from within. For this reason, he then advocated limited cooperation with Britain. He became a judge and in 1899, with British backing, he was appointed Grand Mufti of Egypt. He taught and wrote with the political activist Rashid Rida, who is discussed below. Abduh also organized schools, helped reform al-Azhar, learned French so that he could master modern European thought, and traveled to Europe.

Like al-Afghani, Abduh decided that a basic reason for Islam's inner stagnation was the gap between reason and faith. Although as Egypt became more secularized its reliance on reason had been growing, Abduh was convinced that because Egyptian society was ultimately based on faith rather than reason, it could never be wholly secularized — nor did he wish it to be. He believed that Islam contained the rationality and morality needed to form a modern society but that Islamic thought itself needed to be liberated.

As he put it in his autobiography, this is what Islam needed:

[to be free from] from the shackles of *taqlid* [blind imitation], and understand religion as it was understood by the elders of the community before dissension appeared; to return, in the acquisition of religious knowledge, to its first sources, and to weigh them in the scales of human reason ... and to prove that ... religion must be accounted a friend to science, pushing man to investigate the secrets of existence, summoning him to respect established truths, and to depend on them in his moral life and conduct. All this I [Abduh] count as one matter, and in my advocacy of it I ran counter to the opinion of two great groups, of which the body of the *umma* [the Islamic religious community] is composed — the students of the sciences of religion, and those who think like them, and the students of the arts of this age, with those who are on their side.[25]

Abduh had thus seriously underestimated the power of the political and religious conservatives. For example, when a university professor named al-

Khawli was so inspired by Abduh that he began a literary and therefore, from an orthodox point of view, a critical study of the Quran, he was quickly removed from office by the joint forces of the conservative politicians of Cairo and the *ulama* (religious scholars) of al-Azhar.

In this and in other cases, Abduh felt strongly that the *ulama* were making a grave error. In his view, they invariably refused to make a crucial distinction between the religious essence of Islam, on the one hand, and its supercargo of intricate but ultimately less important social laws, on the other. This "excess of adherence to the outwardness of the law," as he put it, led to blind imitation — the exact opposite of the intellectual freedom he saw in genuine Islam.

Abduh did his best to reform the *sharia* rules governing family relations, ritual duties, and personal behavior. He tried hard to break down the inflexible patterns of scholastic thought traditionally upheld by orthodox Islamic jurists and scholars. Where necessary, he would even go so far as to disregard the literal text of the Quran itself— if doing so would lead to common sense solutions and promote fairness and the public welfare. A good example of Abduh's liberated thought is that, as Grand Mufti, he approved earning interest on bank deposits.

He also held that the legal system was a crucially important factor in any country's prosperity: laws could and, indeed, *must be changed* to reflect changing circumstances. Searching for a cohesive legal methodology for the *sharia*, Abduh argued that jurists should "piece together" (*talfiq*) judgments from the four Sunni legal schools to make laws relevant to modern times.[26] *Talfiq* involves bringing together elements from two or more Islamic legal schools and using them to create new and different doctrines. Modernist reformers have used this practice extensively on matters involving personal status, succession, and *waqf* (religious endowments.) Abduh himself revered the Quran but he would never follow the holy text blindly. As he explained in *The Unity of Theology,*

> The Qur'an came and took religion by a new road, untrodden by previous Scriptures, a road appropriate and feasible alike to the contemporaries of the revelation and to their successors.... The Book gives us all that God permits us, or is essential for us, to know about His attributes. *But it does not require our acceptance of its contents simply on the ground of its own statement of them. On the contrary, it offers arguments and evidence.... It spoke to the rational mind and alerted the intelligence.*[27]

Making the Sharia Fit Modern Times: Rashid Rida (1865–1935)

A Syrian-born author, editor and political activist, Rashid Rida lived and worked in Egypt. He was one of the first Muslim intellectuals to call for a reformed *sharia*, which in his view would form the cornerstone of a strong, modernized but thoroughly Islamic state. The reformist ideals of al-Afghani and especially those of Abduh heavily influenced him. Indeed, Rida's highly regarded magazine, *Al-Manar* (*The Lighthouse*), published for 37 years (from 1898 to 1935), was in essence a call for Islamic reforms according to the teachings of Abduh.

Rida was convinced that Islam was well suited for the modern age. According to the modern scholar Albert Hourani, Rida believed that

> The teachings and moral precepts of Islam are such that if they are properly understood and fully obeyed, they will lead to success in this world as well as the next — and success in all the forms in which the world understands it, [namely] strength, respect, civilization, happiness. If they are not understood and obeyed weakness, decay, barbarism are the results....
>
> What are the principles which are contained alike in Islam and modern civilization? First of all comes activity: positive effort is the essence of Islam and this is the meaning of the term *jihad* in its most general sense ... the second distinguishing sign of Islam is that it has created a single community, a body of men linked by faith and worship yet separated by their natural characteristics, but a community in every sense.... Possession of the truth is the third and most fundamental sign of Islam, and the true Islam is that taught by the Prophet and the "Elders...."[28]

Rida favored the teachings of the Hanbali school of law but was in fact remarkably flexible in his own thought. He held, for example, that when the holy texts were ambiguous or contradictory, Muslims should use reason to find the course of action that was most in accord with the spirit of Islam and that would most help the Muslim community as a whole. He also broke new ground on a fundamental principle of Islam, namely, the consensus of scholars (*ijma*). Here he argued that Muslim religious leaders should exercise not only judicial and political power, but legislative power as well.

Following Ottoman legal practice, Rida said they could do this by creating a body of positive secular administrative law (*kanun*). This would ultimately derive its authority from the general principles of Islam and would be valid as long as it did not conflict with the *sharia*. This process of forging secular law was critically important, Rida believed, because it was the right and indeed the duty of every Islamic state to work out "a system of just laws appropriate to the situation in which its past history has placed it."[29] This, he said, was in fact how law was originally made in the early days of Islam.

The intellectual stagnation and military weakness of the Islamic world of Rida's time was so evident to him that he called for drastic measures. The duty of *jihad* (in this context, defensive efforts to protect Islam) was, he said, binding on all Muslims. But if the Islamic world was weak, it could not discharge this duty successfully. It was therefore essential for the Islamic world to become strong once more. The only way to accomplish this, he stressed, was by adopting the sciences and technology of the West. Since what is an indispensable condition for discharging a duty is itself a duty, Rida held that young Muslims had no choice but to learn how to use the tools of the West.

Toward this end, Rida broke with early Islamic tradition, which prohibits the taking of interest, and said that businessmen should be permitted to charge interest. (Interest had in fact been legally permitted by the Ottomans since the sixteenth century, but they had capped the maximum rate at 10 percent.) Rida now argued that the danger that Western capitalism would take over Islamic lands was so great that this drastic step was justified and, indeed, quite necessary. It could legitimately be justified under the Islamic doctrine of necessity. As Hourani explained, Rida concluded that

> The principle of necessity can therefore be invoked: necessity makes legal what would otherwise be forbidden, and in this case it may compel Muslims to depart from their traditional interpretation of the law and built their economic life on the same basis as the western nations.[30]

Rida's most radical contribution to the theory of Islamic law was what the modern scholar Wael B. Hallaq has called "utilitarianism."[31] This concept was based on the traditional idea of the public interest (*maslaha*) which, as we noted earlier, was also put forward by Ibn Taymiyya in the fourteenth century. Although the notion of the public interest was a familiar one to earlier Islamic jurists, it had only limited importance to them and, to use a bit of modern journalistic jargon, did not have legs. In other words, it could not stand alone but was rather considered to have only a minor role in the vast play of medieval legal thought.

Rida decided that by jettisoning some of the outmoded and counterproductive legal concepts of Islamic law, he could elevate the public interest to a commanding position as a new justification for legislative acts. It could serve, in short, as the intellectual foundation for a reformed body of Islamic law. Hallaq has clearly outlined the interesting successive steps in the evolution of Rida's thought. Most are too detailed to be repeated here, but one can usefully be cited. Hallaq tells us Rida believed that

> The common Muslim individual stands helpless before the formidable and intricate doctrines elaborated by jurists, for their hair-splitting resulted in a highly technical law that is so difficult to comprehend as to render adherence to it a burdensome task.[32]

Hallaq then adds his own conclusion to Rida's. He tells us:

> The contemporary phenomenon of setting aside the *Sharia* in favor of a wholesale importation of foreign laws is but one consequence of the inherited legacy of legal complexities in the traditional system. The technically elaborate nature of traditional legal doctrine is further compounded by the immense detail generated by explaining specific and minute positive legal rulings.[33]

By selectively citing earlier jurists, Rida tried to prove that the public interest (*maslaha*) was a key concept solidly based on revealed sources, i.e., on the Quran, the *sunna*, and scholarly consensus (*ijma*), and that it could therefore be used to reform Islamic law. Appealing as this interpretation may have been to liberals, Rida's doctrine may have been seen by conservatives as negating too much of Islam's legal theory.[34] Perhaps for this reason, it had little chance of success. Rida's ambitious reforms were never put into practice. He died in Syria in 1935.

6

The Sharia *and* Jihad

As we noted earlier, *jihad* is an Arabic word that means "to exert effort, i.e., to struggle or to fight, towards a specific objective." The verb *jahada*, from which the verbal noun *jihad* is derived, and its grammatical derivations appear 41 times in 36 Quranic verses. To see how 10 translators have handled this concept as it appears in one verse, see Appendix 2: Translating the Concept of *Jihad*.

Jahada and its derivatives can refer to a range of activities. Under the Sunnis' general doctrines and historical traditions of the *sharia*, however, *jihad* classically consists of *military actions designed to expand or to defend the territory of Islam.*[1] The theological underpinning of *jihad* is the orthodox belief in a struggle to bring the whole world under Islamic rule.

It is true that some Islamic jurists, especially among the Shiites, have drawn a distinction between the "greater" or "spiritual" *jihad*, on the one hand, and the "lesser" or "physical" jihad, on the other. The former is an internal struggle and refers to a Muslim's efforts to lead an upright, religious life in the face of his own lustful or base impulses. The latter is an external struggle against a tyranny or violent oppression that prohibits the right to practice Islam.

The *Encyclopaedia of Islam* tells us, however, that when the term *jihad* is used, it normally refers to a physical, external struggle, not a struggle against base impulses.[2] Western experts confirm that, in medieval legal discussions, *jihad* normally means "war against infidels": there is nothing inherently *defensive* about it. The indignation of some Muslim scholars over this translation may represent their hope of reinterpreting a long-standing tradition and thus removing offensive war from the quiver of Islamic thought. While doing away with offensive war is certainly a noble objective, rewriting the historical record is another matter entirely.

It is difficult to generalize about the concept of *jihad* because there has been — and still is — so much diversity and complexity in the Islamic world that what may have been true in one time and place may not have been true in another.

One of the reasons that *jihad* can mean different things to different people, both Muslims and non–Muslims, is that it appears in divergent and even contradictory Quranic texts. Doctrinally, these texts reflect four successive categories in the evolution of Muhammad's own thought. They echo the growth of Islam from its early, feeble beginnings in Mecca (610–622) to its later dominant position in Medina (622–632). The four categories are:

- Those which encourage potential converts, by peaceful persuasion, to become Muslims
- Those which enjoin defensive fighting to ward off aggression
- Those which approve, within certain limits, taking the initiative in launching attacks
- Those which urge the faithful to attack at all times and in all places.

A solution to any apparent textual contradictions about *jihad* was found in the traditional doctrine of abrogation (*naskh*), by which later texts were held to abrogate earlier texts. What this meant in practice was that only the last — and in this context the most belligerent — texts about *jihad* remained valid. As the *Encyclopaedia of Islam* concludes, "Accordingly, the [doctrinal] rule on the subject may be formulated in these absolute terms: 'the fight [*jihad*] is obligatory even when they [the nonbelievers] have not themselves started it.'"[3]

Although *jihad* has classically been seen as a duty which is laid permanently on all able-bodied Muslim men (it is permanent because it is held to remain in force until the universal domination of Islam is at last achieved), this obligation is not a simple one. It has two aspects. The first is a *collective obligation* to wage *jihad*. The Islamic community as a whole bears this responsibility.

The second aspect is that *jihad* becomes a mandatory *individual duty* whenever a Muslim's personal participation is necessary to defend the Islamic community as a whole, e.g., when he lives in the territory nearest to the enemy or when his own town is being attacked.[4] Osama bin Laden has hammered away this point. In a *fatwa* of 1998, for example, he asserted that *jihad* is an unavoidable individual duty. According to him, it is not a collective duty which a devout Muslim can ignore on a personal basis, simply assuming that Islam is being adequately defended by the official representatives of the Islamic community, i.e., political leaders and professional soldiers.

To add a further complexity to all this, not all conflicts that the combatants call *jihad* are in fact fought over matters of principle and belief. Motives for fighting vary considerably. Muslims often invoke *jihad* purely as a political and a propaganda weapon, just as American often use "war" to mean an organized drive against medical or social failings, such as cancer, poverty or drunk driving. The politically motivated clashes between India and Pakistan over Kashmir are another good case in point.[5]

Finally, it should also be noted that, historically, Islamic interpretations of what is meant by *jihad* have changed significantly over time.[6] In the nineteenth century, some Muslim writers, particularly those living under the Raj (British colonial rule) in India, claimed that the Quran and *hadith* allowed war only for self-defense against persecution and aggression. The medieval understanding of *jihad* as justifying expansionist war was, they argued, simply wrong.

Later apologists saw a need for further changes. They pointed out that the simple bipolar division of the world into *Dar al-Harb* and *Dar al-Islam* is found nowhere in the Quran or *hadith*. Trying to bring the concept of *jihad* into conformity with modern international legal standards, these writers argued that it was merely the Islamic equivalent of a "just war" in Western terms, namely, one fought for defensive purposes and in order to resist external aggression.

The third and most recent interpretation, however, brings the wheel to full circle. Violence-prone Islamic radicals today say that, in the final years of the prophet's life, *jihad* clearly meant a struggle to bring the whole world under Islamic rule. They therefore assert that the first task of Muslim activists now is to overthrow the corrupt, hypocritical and, in their view, totally *un-Islamic* regimes that currently rule Saudi Arabia and other Muslim countries. Only when these leaders have fallen, say these radical elements, can the external *jihad* resume.

This much is clear enough. What is not clear, however, is why some young men (and a few young women) are so willing to become suicide bombers. In historical terms, Muslim suicide attacks are a very recent development, arguably dating from the first suicide bomb attack on the American Embassy in Beirut in 1983. Many theories have been put forward in the West to explain this phenomenon, but none of them alone — and no combination of them — is entirely persuasive. In this case, at least, too many theories are worse than none at all. Perhaps the most honest thing for Western commentators to do is to admit that they do not fully understand the reasons for these increasingly common suicide attacks.

The Relationship Between the Sharia *and* Jihad

There can be no doubt that *jihad* forms a significant part of the *sharia* and is addressed in books on Islamic jurisprudence. At the same time, however, there is considerable doubt about what this theory really means today.[7] Should we try to understand it the light of medieval Islamic practices? Should we interpret it in the light of the requirements of the modern international legal and political system? Or should we, as President Bush would have it, simply dismiss *jihad* as the posturing of "those who hate freedom"?

A modern scholar, Noga Hartmann, makes the point that the meaning of *jihad* now lies entirely in the eye of the beholder.[8] In other words, since there is no agreed definition of what *jihad* means or should mean, anyone who has something to say about it is free to voice an opinion. If he is a Muslim activist or thinker, he is also free to issue a *fatwa* and hope that his own followers, and perhaps others as well, will follow it. There is, in short, no clear party line on what constitutes *jihad*. Amid all this confusion, however, one thing is certain: from now on, the West can ignore the concept of *jihad* only at its own peril.

The classical medieval theory of *jihad* contained elaborate rules for the onset, conduct, interruption and cessation of war, for the use of weapons, and for the treatment of prisoners.[9] No war could be considered a *jihad* unless it was formally authorized and led by the legitimate religious and political authorities. Islam's enemies were to be given fair warning before they were attacked. If they refused to fight and at the same time also declined to embrace Islam, they were to be offered the semi-autonomous status of "protected minorities" (*dhimmi*)— in return for tax payments to their Muslim rulers. Noncombatants, e.g., women, children, and aged or ill men, were to be spared whenever possible. Enemy property was not to be destroyed wantonly.[10]

Today, however, the relationship between the *sharia* and *jihad* has become murky indeed. Some terrorist acts — the bombings of London's tube (subway) in 2005 is an excellent example here — cannot easily be explained by medieval doctrines. Yet because the *sharia* is not set in stone, many interpretations are possible. A violence-prone Islamic fundamentalist, for example, could argue that Britain, because of its active participation in the American-led occupation of Iraq, is in fact at war with Islam. Such a fundamentalist might conclude that since Britain is a democratic country and the British people have repeatedly voted for the government of Tony Blair, they are not innocent and may therefore legitimately be attacked.[11]

Thus the relationship between the *sharia* and *jihad* is rather complicated. Some Western scholars claim that Islam itself generates violent personalities who produce *jihad*. They claim that repressive social and economic conditions in much of the Islamic world, coupled with political oppression there, generates in young men such acute feelings of humiliation, helplessness and frustration that violence is the inevitable result. Still other Western observers, however, believe that violence is only part of a political vocabulary used to mobilize Muslims. Palestinian jihadists, for their part, claim they are fighting Israel's illegal occupation of their land and are thus legitimate resistance fighters. The jury is still out on the exact relationship between the *sharia* and *jihad* today. It seems likely, however, that there is some truth in each of the above assertions.

Opinions of Selected Islamic Thinkers, Jurists and Political Activists

For more than 1,200 years, Islamic thinkers, jurists and activists have put forward their considered opinions on the *sharia* and *jihad.* Their extensive verbatim accounts, some of which are quoted here, give a much richer appreciation of their historic times than any modern paraphrases possibly can. Fifteen of these men are discussed below. Many of them have already been mentioned earlier in this book: if this is the case, their names are marked with asterisks for ease of reference.

Martyrdom in God's Cause: The Quran and Muhammad* (c. 570–632)

Although devout Muslims consider that God, not Muhammad, is the ultimate source of the Quran, they all agree that this holy scripture was revealed to the prophet by God. They further believe that it was not revealed for the prophet alone, but for the sake of all humanity: Muhammad was merely the recipient and the transmitter of this divine message. Purely for the sake of literary convenience, however, here we will attribute the Quran to Muhammad himself.

Among many other relevant passages about *jihad,* the Quran has this to say about martyrdom in the cause of *jihad*:

- "Let those who would exchange the life of this world for the hereafter, fight for the cause of God; who fights for the cause of God, whether he dies or triumphs, on him We shall bestow a rich recompense" (*sura* 4:74).
- "As for those who are slain in the cause of God, He will not allow their works to perish. He will vouchsafe them guidance and ennoble their state; He will admit them to the Paradise He has made known to them" (*sura* 47:5).
- "If you should die or be slain in the cause of God, His forgiveness and His mercy would surely be better than all the riches they [the infidels]

amass. If you should die or be slain, before God shall you all be gathered" (*sura* 3:157).

- "Never think that those who were slain in the cause of God are dead. They are alive, and well provided for by their Lord; pleased with his gifts and rejoicing that those they left behind, who have not yet joined them, have nothing to fear or to regret; rejoicing in God's grace and bounty. God will not deny the faithful their reward." (*sura* 3:169)
- "He that leaves his home in the cause of God shall find many a refuge in the land and great abundance. He that leaves his dwelling to fight for God and His apostle and is then overtaken by death shall be recompensed by God. Surely God is forgiving and merciful." (*sura* 4:100)

Along "The Beaten Path" with Malik ibn Anas* (d. 795)

Malik's great work, *Al-Muwatta (The Beaten Path)*, is one of the oldest books on Islamic jurisprudence. Containing contemporary accounts of Muhammad's life and of the sayings of the first caliphs, it was written to encourage and inspire the faithful. The quotations selected here have been shortened to improve their readability, e.g., by deleting such pious phrases as "may Allah bless him and grant him peace," but otherwise they are quoted verbatim. If they are not always entirely clear, they are at least valuable for their tenor.[12] *The Beaten Path* claims that, according to reliable first-hand reports, the Messenger of Allah (Muhammad) made the following statements:

- "Someone who does *jihad* in the way of Allah [i.e., for God's cause] is like someone who fasts and prays constantly and does not slacken from his prayer and fasting until he returns."
- "Allah guarantees either the Garden [paradise] or a safe return to his home with whatever he has obtained of reward or booty for the one who does *jihad* in His way, if it is solely *jihad* and trust in the promise that brings him out of his house."
- "Shall I tell you who has the best degree [the highest social standing] among people? A man who takes the rein of his horse to do *jihad* in the way of Allah."
- "By He in whose hand myself is! I would like to fight in the way of Allah and be killed, then brought to life again so I could be killed, and then be brought to life again so that I could be killed."
- "None of you is wounded in the way of Allah — and Allah knows best who is wounded in His way — but that when the Day of Rising [resurrection] comes blood will gush forth from his wound, but its scent will be that of musk."

The Beaten Path also relates these stories about Muhammad:

- "The Messenger of Allah was sitting by a grave which was being dug at Medina. A man looked into the grave and said, 'An awful bed for the believer.' The Messenger of Allah said, 'Evil? What you have said is absolutely wrong.' The man said, 'I didn't mean that, Messenger of Allah. I meant being killed in the way of Allah.' The Messenger of Allah said, 'Being killed in the way of Allah has no like! There is no place on earth where I would prefer my grave to be than here [Medina].' He repeated it three times."
- "[During a lull in a battle], the Messenger of Allah was stimulating people to do *jihad*, mentioning the Garden. One of the Ansar [this term, which means "helpers" in Arabic, is an honorific applied to the Medina clans that supported Muhammad at an early date] was eating some dates he had in his hand, and said, 'Am I so desirous of this world that I should sit until I finish them?' He threw aside what was in his hand and took his sword and fought until he was slain."

Jihad as a Hidden Source of Legal Knowledge: Muhammad ibn Idris al-Shafi'i* (767–820)

In his definitive work, the *Risala* ("epistle"), al-Shafi'i explains to the reader that there are three categories of legal knowledge. The first category consists of easily found and easily understood Quranic rules and regulations. The second category involves obligatory duties that can be derived and understood, though with considerable difficulty, from certain *hadith* or from reasoning by analogy (*qiyas*). These two categories are discussed in Appendix 1.

The third category is, according to Shafi'i, by far the hardest to master and is the most relevant for our purposes here. The following account had been lightly edited. It is especially interesting because of the authoritative light it sheds on early Muslim legal thinking about *jihad*. Asked to describe this elusive third category of knowledge, Shafi'i tells his fellow jurists:

> The public is incapable of knowing this kind of knowledge, nor can all specialists obtain it. But some of those who do obtain it should not all neglect it. If some can obtain it, the others are relieved of this duty [of obtaining it]; but those who do obtain it will be rewarded.[13]

Pressed for a further explanation, Shafi'i first gives his own view and then backs it up with Quranic quotations:

> God has imposed the [duty of] *jihad* as laid down in His Book and uttered by His Prophet's tongue. He [God] stressed the calling [for] the *jihad* as follows:

- "God has purchased from the faithful their lives and worldly goods, and in return has promised them the Garden. They will fight for the cause of God; they will slay and be slain. Such is the true promise which He has made them in the Torah, the Gospel and the Koran. And who is more true to his pledge than God? Rejoice then in the bargain you have made. That is the supreme triumph." (*sura* 9:112)[14]
- "But you may fight against the idolaters [during all 12 months of the year, i.e., including the four months held by Muslims to be sacred], since they themselves fight against you in all of them. Know that God is with the righteous" (*sura* 9:36).
- "When the [four] sacred months are over, slay the idolaters wherever you find them. Arrest them, besiege them, and lie in ambush everywhere for them. If they repent and take to prayer and render the alms levy, allow them to go their way. God is forgiving and merciful" (*sura* 9:5).
- "Fight against such of those to whom the Scriptures were given as believe in neither God nor the Last Day, who do not forbid what God and His apostle have forbidden, and do not embrace the true Faith, until they pay tribute out of hand and are utterly subdued" (*sura* 9:29).

Shafi'i then quotes this Prophetic *hadith*:

I [Muhammad] shall continue to fight the unbelievers until they say: "There is no god but God." If they make this pronouncement [and thereby become Muslims themselves], they shall be secured in their blood and property, unless taken for its price, and their reward shall be given by God.

After quoting two more Quranic verses to make his points, Shafi'i then says:

These communications mean that the *jihad*, and rising up in arms in particular, is obligatory for all able-bodied [believers], exempting no one, just as prayer, pilgrimage, and [payment of] alms also are performed and no person is permitted to perform the duty for another, since performance by one will not fulfil the duty for another.

They may also mean that the duty of *jihad* is a collective duty different from that of prayer: Those who perform it in the war against the polytheists will fulfil the duty and receive the supererogatory merit, thereby preventing those who have stayed behind from falling into error.

But God has not put the two [categories] of men on an equal footing for He said:

- "The believers who stay at home — apart from those that suffer from a grave disability — are not the equals of those who fight for the cause of God with their goods and their persons. God has exalted the men who fight with their goods and persons above those who stay at home. God has promised all a good reward; but far richer is the recompense of those who fight for Him: [they shall receive] ranks of His own bestowal, forgiveness, and mercy (*sura* 4:97).[15]

In his book, Shafi'i writes about *jihad* at much greater length but his conclusion is short, simple, and unequivocal. He tells the faithful: "The literal meaning of this communication is that the duty [of *jihad*] is obligatory on all men."[16]

The Hanbali Law of War: Ibn Hazm* (994–1064)

As mentioned in an earlier chapter, the jurist and theologian Ibn Hazm was famous for his inflexible interpretations of Zahiri, i.e., "literalist" law. This school of thought was named after Dawud al-Zahiri, a jurist who died in Baghdad in 844. Hanbali law generally urges restraint and Ibn Hazm's zeal marks an extreme point in the spectrum of Sunni legal opinion. He was so notorious, in fact, that al-Nawawi, a later medieval jurist (d. 1277), denounced his work as "the ugliest example of hardened literalism."[17]

Nevertheless, Ibn Hazm's 11-volume legal treatise, *Al-Muhalla* (*The Book of Ornaments*), does contain vigorous, clear explanations of some of the classical juridical problems of Islam. His chapter on *jihad* is worth reviewing here.[18] In this chapter, Ibn Hazm lays out, sequentially, the Hanbali rules of war. He begins by drawing the familiar distinction between a collective duty which must be discharged by someone if the community as a whole is to escape divine retribution, e.g., praying over a dead Muslim, and an individual duty incumbent on all Muslims, e.g., to pray five times day. Ibn Hazm takes the position that

> *Jihad* is an obligation incumbent on the Muslims [i.e., it is a collective duty]. If someone undertakes it who repulses the enemy, carries out raids of their territory and protects the borders [i.e., if he undertakes *jihad* as his individual duty], the rest are no longer under obligation.

He then goes on to reiterate a Hanbali tradition: a man must participate in *jihad* as soon as he is summoned to do so. He tells the faithful: "Whomever the commander of the *jihad* commands to go to the House of War, it is incumbent on him to obey him in that [i.e., he must follow the order] unless he has a compelling excuse." Another Hanbali tradition is that individuals (but not strong, well-armed and well-mounted groups) who want to set out on a *jihad* raid first need their imam's permission. "It is not permissible," says Ibn Hazm, "for everyone to undertake raiding on his own, nor for one to enter the House of War without the imam's permission."

Today, some modern revisionists argued that the concept of *jihad* covers only defensive — not offensive — war and that it is really designed to help believers overcome internal psychological challenges, i.e., their base desires. It is true that the Hanbali school makes defensive warfare a more important duty than offensive warfare. But this should not surprise us: the physical survival of a community is always more urgent than campaigns to fulfill its expansionist ambitions.

Taken as a whole, Hanbali tradition does not support the cardinal importance of the "base desires" thesis. As Ibn Taymiyya (discussed below) states, "The command to *jihad* includes [motivations] by the heart, by summons, by argument, by demonstration, by advice, by direction, and by the body. It is incumbent to the full extent of one's ability." He makes no mention here of internal psychological struggles.

Both the Quran and Ibn Hazm offer concise advice on the military tactics to be used in *jihad*. The Quran tells the soldiers of Islam:

> God has now lightened your burden, for He knows that you are weak. If there are a hundred steadfast men among you, they shall vanquish two hundred; and if there are a thousand, they shall, by God's will, defeat two thousand. God is with those that are steadfast[19] [*sura* 8:66].

Ibn Hazm himself, however, takes a much more uncompromising line. He admonishes the troops: "It is not permissible for a Muslim to flee before a polytheist or multiple polytheists, however many they may be, unless he returns with a greater number of Muslims." He provides other stern tactical advice as well. Some examples:

- "It is permissible to burn the polytheists' trees, food, crops, and houses to the point of destroying them."
- "It is strictly impermissible to destroy their animals, whether camels, oxen, sheep, horses, fowl ... except for swine."
- "It is not permissible to kill their women or to kill the immature among them, unless one of them should fight. When the Muslim has no alternative but to kill them, he may kill them.... If they are killed in night raids or in the confusion of battle, unintentionally, that is unobjectionable.... It is permissible to kill everyone else of the polytheists, whether a combattant or non-combattant, trader or hireling ... an old man of authority or not, bishop, priest, monk, blind, or disabled or no threat to anyone: however it is also permissible to spare them."

The faithful are specifically permitted to join forces with immoral "reprobates" (in this context, Shiites or other Muslims who want to fight only under their own leaders) if this becomes necessary to achieve common military objectives for Islam. In such a case, moreover, the orthodox must not hold back in any way. Ibn Hazm encourages them with these dramatic words:

> Whenever one fights along with a reprobate, let him kill the unbelievers and ruin their crops, their homes, and their fruits. Let him seize the women and children without hesitation. Bringing them out of the shade of unbelief to the light of Islam is an obligation. The one who omits it, though capable, rebels against God. Every sin is less than leaving them in unbelief and aiding them to remain in it. There is no sin greater than the sin of him who rejects *jihad* against the unbelievers....

"Fighting One's Own Desires": Abu Hamid Al-Ghazali* (1058–1111):

W. Montgomery Watt, a famous scholar of Islam, concluded that the jurist, logician and theologian Abu Hamid al-Ghazali "undoubtedly performed a great service for devout Muslims of every level of education by presenting obedience to the prescriptions of the *Sharia* as a meaningful way of life."[20] One aspect of al-Ghazali's contribution to Islam was the importance he attached to internal *jihad (jihad al-nafs).*

Much to this point is the following selection from al-Ghazali's book, *The Revival of the Religious Sciences (Ihya Ulum al-Din)*. It comes from a chapter mentioned earlier, the "Book of the training of the ego and the disciplining of manners and the healing of the heart's diseases." Al-Ghazali writes:

> Know that the body is like a town and the intellect of the mature human being is like a king ruling that town. All the forces of the external and internal senses he can muster are like his soldiers and his aides. The ego that enjoins evil, that is, lust and anger, is like an enemy that challenges him in his kingdom and strives to slaughter his people. The body thus becomes like a garrison-town and sea-outpost, and the soul like its custodian posted in it. If he fights against his enemies and defeats them and compels them to do what he likes, he will be praised when he returns to God's presence, as [the Quran says] "God has exalted the men who fight with their goods and their persons above those who stay at home" [*sura* 4:95]....[21] The Prophet said: "The fighter against unbelief is he who fights against his own ego in obeying God" [the *sura* for this quote is not identified in the text].

Legal Doctrines of *Jihad*: Ibn Rushd* (1126–1198)

Ibn Rushd became famous in Europe, where he is known by his Latin name of Averroës, because of his achievements as a philosopher. His penetrating, incisive explanations of Aristotle's work helped Jewish and Christian scholars better understand this Greek philosopher. In the Islamic world, however, Ibn Rushd is remembered chiefly as a jurist. The full title of his best-known legal handbook is both sonorous and inviting: "The beginning for him who interprets the sources independently and the end for him who wishes to limit himself" (*Bidayat al-Mujtahid wa Nihayat al-Muqtasid*).

As the modern scholar Rudolph Peters explained in his definitive study, *Jihad in Classical and Modern Islam*, this handbook belongs to a genre of legal treatises in which the controversies between the different schools of law are juxtaposed.[22] Ibn Rushd's handling of this process is unique because he looks dispassionately at the sources (Quran or *hadith*) which other jurists have used to justify their views on *jihad* and does not impose his own opinions on their arguments. As the following excerpts suggest, he discusses *jihad* in considerable depth. Some of his main points are:

- "Scholars agree that the *jihad* is a collective not a personal obligation.... The obligation to participate applies to adult free men who have the means at their disposal to go to war and who are healthy, that is, not ill or suffering from chronic diseases."
- "Scholars agree that all polytheists should be fought. This is founded on [a Quranic verse]: 'Fight them until there is no persecution'" (*sura* 8:39). Here Ibn Rushd is assuming that the reader knows the Quran by heart, so that it is only necessary for him to quote the opening words of a given verse. From memory, the reader will then automatically be able to fill in the rest. The full text of this passage reads, in Dawood's translation:

Make war on them until idolatry shall cease and God's religion shall reign supreme. If they desist [from their mistaken ways], God is cognizant of all their actions; but if they pay no heed, know then that God will protect you. He is the noblest Helper and the noblest Protector.

- "Damage inflicted upon the enemy may consist of damage to his property, injury to his person or violation of his personal liberty, i.e., that he is made a slave and is appropriated.... Most scholars are agreed that, in his dealings with captives, various policies are open to the Imam [i.e., the caliph, head of the Islamic state]. He may pardon them, enslave them, kill them, or release them either on ransom or as [non–Muslims living under Muslim protection], in which latter case the released captive is obliged to pay poll-tax (*jizya*).... As regards injury to the person, that is, the slaying of the enemy, the Muslims agree that in times of war, all adult, able-bodied, unbelieving males may be slain.... Opinions vary as to the damage that may be inflicted on their property, such as buildings, cattle and crops...."
- "According to all scholars, the prerequisite for warfare is that the enemy must have heard the summons to Islam. This implies that it is not

allowed to attack them before the summons has reached them.... Nevertheless it has been related irrefutably that the Prophet repeatedly made sudden attacks upon the enemy at night or at dawn. Some, consequently, maintain, and they are in the majority, that the practice of the Prophet has abrogated his words."

- "The maximum number of enemies against which one is obliged to stand one's ground is twice the number [of one's own troops]."
- "[A truce] is considered by some to be permitted from the very outset and without an immediate occasion, provided that the Imam deems it is in the interest of the Muslims. Others maintain that it is only allowed when the Muslims are pressed by sheer necessity, such as a civil war or the like... Still, there is controversy about the duration of this [truce] period. According to some it amounts to four years, but according to others three or ten years."
- "The Muslims are agreed that the aim of warfare against the People of the Book [those who have a holy scripture of their own, e.g., Jews and Christians] ... is twofold: either conversion to Islam, or payment of the poll-tax.... One famous question remains to be touched upon in this connection: that whether it is permitted to march into hostile territory carrying a copy of the Koran. Most scholars do not consider it allowed because an authoritative rule to this effect has been handed down from the Prophet in an authentic Tradition [*hadith*]. Abu Hanifa, on the other hand, has taught that it is allowed, provided that this is done under the protection of a strong and safe army."

An Early Fundamentalist Calls for *Jihad*: Ibn Taymiyya* (1263–1328)

Ibn Taymiyya was an extraordinarily conservative Hanbali jurist and theologian. He explores the issue of *jihad* in some length in his book on statecraft according to the *sharia*, a work entitled *Governance According to God's Law in Reforming Both the Ruler and His Flock* (*al-siyasa al-shariyya fi islah al ra'y wa al-raiya*). In it, he stresses the religious and moral imperative of taking up the cause of *jihad*. Among the points he makes are the following, which have been lightly edited:

- The command to participate in *jihad* and the mention of its merits occur "innumerable times" in the Koran and the *sunna*. It is therefore the best voluntary act a Muslim can perform.
- Ibn Taymiyya quotes Muhammad as saying: "Him whose feet have become dusty in the way of God [i.e., *jihad*] will God save from hellfire." He also cites another Prophetic *hadith*: "A day and a night

spent in *ribat* [living on the frontier of Islam to be ready to defend its territory against enemies] are better than one month spent in fasting and vigils. If he [the man who performs *jihad*] dies, he will receive the recompense of his deeds and subsistence, and he will be protected by the Angel of the Grave [an angel charged with interrogating a dead person about the deeds he did in his life]."

- Ibn Taymiyya reports that Mohammed said: "Every community has its devotional journeys and the devotional journey of my community is *jihad* in the way of God." Ibn Taymiyya then adds his own views. These are, in brief, that — more than any other act —*jihad* shows love and devotion for God, and that any individual or community that participates in *jihad* is positioning itself between two "blissful outcomes": either victory, or martyrdom and Paradise.

- Finally, Ibn Taymiyya argues that the most important type of *jihad* is the one against the unbelievers and against those that refuse to abide by the prescriptions of the *sharia*.[23]

One remarkable aspect of Ibn Taymiyya's legal thought has been mentioned in an earlier chapter. It remains his most influential impact on Islam today. He was the first jurist to call for legitimate rebellion against nominally Muslim rulers, namely, the Mongols, who were not ruling in accordance with the *sharia*.

The Mongols had converted to Islam but they practiced a very unorthodox version of it. Because they still followed their tribal customs instead of the dictates of Islam, Ibn Taymiyya first denounced them as "infidels" (*kufar*) — an extremely pejorative term — and then advocated *jihad* against them. The modern scholar Sami Zubaida tells us that

> The denunciation of supposedly Muslim rulers — who rule in accordance with man-made laws and abandon what God has revealed — as infidels and their realm as *jahiliyya* [the "state of ignorance" said to exist in Arabia before the rise of Islam] was to become widespread among modern militant Islamists [this term, coined by modern scholars, usually means violence-prone Islamic fundamentalists] ... Ibn Taymiya [sic] became one of the few figures of historical *fiqh* [Islamic jurisprudence] to be revived and adulated in modern Islamism, the mainstream of *fiqh* being too subservient to rulers and their foibles to serve radical directions.[24]

Jihad in Practice: The Followers of Muhammad Ibn Abd al-Wahhab* (1703–1792)

By 1788, the Wahhabi-Saudi *jihad* had won control of most of the Arabian Peninsula. Ibn Abd al-Wahhab himself died in 1792, but this did not slow down the religious-political campaign he had helped to found. In 1801, the Wahhabis and the Saudis attacked the Shia holy city of Karbala and slaughtered its citizens. The next year, during their campaign against Mecca, about 10,000 Wahhabi "bandits," as their opponents labeled them, pillaged the Arabian town of Ta'if. This massacre eventually found its way into a book.

At the beginning of the twentieth century, some mainstream Iraqi Muslims came to believe that "the Wahhabi heresy was knocking at the gates of Baghdad" and that it was essential to try to stem this fundamentalist tide. They therefore asked the Iraqi scholar al-Zahawi (1863–1936) to denounce Wahhabi doctrine and jurisprudence. He did so in a polemic entitled *A True Dawn: A Refutation of Those Who Deny the Validity of Using Means to Allah and the Miracles of the Saints (al-fajr al-sadiq fi al-radd ala munkiri al-tawassul wa al-khawariq).*[25] It was published in 1905 and contains this account of what happened in Ta'if:

> Undoubtedly, one of the worst abominations perpetrated by the Wahhabis ... was the massacre of the people of Ta'if. They killed everyone in sight, slaughtering child and adult, ruler and ruled, lowly and high-born. They began with a suckling child nursing at his mother's breast and moved on to a group studying the Qur'an, slaying all of them, down to the last man. When they had wiped out the people in the houses, they went into the streets, the shops and the mosques, killing whoever happened to be there. They even killed people in prayer until they had annihilated every Muslim in Ta'if and until only some twenty or more people remained....
>
> The Wahhabis cast books into the streets to be blown to and fro, including copies of the Qur'an, volumes [by the famous *hadith* scholars] Bukhari, Muslim and other canonical works of *hadith*, and books of *fiqh* [jurisprudence], all amounting to thousands. Books remained in the streets for several days, trampled on by the Wahhabis. Not one among them made the slightest attempt to remove even one page of the Qur'an from under foot and preserve it from the ignominy and disrespect of this display. Then they destroyed the houses and made what was once a town into a barren wasteland.[26]

The Doctrine of the "Double *Jihad*" in West Africa: Uthman Dan Fodio (1754–1817)

Localized, small-scale *jihad*s flourished in West Africa, beginning in the sixteenth century.[27] The central Sudan later became another focal point of *jihad*. Muslim reformers and clerics there wanted to establish a pure Islamic society along the paths pioneered by the prophet and the early caliphs. Some of these men visited Mecca and Medina. They returned home full of zeal— eager to uphold the rule of the *sharia* and to encourage local Muslims to seek individual salvation. At the same time and contributing to this evangelical fervor, there was great hope throughout West and Central Africa that the early 1800s would witness the once-in-a-century appearance of a "renewer of Islam" (*mujaddid*).

The men who came back to central Sudan from Mecca and Medina taught their countrymen the doctrine of the "double *jihad*." This was a two-fold process. The first step, they explained, was the inner *jihad*, i.e., the struggle against one's base impulses. When these passions had been mastered sufficiently, the next step was the outer *jihad*, that is, military action against neighboring pagan tribal chiefs and against corrupt Muslim rulers and the obsequious *ulama*, who were more interested in pleasing their political masters than in implementing the *sharia*.

In his time, Uthman Dan Fodio was the most influential Islamic scholar in sub–Saharan Africa. He was strongly opposed to corrupt practices and was a firm advocate of *jihad*. He had charisma: not only did he have a deep knowledge of the *sharia*, but he also had visions that persuaded him he could work miracles. Indeed, in one vision, he even ascended to heaven, where he was named the imam of the saints and was presented with the sword of truth. Many of the faithful considered him to be the long-awaited *mahdi*, or messiah, of Islam.

These intellectual and mystical undertakings served a very practical purpose: they gave him the authority he needed, as a lone scholar, to challenge the entrenched religious and political establishment of the region. In 1804, tensions between Uthman Dan Fodio and this elite broke out into the open. He moved to a neighboring region and was elected imam and head of the Muslim community. He promptly declared *jihad*, with such success that by 1808 most of the local rulers had been defeated. Their lands were thus brought under the loose control of Uthman Dan Fodio's regional empire, which was centered in Sokoto in northwestern Nigeria.

When Uthman Dan Fodio died in 1817, his son, Muhammad Bello, succeeded him. The West African *jihad* went from strength to strength. By 1830, it had conquered most of northern Nigeria and northern Cameroon. This movement had some noteworthy accomplishments. It strengthened the practice of the *sharia*; stimulated legal, theological, poetical and other works in the Hausa language; and helped spread Islam into southern Nigeria.

Jihad as a Pacifist Creed:
Sayyid Ahmad Khan (1817–1898)

Sir Sayyid Ahmad Khan was an Indian educator, jurist and reformer. He believed that Islam was entirely compatible with modern science and in 1875 he founded the Muslim Anglo-Oriental College at Aligarh in Uttar Pradesh, India to put this conviction into practice. He hoped that this new institution, which is still going strong today as the Aligarh Muslim University, would become "a Muslim Cambridge in India."

Sayyid Ahmad Khan was convinced that, in order to modernize Islam, it was first necessary to reinterpret the Quran. Independent reasoning (*ijti-had*), rather than blind imitation (*taqlid*) of the thought of long-dead Islamic scholars should, he argued, be encouraged. When reason and a holy text differed, reason must, in his view, prevail. In the wake of the anti–British Sepoy Mutiny of 1857, he argued that *jihad* meant only defensive war and that further resistance to British rule was not justified as long as the British did not interfere actively with the practice of Islam. Indeed, he treated Islam as a private religion, not as a mass undertaking, and depicted it virtually as a pacifist creed fully in conformity with the provisions of international law.[28]

He argued as follows:

> First, what is *jihad?* It is war in defence of the faith.... But it has its conditions, and, except under those, it is unlawful. It must be against those who are not only *Kafirs* [unbelievers], but also "obstruct the exercise of the faith" [here he is referring to *sura* 47:1, which states, "God will bring to nothing the deeds of those who disbelieve and debar others from His path"]. The doctors of the law [*sharia*] in all ages ... have laid down that to constitute the essential conditions for *jihad* on the part of the protected Musalmans as against a Christian power protecting them, there must be *positive* oppression or obstruction in the exercise of their faith; not merely want of countenance, negative withholding of support, or absence of profession of the faith; and further, this obstruction and oppression which justifies *jihad* must be, not in civil, but in religious matters; it must impair the foundation of some of the "pillars of Islam...." [It must not affect only less substantive matters, which are merely] negative abstentions from the faith, not that positive oppression and obstruction to the exercise of the faith which alone can justify *jihad*.[29]

Unfortunately, Sayyid Ahmad Khan had two intellectual weaknesses that were to prove fatal to his efforts to reform Islam. First, the highly traditionalist *ulama* agreed that, because he had never finished his Islamic education, he lacked the academic qualifications necessary to interpret the Quran and *hadith*. Second, a modern biographer, Muzaffar Iqbal, frankly admits that "the shallowness of his knowledge of Western science and its philosophical underpinnings was apparent from his writings."[30]

These serious shortcomings, coupled with his willingness to collaborate with the British (he was knighted by Queen Victoria in 1888) and his opposition to parliamentary democracy in India (he feared it would result in Muslims being dominated by the Hindu majority), cost him the support of the *ulama*. Without their backing, there was no chance that his doctrinal reforms, including his pacifist views on *jihad*, would be put into effect in India.

Calling for Internal *Jihad*: Rashid Rida* (1856–1935)

As noted earlier, Rashid Rida was a reformer, editor and political activist who lived and worked in Egypt. He was one of the first Muslim intellectuals to call for a reformed *sharia*, which would be the foundation of a modernized but fully Islamic state. It was essential, he argued, that such a state be militarily strong in order to compete with the highly armed colonial and other powers that would otherwise threaten it. This new Islamic state, in short, would have to assume responsibility for its own defense.

To justify his position, Rida cited this Quranic verse:

> Let not the unbelievers think that they will ever get away. They have not the power to do so. Muster against them all the men and cavalry at your command, so that you may strike terror into the enemy of God and your enemy, and others besides them who are unknown to you but known to God. All that you shall give in the cause of God shall be repaid to you. You shall not be wronged [*sura* 8:59].

He defined *jihad* purely in defensive terms and did not want any expansionist military policy. He wrote: "Everything that is mentioned in the Koran with regard to the rules of fighting is intended [that is, understood to be] defence against enemies that fight Moslems because of their religion."[31] He did advocate *jihad*, but only in the sense of an internal moral striving for a believer's purity and self-perfection.[32] As noted in an earlier chapter, however, this pacifist doctrine and Rida's other ambitious reforms were never put into effect.

A Modernist Interpretation of *Jihad*: Mahmud Shaltut (1923–1963)

Mahmud Shaltut was an Islamic scholar who received his religious elementary education in Alexandria, Egypt. He then spent many years at al-Azhar University in Cairo, where he rose to become rector of the university. Shaltut was a prolific writer on the *sharia* and on exegesis (*tafsir*).[33] Except for the Quranic quotations, the quotations used here come from his book, *The Koran and Fighting* (*al-Qur'an wa al-qital*), which was published in 1948. Although Shaltut is not as well known in the West as many of the other Islamic scholars mentioned here, his work nevertheless deserves our attention: he lays out his line of reasoning clearly and simply, buttressing it with arguments from the Quran. His citations of the Quranic verses on fighting are exceptionally useful for non–Muslims who want to learn more about the *sharia* and *jihad*.

Shaltut introduces these verses by noting that "The Koran is concerned with two kinds of fighting: the fighting of Muslims against Muslims and the fighting of Muslims against non–Muslims." He deplores the former and quotes an appropriate Quranic verse to make this point: "The believers are a band of brothers. Make peace among your brothers and fear God, so that you are shown mercy" (*sura* 49:10).[34]

The second kind of fighting — Muslim vs. Muslim — is more complicated and gets fuller treatment. Shaltut argues that God revealed the first
Quranic verses on fighting at the perfect moment, i.e., just when the early
Muslim community was feeling despondent and ill-used because of its forced
emigration from Mecca to Medina. These verses, he believed, restored the
confidence of the faithful because they gave them permission to fight:

> Permission to take up arms is hereby given to those who are attacked, because
> they have been wronged. God has power to grant them victory: they have been
> unjustly driven from their homes, only because they said: "Our Lord is God."
> ...whoever helps God shall be helped by Him. God is powerful and mighty: He
> will assuredly help those who, once masters in the land, will attend to their
> prayers and render the alms levy, enjoin justice and forbid evil. God governs the
> destiny of all things [*sura* 22:39–41].

Shaltut justifies this divine permission to fight as corresponding merely
to "the customary practice that people ward each other off so that a certain
equilibrium is attained, oppression is avoided, and adherents of the different
creeds and cults can perform their religious observances and keep believing
in the pure doctrine of monotheism." He then moves on to consider other
Quranic "Verses of Fighting." This is a good example:

> Fight for the sake of God those that fight against you, but do not attack them
> first. God does not love aggressors. Slay them wherever you find them. Drive
> them out of the places from which they drove you. Idolatry is more grievous
> than bloodshed. But do not fight them within the precincts of the Holy Mosque
> unless they attack you there; if they attack you, put them to the sword. Thus
> shall the unbelievers be rewarded: but if they mend their ways, know that God is
> forgiving and merciful. Fight against them until idolatry is no more and God's
> religion reigns supreme. But if they desist, fight none except the evil-doors. A
> sacred month for a sacred month: sacred things too are subject to retaliation. If
> anyone attacks you, attack him as he attacked you. Have fear of God and know
> that God is with the righteous [*sura* 2:190–194].

Shaltut gives a reason for this and similar verses. He explains that Muslims have been ordered to fight simply because of the "aggression directed
against them, expulsion from their dwellings, violation of God's sacred institutions and attempts to persecute people for what they believe." As soon as
the aggression stops and religious liberty flourishes, Muslims must stop fighting.

These same principles, Shaltut continues, can be found in many other
Quranic verses. In the interests of brevity, here we shall cite only some of their
key phrases:

- "And how should you not fight for the cause of God, and for the help-
  less old men, women, and children [of Mecca]...?" (*sura* 4:75).

- "Therefore fight for the cause of God. You are accountable for none but yourself" (*sura* 4:84).
- "If they [your enemies] do not keep their distance from you, if they neither offer you peace nor cease their hostilities against you, lay hold of them and kill them wherever you find them" (*sura* 4:91).

Shaltut then gives his personal, revisionist summary of the true message of the Verses of Fighting by making these three points:

- ...there is not a single verse in the Koran which could support the opinion that the aim of fighting in Islam is conversion."
- "...there are only three reasons for fighting, viz. to stop aggression, to protect the Mission of Islam and to defend religious freedom."
- "...in giving its prescriptions for fighting, the Koran did not admit of avidity, selfishness and humiliation of the poor as motives for it, but intended it as an instrument for peace and tranquility and for a life founded on justice and equality."[35]

Shaltut's modernist reinterpretations of *jihad* continue for another 22 pages of text but they need not detain us here. The general tenor of his remaining comments is apparent from this soaring exhortation he gives to the reader:

> Read all this and you will know the lofty spirit of righteousness, equality, co-operation and affinity that Islam cherishes with regard to its relations with non–Muslims. It is a kind of relationship so magnificent that, compared with it, the most modern principle known to the human mind in international relations wanes into insignificance.[36]

Founder of Modern Islamic Fundamentalism: Sayyid Qutb (1906–1966)

Sayyid Qutb was one of the most influential Islamic thinkers of the twentieth century.[37] He can rightly be called the spiritual father of today's Islamic radical fundamentalists. Most of these men have read Qutb's works or are familiar, at least in general terms, with his basic ideas. His books have been translated into all the major languages of Islamic countries.

By the age of 10, Qutb had memorized the entire Quran. Educated at a teacher's college in Cairo, he was later hired as a teacher by the Egyptian Ministry of Education and in 1948 was sent to the United States to learn about the American educational system. During his two-year stay there, he studied modern systems of education and training at several American colleges, including Wilson's Teachers' College in Washington, D.C.; the Teacher's College, an institute at the University of Northern Colorado; and Stanford University in California. He obtained a master's degree in education from the

Teacher's College. Ironically, his very familiarity with the West became his reason for rejecting it.[38]

During these two years, Qutb was deeply shocked by what he perceived as America's hostility toward Arabs, its unquestioning support for Israel, and its sexual permissiveness — by which he meant that even churches would host dances where young men and women could dance together, holding each other closely. He came to believe that Islam was a superior creed and that the West held a deeply rooted, permanent hatred of Islam. As a result, he concluded, the Islamic world must not try to follow Western models but must reinvigorate itself instead.

When he returned to Egypt in 1951, Qutb became one of the main ideologists of the Muslim Brotherhood, a reformist-revivalist movement that had been founded in Egypt in 1928. When this organization was suppressed by Nasser's regime in 1954, Qutb was arrested, tortured, and held in prison for ten years. Finally released in 1964, he remained totally unrepentant. Eight months later, after his release he was charged with plotting against the Egyptian government and was rearrested. Tried for conspiring to overthrow Nasser (the court found him guilty of "destructive and terrorist activities" and of "encouraging sedition"), he was hanged in 1966 on Nasser's express orders.

Qutb's most incendiary work is entitled *Signposts on the Road*, also known as *Milestones*. It was published in 1964, as soon as he got out of prison, and was almost certainly the reason for his subsequent re-arrest and execution. Its message was indeed revolutionary. *Signposts on the Road* roundly denounced Nasser's government — and, in fact, the whole contemporary Islamic world — as languishing in *jahiliyya*, that state of ignorance held to have existed in Arabia before the rise of Islam. To restore Islam to its former glories, Qutb therefore advocated an all-out *jihad* against secularism, capitalism, and agnosticism. He wanted to establish, through the *sharia*, God's rule on earth (*hakimiyyah*).

Before he became a radical, Qutb was an intellectual who published poems and literary criticism but he was not a trained scholar of Islam. Nevertheless, he was quick to uphold the virtues of the *sharia*. He assured the faithful:

> Islam proclaims the liberation of man on earth from the subjection to something that is not God [e.g., capitalism]. Therefore, Islam has to march out in order to put an end to the actual situation that conflicts with this universal proclamation, by means of both elucidation and action. It has to deliver blows at the political forces that make men the slaves of something that is not God, i.e., that do not rule them according to the *Sharia* and the authority of God, these forces that prevent them from hearing the elucidation and from freely accepting the Creed, without being hindered by any authority. [It has to destroy these forces] in order to establish a social, economic and political order that allows this liberation to

proceed effectively, after having put an end to the dominating power, regardless of whether this is purely political, or obscured by racialism or by the ideology of class-supremacy within one race.[39]

Calling for a Worldwide *Jihad*:
Sayyid Abdul-Ala Mawdudi (1903–1979)

Mawdudi's ideas greatly influenced the course of Islamic nationalism in India.[40] He was an Indian anarchist, reformer and journalist — not a classically trained jurist or a theologian but, rather, a political activist and a passionate believer in Islam. In his reading, he fell under the spell of the strict fundamentalist teachings of Ibn Taymiyya and of Muhammad ibn Abn al-Wahhab. Mawdudi came to believe that the Muslims of his time were living under deplorable spiritual conditions, which nearly amounting to *jahiliyya*, i.e., that "time of ignorance" of the pre–Islamic era. He explained the weaknesses of Islam in India itself as being due to the fact that, in British India, Muslims were being forced to live side-by-side with Hindus.

The best solution to this problem was, according to Mawdudi's 1927 book, *Jihad in Islam*), worldwide Muslim rule. He therefore called not only for restrictions on all non–Muslims currently living under Islamic rule but also, as a true anarchist, he wanted to see a world-wide *jihad* that would overthrow virtually all existing governments, Muslim and secular alike. He explained his goals very clearly:

> For Islam is not concerned with the interest of one nation to the exclusion of others and does not intend to advance one people to the exclusion of others.... Therefore, Islam resists any government that is based on a different concept and program, in order to liquidate it completely.... Its aim is to make this concept victorious, to introduce this program universally, to set up governments that are firmly rooted in this concept and this program.... Islam wants the whole earth and does not content itself with only a part thereof. It wants and requires the entire inhabited world.... In order to realize this lofty desire, Islam wants to employ all forces and means that can be employed for bringing about a universal all-embracing religion. It will spare no efforts for the achievement of this supreme objective. This far-reaching struggle that continuously exhausts all forces and this employment of all possible means are called *jihad*.[41]

Mawdudi wanted to reform Islam so that it would henceforth rely on the Quran and the *sunna* alone. Towards this end, he urged the creation of a truly Islamic state with Islamic governmental, banking and other institutions. On a more liberal note, however, he also favored the use of rational judgments on religious issues so that the basic principles of Islam could be applied intelligently to modern societies.

It was on the basis of these ideas that Mawdudi founded, in 1941, the militant Community for Islam (*Jamaat-i Islam*). Although classically trained

Islamic scholars denounced him as an extremist, his anti–Hindu teachings and his advocacy of violent revolution struck a responsive chord among Indian Muslims. Mawdudi's fiery views helped fuel Hindu-Muslim tensions over the status of Kashmir. Indeed, they ultimately contributed to the partition of British India and to the creation of the independent Islamic state of Pakistan.

A Rage-Driven *Jihad*: Osama bin Laden (1957–)

Raised in Saudi Arabia to be a strict, devout Muslim, bin Laden earned a degree in economics and public administration in 1981 from the highly conservative King Abdul-Aziz University in Jeddah. There he also studied the *sharia* under Mohammad Qutb, brother of the fundamentalist Sayyid Qutb, who had been executed in Egypt in 1966. After graduating from the university, he fought with the *mujahidin* (literally "those that do *jihad*") resistance against the Soviet invasion of Afghanistan. It must be stressed that bin Laden is not an Islamic scholar, a jurist or a deep thinker. He does not speak for the world of Islam. Nevertheless, he has played a decisive role in bringing the concept of *jihad* to the forefront of the consciousness of the Western world.

Beginning in about 1995, bin Laden began to produce policy statements calling for the overthrow of the royal family of Saudi Arabia and for an unrelenting *jihad* against the Americans. The need for and justification of *jihad* was a recurrent theme. Here are some examples:

- In a 1996 "Declaration of War Against the Americans Occupying the Land of the Two Holy Places," i.e., the mosques of Mecca and Medina in Saudi Arabia, he argued that Ibn Taymiyya would certainly have agreed that using *jihad* to expel the Americans from Saudi Arabia is a primary duty for Muslims today. Bin Laden said:

If there is more than one duty to be carried out, then the most important one should receive priority. Clearly, after Belief there is no more important duty than pushing the American enemy out of the holy land. No other priority, except Belief, could be considered before it ... Ibn Taymiyya stated, "to fight [*jihad*] in defense of religion and Belief is a collective duty; there is no other duty after Belief than fighting the enemy who is corrupting the life and the religion. There are no preconditions for this duty and the enemy should be fought with one's best abilities."[42]

- In "The New Powder Keg in the Middle East," an interview published in 1996 by a militant–Islamist Australian magazine, bin Laden was asked by the interviewer:

As part of the furious international campaign against the Jihad movement, you were personally the target of a prejudiced attack, which accused you of financing terrorism and being part of an international terrorist organization. What do you have to say to that?

Bin Laden replied:

After the end of the cold war, America escalated its campaign against the Muslim world in its entirety, aiming to get rid of Islam itself. Its main focus in this was to target the scholars and the reformers who were enlightening the people to the dangers of the Judeo-American alliance.... However, our gratitude to Allah, their campaign was not successful, as terrorizing the American occupiers is a religious and logical obligation. We are grateful to Allah Most Exalted in that He has facilitated Jihad in his cause for us....[43]

- In a 1997 Cable News Network (CNN) interview, bin Laden said:

We declared *jihad* against the U.S. government, because the U.S. government is unjust, criminal and tyrannical. It has committed acts that are extremely unjust, hideous and criminal, whether directly or through its support of the Israeli occupation.[44]

- In a 1998 *Time Magazine* interview, bin Laden said:

The International Front for Jihad against the U.S. and Israel has, by the grace of God, issued a crystal-clear fatwa calling on the Islamic nation to carry on *jihad* aimed at liberating the holy sites [the mosques of Mecca and Medina].[45]

- In 2002, bin Laden's "Letter to the American people" appeared in Arabic on the Internet. Translated and circulated by Islamists in Britain, it opened by quoting the "permission to take up arms" Quranic verse (*sura* 22:39), which we have already cited earlier in this book. Bin Laden asked rhetorically: "Why are we fighting and opposing you [the Americans]?" He gave two answers. The first answer was: "Because you attacked us and continue to attack us." Bin Laden goes on to list what he sees as the many American offenses against Islam. The second answer was: "These tragedies and calamities are only a few examples of your oppression and aggression against us. It is commanded by our religion and intellect that the oppressed have a right to return the aggression. Do not await anything from us but Jihad, resistance and revenge."

This interview continued at greater length, but we shall close here with bin Laden's two basic points:

- "If you fail to respond to all these conditions [e.g., that the U.S. must stop supporting Israel], then prepare for [a] fight with the Islamic Nation. The Nation of Monotheism that puts complete trust on Allah and fears none other than Him."
- "If the Americans do not respond [to bin Laden's conditions], then

their fate will be that of the Soviets who fled from Afghanistan to deal with their military defeat, political breakup, ideological downfall, and economic bankruptcy. This is our message to the Americans, as an answer to theirs."[46]

When this was written, bin Laden was still at large. The continuing importance of his *jihad* is evident. Then-CIA Director Porter Goss, for example, said that the United States had a good idea of where bin Laden was hiding, but that Pakistan would not let the Americans mount a proper manhunt for him. Goss' statement confirmed the widespread belief that bin Laden was hiding in the mountains of northern Pakistan but that, fearing the hostile reaction of Islamic militants in his own country, Pakistan's president, Pervez Musharraf, was not eager for him to be captured. Musharraf himself said: "One would prefer that he's captured somewhere outside Pakistan. By some other people."[47]

7

The Sharia *in the World Today*

Having reviewed the background and history of the *sharia*, it is now time to look very briefly at the different versions and interpretations of the *sharia* in 29 selected countries today. With the sole exception of India, where only about 13 percent of the population is Muslim, in each of the other countries at least half of the citizens are Muslims. These countries, together with estimates of the percentage of Muslims in each country, are also listed in Appendix 3 for ease of reference. They tend to fall into five broad categories:

- Countries where various interpretations of the *sharia* are fully applied. The best examples here are Saudi Arabia and Iran.
- Countries where the judicial system includes both the *sharia* and secular law. A good example is Egypt.
- Countries that have accepted, copied or adopted European laws and have abolished the *sharia* entirely. The best example is Turkey.
- Countries where the security situation is so tenuous that there is virtually no nationwide rule of law. Afghanistan and Iraq are excellent examples.
- Countries where Islam is not a uniform culture and where the legal systems are conflations of customary, colonial, and Islamic law.[1] The states of West Africa are the best examples, but in the interests of brevity only a few of them will be discussed here.

Today, each country's legal code is complicated, unique, and reflects a range of local historical and cultural events. The brief surveys that follow try to put each country into a simple historical perspective and provide a snapshot of legal conditions there today. These surveys are written for the general reader: they do not pretend to be scholarly dissertations aimed at the expert.

They should therefore be considered only *illustrative*, not definitive.

An important caveat must be mentioned as well. Despite our best efforts, it has not been possible to find up-to-date, 100 percent reliable information about *sharia*-based legal systems in all these countries today. Data about trials and sentences by *sharia* courts are, in particular, nearly impossible for non-resident foreigners to obtain. Our repeated efforts to elicit information from scholarly e-mail lists specializing in Islam have produced little of value. Islamic institutions have been similarly unresponsive.

As a result, much of our information comes perforce from published sources that are, by their very nature, somewhat dated. These include the U.S. State Department's annual *Background Notes* and its *Country Reports on Human Rights Practices*; the Central Intelligence Agency's *World Factbook*; the draft legal surveys written by Emory University's law school before 2002; and, in some cases, the Carnegie Endowment's *Arab Political Systems: Baseline Information and Reforms*. Given the inherent limitations of these sources, we believe that the following descriptions were accurate at the time of writing.

Afghanistan

Afghanistan is an Islamic country (99 percent of the population is Muslim) where the *sharia* has long been extremely important. An estimated 80 percent of the population is Sunni and follows the Hanafi school of jurisprudence. Most of the remainder of the population is Shia. Islamic practices pervade all aspects of Afghan life. According to Article 3 of the new constitution of 2004, "In Afghanistan no law can be contrary to the beliefs and provisions of the sacred religion of Islam." It is not yet clear what this will mean in practice. Perhaps a straw in the wind was the case of Abdul Rahman in 2006.

Western press accounts are sketchy but it appears that Rahman, after a divorce, tried to get custody of his daughters in Kabul. His wife's family bitterly opposed this plan. Indeed, they told the court that he was unfit to care for his children because, 16 years earlier, he had converted from Islam to Christianity while working with a foreign aid group in Pakistan. Learning about this case, an ambitious Afghan prosecutor promptly charged Rahman with apostasy, a crime punishable by death under some interpretations of the *sharia*.

Things might have gone very badly indeed with Rahman if the international media had not picked up the case and if Western leaders, including Pope Benedict XVI, had not made very strong protests to the government of Afghanistan.[2] Ostensibly, due to lack of evidence and to Rahman's alleged mental problems, the case was returned to the prosecutors "for more investigation." In practical terms, this meant it was being dropped permanently.

Rahman, who had first been held in a detention center in central Kabul but was later moved to the notorious Policharki Prison just outside of Kabul after other inmates made threats against him, was soon released from jail. Angry fundamentalists, however, immediately took to the streets to demand his death, however, so his survival remained problematical. The best — and, indeed, the only — solution was for him to leave Afghanistan. Italy granted him asylum. He arrived there safely without any mishap.

Afghanistan's recent history has been one of unrelenting violence — a story of invasion, civil unrest and political instability. This process continues today. The Soviet Union invaded Afghanistan in 1979, but was forced to withdraw 10 years later by *mujahidin* forces (including a young fighter named Osama bin Laden), which were largely supplied by the United States. The Communist regime in Kabul collapsed in 1992. Conflicts subsequently erupted among rival factions and gave rise to the fundamentalist Taliban (literally "religious students") movement, which seized Kabul in 1996 and then captured about 90 percent of the country.

In 1997, the Taliban issued an edict renaming the country the Islamic Emirate of Afghanistan and granting its leader Mullah Omar ultimate authority as head of state and Commander of the Faithful. Under his rule, a very strict interpretation of the *sharia* was imposed. Public executions and punishments, e.g., flogging, became regular events at Afghan soccer stadiums. According to the U.S. State Department,

> The Taliban had risen to power in the mid 90s in reaction to the anarchy and warlordism that arose after the withdrawal of Soviet forces. Many Taliban had been educated in madrasas [theological colleges] in Pakistan.... The Taliban sought to impose an extreme interpretation of Islam — based on the rural Pashtun tribal code — on the entire country and committed massive human rights violations, particularly directed against women and girls.[3]

After the 11 September 2001 terrorist attacks against New York and Washington, the U.S. and its allies toppled the Taliban regime because it had been sheltering Osama bin Laden and serving as a safe base for terrorist training camps. An international conference in Germany led to the adoption of a new constitution in 2004 and to the election of Hamid Karzi as the first democratically elected president of Afghanistan. Elections for the new government's legislative body, the National Assembly, were held in 2005.[4]

Afghanistan has had some seven constitutions in the last one hundred years. The present Afghan government remains exceptionally weak and highly dependent on American and other Western support. It will probably not be able to discharge all — or perhaps any — of the heavy responsibilities laid on it by the new constitution. According to the U.S. Central Intelligence Agency, these burdens are as follows:

...the state is obliged to create a prosperous and progressive society based on social justice, protection of human dignity, protection of human rights, realization of democracy, and to ensure national unity and equality among all ethnic groups; the state shall abide by the UN charter, international treaties that Afghanistan signed, and the Universal Declaration Human Rights.[5]

Afghanistan's long term prospects are clouded. It remains violent, politically fragmented, extremely poor, landlocked, and highly dependent on foreign aid and on farming (it is the world's largest producer of opium). The new constitution set up a Supreme Court, High Courts and Appeals Courts, a Ministry of Justice, and a separate Afghan Independent Human Rights Commission. It is uncertain whether any of these will have much power.

Personal and group behavior in Afghanistan — and the settlement of disputes — continues to be governed largely by Islam and by traditional tribal and ethnic customs. On the nascent legal front, there is also the problem of accountability for crimes committed during recent conflicts. It is too early to predict what exact role the *sharia* will play in Afghanistan in the future, but it is very likely to be a considerable one.

Algeria

After 132 years of French rule, Algeria finally won its independence in 1962, after a long, bitter, bloody war that began in 1954. A new constitution, adopted in 1989, allowed the formation of political parties. However, when a militant Islamist party, the Islamic Salvation Front, won the first stage of national elections in 1991, the Algerian army, with the support of Western governments, promptly canceled the second round of elections to prevent a radical Islamic government from coming to power. This action sparked a violent reaction by the Islamists: since 1991, terrorist violence and civil strife in Algeria have resulted in between 100,000 and 150,000 deaths. Although the security situation has improved markedly in recent years, an estimated 40 to 50 Algerians are still killed each month in terrorist-related violence.

About 32 million people live in Algeria; 99 percent of them are Sunni Muslims. Their legal system is based on French and Islamic (chiefly Maliki) law. Judicial review of legislative acts is provided by a Constitutional Council, composed of Supreme Court justices and other officials. Article 2 of the constitution provides that Islam is the religion of the state. The constitution calls for an independent judiciary, but in practice the judicial process is severely restricted by the pervasive influence of the executive branch and by its own internal judicial inefficiencies. Despite some legal reforms, prolonged pretrial detention and long trial delays remain problems today.

After several years of debate, discussion and protest, a Family Code was enacted in 1984. Article 222 of the Code defines the *sharia* as the residuary source of law. This fact gives Algerian litigants a range of options. They can use interpretations from whatever legal schools they favor. They can draw on original Islamic sources, e.g., the Quran and the *sunna*. They can also quote secondary scholarly and juristic sources. The Family Code places limits on women's civil rights. Women in Algeria face discrimination on other fronts as well.

Bahrain

In the 1830s, the ruling Al Khalifa family signed the first of many treaties making Bahrain a British Protectorate. Independent from Britain since 1971, Bahrain is now a constitutional hereditary monarchy; an oil and gas producer, processor and refiner; and a major international Islamic financial center. It currently has 28 Islamic banks — the largest concentration of Islamic financial institutions in the world.[6]

The total population is about 688,000 people, an estimate that includes some 235,000 non-nationals. Ninety-eight percent of the Bahrainis are Muslims. Although more than two-thirds of the population is Shiite, the ruling family and most of the government, military, and business leaders are Sunnis.

Bahrain has a complicated system of courts, which are based on diverse juridical sources. These include the Sunni *sharia*; the Shiite *sharia*; tribal laws; Egyptian codes; and the civil codes and regulations drawn up by the British, following English common law, in the early twentieth century. Shiites follow the Ja'fari school of legal thought; Sunnis prefer the Shafi'i or the Maliki schools. Personal status law remains uncodified and is administered by *sharia* courts, as regulated by the Judicature Law of 1971. This directs judges to consult the following residuary sources of law, in the following order of precedence: principles of the *sharia*, custom, natural law, or principles of equity and good conscience.

In 2001, the emir (now king) Abdullah bin Khaled Al Khalifa created a Supreme Judicial Council to regulate the courts and separate the judicial and the administrative branches of the government. The senior court is the High Civil Appeals Court. A new constitution was issued in 2002.

Bangladesh

The CIA World Factbook describes Bangladesh as "a poor, overpopulated, and ill-governed nation."[7] Many people are landless and are forced to live on and cultivate lands which flood annually during the monsoon rainy season. Now a parliamentary democracy, Bangladesh came into being in 1971, when Bengali East Pakistan seceded from its union with West Pakistan. (See the section on Pakistan, below.) The population now totals about 144 million people; some 88 percent are Muslims (the majority is Hanafi) and 10 percent are Hindus.

A 1977 amendment to the constitution of 1972 deleted the principle of secularism and replaced it with the concept of "absolute trust and faith in Almighty Allah." As further amended in 1988, the constitution now declares, in Article 2(a), that "the state religion of the Republic is Islam, but other religions may be practised in peace and harmony in the republic."

The civil court system is based on the British model, i.e., on English common law. The judiciary is organized at two levels, with subordinate courts and a Supreme Court with Appellate and High Court Divisions. Islamic family law is applied through the regular court system. The Family Courts are courts of first instance, i.e., courts where lawsuits first begin, for personal status cases of all religious communities; different religious communities are governed by their own personal status laws. The Family Courts Act of 1985 governs the jurisdictions and functions of these courts. Their jurisdiction is limited to civil suits; criminal offenses fall under the jurisdiction of Criminal or Magistrates Courts.[8]

In many respects, the legal system of Bangladesh appears to be dysfunctional. There is a large judicial backlog of cases; lengthy pretrial detention is common in criminal cases; and, while fees for using the Family Courts are nominal, lawyers' and notaries' charges there considerably increase the costs of going to court. Nevertheless, much legal development has occurred through family case law. Some cases in point[9]:

- In *Hasina Ahmed v. Syed Abdul Fazal* (1980), a Family Court ruled that a woman may be granted a *khul'a* divorce by a judicial decision, without the husband's consent. As noted earlier, such a divorce requires a woman to forego all her financial rights from the marriage.
- In *Nally Zaman v. Giasuddin Khan* (1982), a Family Court judged that, with the passage of time, a husband could not unilaterally sue for forcible restitution of conjugal rights against an unwilling wife.
- In *Muhammad Abu Baker Siddique v. S.M.S. Baker & others* (1986), the court overruled the classical Hanafi position that a divorced mother's custody over her son ends when the boy is 7 years old. The court justified its ruling on the grounds that "the paramount consideration should be the child's welfare."
- In *Rusom Ali v. Jamila Khatun* (1991), the court followed classical

Hanafi law by holding that a wife is not entitled to arrears of maintenance. Hanafi law says that maintenance is required only from the date the suit is brought before the Family Court until three months from the decree of dissolution of marriage. The former wife or child may not claim past maintenance unless the parties have a previously established agreement.

Egypt

Egypt is the most populous country in the Arab world. Estimates of the religious makeup of the Egyptian population vary substantially, but it is likely that about 90 percent of Egyptians are Muslims. Coptic Christians and others make up the remainder. More than 90 percent of Egyptian Muslims are Sunnis.

Egypt's judicial system is derived from English common law, French law (the Napoleonic codes), and the *sharia*. Marriage and personal status law (family law) are primarily based on the *sharia*. The Egyptian Civil Code 131 of 1948 permits recourse to Hanafi jurisprudence where an issue is not sufficiently legislated by other means. Egypt, however, has traditionally favored a flexible approach to Islamic law: this has resulted in the assimilation of the doctrines of other schools of law as well. The *sharia* courts were integrated into the National Courts in 1956 by the Sharia Courts and Community Tribunals (Abolition) Act of 1955. A secular Supreme Constitutional Court has the final say in legal matters.

The constitution was adopted in 1971 and was amended by referendum in 1980. Article 2 reads in full: "Islam is the religion of the State and Arabic is its official language. Islamic jurisprudence is the principal source of legislation." The constitution provides for an independent judiciary; in practice, however, the judiciary is subject to the wishes of the government of President Hosni Mubarak. An Emergency Law of 1981 has further undermined judicial independence. Egyptian laws on marriage and personal status correspond to an individual's religion. Judges trained in *sharia* proceedings preside over family law cases in the courts.

The Procedural Personal Status Law of 2000 provides for *khul'a* divorce, which allows a Muslim woman to get a divorce without her husband's consent — provided that she foregoes all her financial rights from the marriage, e.g., alimony, dowry, and other benefits. Some judges, however, have not applied this law fairly or correctly, thus causing long bureaucratic delays for thousands of women who have filed for such divorces.

Under Islamic law in Egypt, Muslim female heirs receive half the amount of a male heir's inheritance. A sole female heir receives half of her parents' estate; the other half goes to male relatives. A sole male heir inherits all of his parents' property. Male Muslim heirs are traditionally expected to provide for all family members who are in need but, in practice, this assistance is not always forthcoming. This uneven distribution of wealth through the male line also fails to recognize that more women are now working outside the home and that the nuclear family is becoming more independent of the traditional extended family structure.

One interesting case involving Islamic law is worth recounting here. As stated earlier, *hisba* ("personal accountability") means, in practice, the responsibility of every Muslim "to promote what is right and to prevent what is wrong." In the 1990s, Nasr Abu Zayd, a professor at Cairo University, was accused of apostasy by his neo–Salafi (Islamic fundamentalist) opponents.[10] They claimed that his writings denied the divine quality of the Quran because he treated the holy book as a literary work based on religious myth. Although he continually stressed that he was a believing Muslim and that he considered the Quran to be the word of God, this still meant, in their eyes, that he was an apostate.

If this were indeed the case, under the terms of the *sharia*, Nasr Abu Zayd's Muslim wife could no longer be legally be married to him. For this reason, a court soon divorced them: Islamic law provides that a Muslim woman cannot be married to a non–Muslim man. Moreover, the doctrine of *hisba* provides that any Muslim may take legal action when Islam itself is wronged. Nasr Abu Zayd's opponents therefore took the case to court in 1993. An unfriendly, ambitious lawyer pushed this case to make himself better known and foster his own career.

In 1995, to the surprise and consternation of Cairo's intellectual elite, the Supreme Court ruled in favor of the plaintiffs. As a result, Abu Zayd and his wife were obliged to leave Egypt. They resettled, in exile, in the more tolerant Netherlands, where he became a professor of Arabic in Leiden, a great center of Western scholarship on the Islamic world. In 1996 the Egyptian government decided that *hisba* could no longer be used in this manner as a legal tool. Egyptian law now prevents claims by private individuals based on *hisba*.

India

Although 83 percent of India's population is Hindu, more than 120 million Muslims, i.e., about 13 percent of the total population, also live there. This is one of the largest Muslim populations in the world. About 90 percent of the Muslims are Sunnis. According to its 1950 constitution, India is a "sovereign, socialist, secular, democratic republic." Its central government is patterned after the British parliamentary system. India's legal system includes personal status laws for its many different religious communities.[11]

In 1947, murderous hostility between Hindus and Muslims led Britain to partition British India by creating two new Muslim-majority states — East and West Pakistan. Today there remains a constant potential for renewed Hindu-Muslim violence within India itself, e.g., feuding over the construction of mosques several centuries ago on sites where Hindus believe that their temples previously stood. Moreover, attacks by Muslim militants trying to end Indian rule in Jammu and Kashmir have driven almost all Hindus out of the Kashmir valley.

India's modern judicial system began under the British and is based, in part, on English common law. Separate codes of personal law apply to Muslims, Christians and Hindus. The status of minority communities' personal laws has been the subject of continuing debate in India. Article 44 of the constitution puts forward the goal of gradually establishing legal uniformity in India, particularly in terms of adopting a uniform civil code. This Directive Provision, as it is called, states that the government of India "shall endeavour to secure for the citizens a uniform civil code throughout the territory of India." The establishment of such a code, however, is seen by many religious communities (e.g., Muslims, Christians, Zoroastrians, Jews, Hindus, Buddhists, and Sikhs) as seriously threatening their own legal autonomy. They wish to continue to be governed in family matters by their own personal laws, as applied within the superstructure of the Indian legal system. Thus Article 44 is not likely to be implemented any time soon.

Under British rule, colonial courts were directed to apply "indigenous legal norms" in cases relating to family law and religion, with "native law officers" serving as expert advisers. Muslim personal status law, based largely on Hanafi jurisprudence, still governs many non-criminal matters involving Muslims, e.g., family law, inheritance, and divorce. Some Indian commentators on this indigenous system of law, formerly known as "Anglo-Muhammadan law" and now termed "Indo-Muslim law" have expressed unhappiness over the authoritative position gradually assumed by this law over the years. Among the problems they cite are the quality of translations, the lack of judicial expertise in Muslim law, the introduction of English legal principles and procedures, and the provisions of customary law.

Muslim personal law is now applied by the regular court system. There are four levels of these courts. The first are the civil courts, with jurisdiction over arbitration, marriage and divorce, guardianship, probate, etc. The next level of courts is in the district level of each state. The third level consists of the State High Courts in each of India's 18 states. At the last level, the Supreme Court has the final legal say.

The courts of first instance for personal status are generally the Family Courts, organized under the Family Courts Act of 1984. They are the equivalent of any district or subordinate civil court and address a range of issues: decrees of nullity, restitution of conjugal rights, judicial separation or dissolution, validity of marriage, matrimonial property, orders or injunctions arising out of marriage, legitimacy, maintenance, guardianship, custody, and access to minors.[12]

With the exception of a few enactments, most of the personal law applicable to Muslims is uncodified and is administered by state courts on the basis of Indo-Muslim precedents. Most of the legislation on Islamic family law dates from the period of British colonial rule. Some examples are the Registration of Muhammadan Marriages and Divorces Act (1876); the Child Marriage Restraint Act (1929); the Muslim Personal Law (*Sharia*) Application Act (1937); and the Dissolution of Muslim Marriages Act (1939).

Two illustrative cases from Muslim personal law may be of interest here:

- Polygamy is still governed by the traditional provisions of the *sharia*, but the Indian Criminal Procedure Code provides that a woman who refuses to live with her husband on "just grounds" is still entitled to maintenance. "Just grounds" are defined as including the husband's contracting a polygamous marriage. In the c. 1960 case of *Itwari v. Asghari*, for example, the burden of proof was on the husband to show that his subsequent marriage did not constitute insult or cruelty to his first wife. Even where, as in this case, there was no proof of cruelty, the court would not pass a decree for restitution of conjugal rights. The court felt that it would be unjust and inequitable to compel to the former wife to return to her ex-husband under these circumstances.

- In the celebrated 1986 case of *Muhammad Ahmad Khan v. Shah Bano Begum*, the court held that there is no conflict between the classical Hanafi requirement that a man must maintain his divorced wife during her *idda* (the three month waiting period before she can remarry) and the broader obligation to support financially her until such time as she might become self-supporting again, e.g., by remarrying. Shah Bano was an indigent woman in her 60s, who had been divorced by her husband by triple *talaq* (saying "I divorce you" three times) after 40 years of marriage.[13] In her case, this ruling meant that her ex-husband had to support her for the rest of her life, since she had virtually no chance of ever marrying again. The ruling met with fierce protest from conservative Muslim groups, who argued that it constituted gross interference in Islamic personal status laws. The upshot of the controversy was the passage of the Muslim Women (Protection of Rights on Divorce Act) of 1986, which in essence upheld the broader obligation of financial support. Although the court upheld Shah Bano's right to support, its ruling was so unpopular that her own community put great pressure on her to abandon her claim. In the ensuing debates, she denounced the Supreme Court in a letter, arguing that its judgment was contrary to the Quran and the *sunna* and that it constituted undue interference with the requirements of Muslim personal law.[14]

Indonesia

Indonesia consists of more than 17,000 islands, only 1,000 of which are permanently settled. It is officially a secular state but it has the world's largest Muslim population: about 88 percent of its roughly 213 million people are Muslim, mainly adherents of the Shafi'i school of jurisprudence.

Beginning in 1602 when the Dutch East India Company was formed, the Dutch established themselves as the rulers of present-day Indonesia by gradually dominating its many small kingdoms. Dutch rule lasted 300 years; during that time, the Netherlands East Indies became one of the world's richest colonial possessions. Dutch scholars identified and classified 19 different systems of customary law in the region. The first modern legislation in Indonesia relating to the application of Islamic law was a Royal Decree of 1882, which established a "Priest Court" for the islands of Java and Madura.

Occupied by Japan during World War II, Indonesia proclaimed its independence in 1945. The 1945 constitution does not endorse any specific religion but provides that "the State is based upon the belief in the One, Supreme God." The constitution also guarantees freedom of religion and embodies five principles of state philosophy known as the Pancasila. These principles are monotheism, humanitarianism, national unit, representative democracy by consensus, and social justice. The highest court is the Mahkamah Agung (Supreme Court). The constitution provides for an independent judiciary; in practice, however, the courts are subject to political influence from the executive branch of the government.

Indonesia's legal system is based on Roman-Dutch law, substantially modified by Islamic law, custom, and new criminal procedures and election codes.[15] The wellsprings of Indonesian law are official compilations of Islamic law, statutory legislation, and presidential instructions. Indonesia allows its 30 provinces the option of applying aspects of the *sharia*.

The Basic Law on Judicial Power (1970) provides for general, religious, military, and administrative courts. Religious courts (Pengadilan Agama) are established side by side with District Courts. Religious courts are at two levels: there are about 300 courts of first instance in the districts, and about 25 appellate courts in the provinces. These courts have jurisdiction over civil cases between Muslim spouses on matters concerning marriage, divorce, reconciliation, and alimony. Appeals from the religious appeals court go to the Supreme Court.

A new Marriage Law, passed in 1974, generated much controversy over polygamy and divorce. The government had to compromise by increasing the jurisdiction of *sharia* courts and by eliminating registration as a requirement for marriage. The Marriage Law is applied by the regular court system for non–Muslims and by *sharia* courts for Muslims.

Following the controversy over the Marriage Law, since the mid–1980s Indonesia's Ministry of Religion and the Supreme Court judges have produced regulations known as the Compilations of Islamic Law in Indonesia. These are based on arguments from various schools of law, on the application of Islamic law in other countries, and on decisions from religious courts. The Compilations are used to clarify points of personal law and inheritance for application by *sharia* courts.

Monogamy is legally considered to be the basis of marriage, but the Marriage Law does not prohibit polygamy for religions that allow it, e.g., Islam, Hinduism, and Buddhism. Polygamy is permissible with the consent of the existing wife or wives and with judicial permission. The Marriage Law provides that divorce shall be carried out only before a Court of Law, after the Court has tried to reconcile the parties. Property acquired during marriage is considered joint property; the Marriage Law only directs that division is according to the laws applicable to the parties. The court may order alimony for children or maintenance for the former wife. Succession is governed by classical Islamic law. The Supreme Court has often tried to equalize the rights of male and female inheritors.

Iran

Ninety-nine percent of Iran's population of 68 million people is Muslim. Most of them (89 percent) are Shiites; Sunnis comprise only 9 percent of the population. The central feature of Iran's political-religious system is rule by a Shiite "religious jurisconsult." Its senior leadership consists of Shia clergymen, including the supreme leader of the revolution, the president, the head of the judiciary, and the speaker of parliament.[16]

Conservative Shiite domination of Iran dates from 1979. That year, the charismatic religious leader Ayatollah Ruhollah Khomeini (1902–1989) returned from exile in France to lead a popular revolution that resulted in a new, theocratic republic guided by Shiite Islamic principles, e.g., the expected return of the *mahdi* (messiah). His regime was termed "the rule of the jurisprudential scholar" (*wilayat al-faqih*). It was the first attempt in modern times to create a purely Islamic state, or, more precisely, a Shiite state constructed along socialist lines. Such a state had no precedent in Islamic history.

Khomeini himself was a great believer in Islamic justice, not only for theological reasons but also because trials could be short and punishment could be implemented very quickly. As he put it very clearly,

> Islamic justice is based on simplicity and ease. It settles all criminal and civil complaints and in the most convenient, elementary, and expeditious way possible. All that is required is for an Islamic judge, with pen and inkwell and two or three enforcers, to go into a town, come to his verdict in any kind of case, and have it immediately carried out.[17]

The 1979 Iranian constitution codified Islamic principles of government. Article 4 states that "all civil, penal, financial, economic, administrative, cultural, military, political, and other laws and regulations must be based on Islamic criteria." Article 12 declares that Shia Islam of the Twelver (Ja'fari) sect is Iran's official religion. Judicial authority is constitutionally vested in the Supreme Court and the four-member High Council of the Judiciary. Together, they are responsible for the enforcement of all laws and for establishing judicial and legal policies.

The constitution stipulates that "the judiciary is an independent power" but in the past Iranian lawyers have joked that "a judge's verdict is sold by the kilo."[18] The judiciary is also seen as biased against reform and as the servant of Iran's highly conservative government. Both the chief of the Supreme Court and the Prosecutor-General must be scholars of Islamic law permitted to use independent reasoning on doctrinal issues. Article 167 of the constitution states that, in the absence of a clear written legal code to cover the case at hand, judges must either use their own independent reasoning or must consult accepted sources, i.e., usually Khomeini's books on Islamic jurisprudence.[19]

All bills passed by the National Assembly must be approved by the Council of Guardians (a group of senior clerics) to make sure that they conform to Islamic principles. Special Civil Courts were established in 1979 to adjudicate cases involving family law, succession, and pious foundations.

A 12-article law on marriage and divorce, passed in 1986, allows the wife the right to obtain a divorce if the husband marries another wife without her permission or if, in the court's assessment, he does not treat his wives equally.

Divorce is governed by classical Shiite law, requiring a specific formula and two male witnesses. A 1992 amendment expanded a wife's access to divorce if her husband is deficient in certain areas, e.g., failing to support here, keeping bad company, contracting an incurable disease or madness, etc. The Shiite law of inheritance is also in force, which usually means that a woman inherits the same share as a man.

In an effort to curtail "un–Islamic behavior" among young Iranians, the government in 2002 formed a "religious police" force, similar to the one in Saudi Arabia, to assist the existing "morality police." The mission of the new force was to help enforce Iran's strict rules of moral behavior. Press reports say that members of this force have beaten people in the street for such offenses as listening to music or, in the case of women, wearing makeup or immodest clothing.

It is nearly impossible for outsiders to get reliable information about current legal conditions in Iran today, but it seems clear that traditional Islamic punishments are still being applied. In its 2004 report, for example, Amnesty International stated that

> At last 108 executions were carried out [in 2003], including of long-term political prisoners and frequently in public. At least four prisoners were sentenced to death by stoning while at least 197 people were sentenced to be flogged and 11 were sentenced to retaliatory amputation of fingers and limbs. The true numbers may have been considerably higher.[20]

According to the 2005 U.S. State Department human rights report for Iran, a 16-year-old girl, Ateqeh Rajabi, was hanged in public in 2004 for "acts incompatible with chastity." She was not believed to be mentally competent and had no access to a lawyer. The Iranian Supreme Court upheld her sentence. An unnamed man arrested with her received 100 lashes and was released.[21]

Iraq

During World War I, the British artificially put three provinces of the Ottoman Empire together as "Iraq." These former provinces remain potential fault lines, along which Iraq may some day fragment. When Iraq was declared independent in 1932, the Hashemite family, which also ruled Transjordan, governed the country as a constitutional monarchy. After a long string of political upheavals in Iraq, Saddam Hussein came to power in 1979. His Baath party was a purely secular party. It did not rely on Islam but was based instead on a mixture of militaristic ideas; socialism; and Leninist drama, i.e., the heroic "pioneer" (Saddam himself) who purifies society.

Today there are about 26 million Iraqis, 97 percent of whom are Muslims. Some 60 to 65 percent are Shias and 32 to 37 percent are Sunnis. Under Saddam Hussein, the Sunnis were dominant and treated the Shiites badly — not so much because they were Shiites but because he favored his own "tribes." As a result, the Shiites feel ill-used and will have a major voice in future governments.

When this book was written, Iraq was still a war zone. It had no effective rule of law beyond that imposed — only locally and only temporarily — by armed forces, usually American. Optimists, led by President Bush, claimed that that Iraqi leaders would be able to forge a viable, effective, representative "national unity" government. Pessimists, on the other hand, forecast an eventual partition of the country into different sectarian enclaves. As the journalist Patrick Cockburn wrote presciently in the spring of 2006,

> Iraq is splitting into three different parts. Everywhere there are fault lines opening up between Sunni, Shia and Kurd.... The moment when Iraq could be held together as a truly unified state has probably passed.... The real question now is whether Iraq will break up with or without an all-out civil war.[22]

When this was written, Iraq was still in too much turmoil to permit any responsible estimate of what its legal system might eventually be. In 1959, Iraq drastically modified its *sharia*-based family law system and became one of the Middle East's least religious states. Whether the *sharia* should be more strictly applied in post–Saddam Hussein Iraq will be one of the most difficult and most divisive questions facing any new Iraqi government. Perhaps all we can do is to mention some important provisions of Iraq's new constitution, which was adopted in 2005 and which contains 139 articles.

The first chapter of the constitution outlines its basic principles. These include the following:

- Islam is the national religion and a basic foundation for the country's laws. Freedom of religion, however, is upheld.
- Iraq is defined as being part of the Islamic world; its Arab citizens are part of the "Arab nation."
- The constitution is the highest law of the land. No law may be passed that contradicts the constitution itself; the "established" rules (or the "fixed" or "undisputed" rules, according to various translations) of Islam; or the principles of democracy.

It seems very likely that questions of personal status, e.g., marriage, divorce, inheritance, adoption, etc., will eventually be handled by Iraq's different communities in accordance with their own traditions. There will almost certainly be a religious court system similar to the one in Lebanon. This means that the *sharia* will be implemented in the realm of family law, regardless of whether Iraq eventually becomes a Balkanized or a unified country.

Jordan

What is now known as Jordan was part of the Ottoman Empire until World War I. First called "Transjordan," it was established as compensation for the Arabs of the region, who did not get the independent Arab state promised by the British during the war. After a period of indirect British Mandate rule, it became independent as a constitutional monarchy in 1946. It was first governed by King Hussein (1953–1999) and since then by his son, King Abdullah II. Jordan's population of 5.8 million people consists of Sunni Muslims (92 percent), Christians (6 percent), and small Shiite and Druze communities (2 percent). The Druze are a small, distinct community, most prominent in Lebanon and Israel, whose religion resembles Islam but is influenced by other religions. Jordan also is home to 1.7 million Palestinian refugees and 800,000 persons displaced by the 1967 Arab-Israeli war — a fact which often causes tensions in Jordan.

Jordan's legal system is based on legislation, constitutional law, religious laws, and customary law. Judges are appointed and dismissed by royal decree. The constitution, last amended in 1984, declares Islam to be the religion of the state. It does not formally identify the sources of legislation, but provides that "the *sharia* courts in the exercise of their jurisdiction shall apply the rulings of the *sharia* law." The constitution also provides for the establishment of separate civil and religious courts.

Jordan's Civil Code and its Law of Personal Status, both approved in 1976, were influenced by French law and by Egyptian and Syrian legal developments. The Hanafi school of law remains dominant in Jordan. The Jordanian legal system draws from its Ottoman heritage by giving the religious courts of different communities jurisdiction over matters of personal status. Its civil court system follows the French model. The religious courts are of two kinds: *sharia* courts and tribunals of other religious communities. The *sharia* courts have jurisdiction in three types of cases: those involving the personal status of Muslims themselves; those involving the payment of blood money; and those in which one party is Muslim and the non–Muslim party agrees to have the case heard by a *sharia* court. Appeals can be made to the *Sharia* Court of Appeal in Amman. A special court appointed by the civil Court of Cassation, i.e., the court of last resort, adjudicates any disputes between two religious courts and between a religious court and a civil court.[23]

In the past, Jordanian law dealt leniently with those convicted of an "honor crime," e.g., the murder or attempted murder — by her relatives — of a woman suspected of sexual misconduct. Responding to criticism from human rights activists, in 2001 the government passed a law that removed an article exempting perpetrators of honor crimes from the death penalty. The government also plans to cancel other articles that reduce the sentence for crimes committed in a fit of fury.[24] (It should be noted that the concept of lenient sentences for such crimes springs from French, i.e., Napoleonic, penal law, not from Islamic law itself.)

In one notable *sharia* case, a first instance *sharia* court of south Amman ruled on an apostasy charge in 1989. Toujan al-Faisal, a journalist and a candidate for parliament, was accused of apostasy — even though Jordan has no apostasy law. The plaintiffs argued, nevertheless, that she should be declared an apostate and should be divorced from her husband. The court eventually ruled that it had no jurisdiction in this case. Later, the *sharia* court of appeal held that there was no evidence of apostasy and therefore dismissed the case.[25]

Kuwait

The Ottoman Empire governed present-day Kuwait as part of Iraq's Basra province from the late seventeenth to the late nineteenth century. In 1899, a Treaty of Protection placed Kuwait under British control, via the ruling Al-Sabah dynasty, until 1961. Kuwait is now a constitutional hereditary emirate and has 10 percent of the world's oil reserves. Attacked and overrun by Iraq in 1990, it was liberated in four days by an American-led coalition in 1991.

The population of Kuwait is about 2.3 million, including 1.2 million non-nationals, many of them Arabs from neighboring states. They usually work in low-paying jobs in the petroleum sector or as servants. Eighty-five percent of the Kuwaitis are Muslims. Seventy-five percent of them are Sunnis; the remainder are Shiites. Members of other faiths — Christians, Hindus, Parsis (fire-worshipers who are devotees of the Persian prophet Zoroaster) — make up the remainder.

In 1959, the emir Abdullah al-Salim al-Sabah enlisted the services of a renowned Arab jurist, Abd al-Razzaq al-Sanhuri (d. 1971), to draft a number of codes that would be inspired by Egyptian and French models. Matters relating to civil and commercial law were codified in the 1960s, but it was not until 20 years later that the Civil Code (1980) and the Kuwaiti Code of personal status (1984) were finally enacted.

The judicial system today consists of a civil law system and, for personal matters, the *sharia* as interpreted by the Maliki school.[26] Article 2 of the 1962 constitution states that "the religion of the State is Islam, and the Islamic *Sharia* shall be a main source of legislation." Article 1(2) of the Civil Code directs that, in the absence of a specific legislative provision, judges are to make decisions according to custom. In the absence of an applicable principle of custom, they are to be guided by principles of Islamic jurisprudence (*fiqh*) most appropriate under the general and particular circumstances.

Kuwaiti courts can rule on all disputes concerning personal status and civil, commercial, and criminal matters. There are three levels of courts: courts of first instance, which have personal status and other divisions; the High Court, which can also address personal status issues; and the Supreme Court, with two divisions — High Appeal and Cassation. Courts dealing with personal status law are divided into Sunni, Shiite, and non–Muslim sections.

Lebanon

Following the collapse of the Ottoman Empire after World War I, the several Ottoman provinces that now constitute Lebanon were mandated to France. Independent since 1943, Lebanon has experienced alternating periods of prosperity and conflict. Civil war variously raged or simmered from 1975 to 1989, ending only with the Ta'if Agreement of 1989. The United States intervened militarily in Lebanon in 1982–1984 after the 1982 Israeli invasion of that country. One result was the suicide bombing of the American Embassy in 1983, which marks the beginning of Islamic suicide attacks against Western targets. An uneasy calm has generally prevailed in Lebanon since the Ta'if Agreement but it was seriously marred by the 2005 assassination of former Prime Minister Rafiq Harriri.

About 60 percent of the 3.8 million people now living in Lebanon are Muslims. Christians account for some 39 percent, and other faiths make up the remainder. About 19 religious groupings are recognized officially. All of these sects have different personal status regulations and most have their own courts and judges. Lebanon's constitution was initially passed 1926. No official census has been taken since 1932, a remarkable fact that reflects the very high sensitivity of the Lebanese to confessional, i.e., religious, balance in the political process. Under this balance, first outlined in 1943 as an unwritten national pact, the president of Lebanon must be a Maronite Christian; the prime minister, a Sunni; and the speaker of parliament, a Shiite.

The Lebanese government accords recognition to legally recognized sects, which are free with respect to their personal affairs, freedom of belief, exercise of religious rituals, and freedom of religious education. Today, Lebanon's legal system includes both secular and religious courts, which apply a combination of Ottoman law, canon law, the Napoleonic code, and civil law.

There are four Courts of Cassation (three courts for civil and commercial cases, one for criminal cases). A Constitutional Council rules on the constitutionality of laws. The Supreme Council hears charges, should any arise, against the president and the prime minister. There is no official state religion or recognition of the *sharia* as a source of legislation.[27]

There are, however, two levels of *sharia* courts for Muslims on matters of personal status: the Courts of First Instance, which have Sunni and Ja'fari (Shiite) judges, and the Supreme *Sharia* Court in Beirut, which has three *qadis* (judges) and a civil judge, who acts as Attorney-General. The Law of the Rights of the Family (1962) applies Hanafi doctrines to most Sunni personal status cases, and Ja'fari *fiqh* (jurisprudence) to similar Shiite cases.

For Muslims in Lebanon, the Hanafi Ottoman family law that was passed in 1917 is still valid today. It is based on the family law regulations drawn up by Muhammad Qadri Pasha (d. 1889), an Egyptian jurist and Minister of Justice who codified these regulations for the first time in the second half of the nineteenth century. Additional laws were passed for the Druze in 1948 and for the Sunnis and Shiites in 1962.

There have been several initiatives in the history of modern Lebanon to introduce an optional civil marriage for those Lebanese who would like to get married under the provisions of the same civil family code. However, the deeply-rooted sectarian divisions within Lebanese society as a whole, and especially among Lebanese religious leaders, have thus far prevented adoption of such a civil marriage procedure.

Libya

Libya was part of the Ottoman Empire from 1551 until 1911. The Italians invaded Libya in 1911 and annexed it as a colony in 1934. It finally became independent in 1951. The *sharia* was made subordinate to secular law in 1954, but this caused so much popular protest that separate religious and secular jurisdictions were reestablished in 1958. Colonel Qadhafi came to power in 1969 by leading a coup against King Idris.

The current legal system is based on the *sharia* and on French and Italian law. However, like many other aspects of life in Libya today, its implementation in important cases depends chiefly upon the wishes of Colonel Qadhafi himself. He has long seen himself as a revolutionary future-oriented leader. Indeed, he espouses an entirely new system of government. Labeled the "Third Universal Theory," this unique combination of Islam, socialism, and tribal practices is supposed to be implemented by the Libyan people as part of Qadhafi's concept of "direct democracy." He has laid out his theories in what is known as the "Green Book."

Colonel Qadhafi believed that the two-track (religious and secular) legal decision of 1958 not only violated the Quran but also regulated the *sharia* to a secondary status. He therefore decided in 1971 to make all Libyan laws conform to the *sharia*. Two years later, the religious judicial system of *qadi* courts was abolished. The secular court system now includes religious matters in its jurisdiction.

This decision has raised some interesting problems. Consider, for example, the Quranic dictum that the appropriate punishment for theft is retaliatory amputation of one of the thief's hands. Debates arose in Libya over whether "amputation" should mean physical amputation or, rather, simply removing the financial needs or the temptations which had driven the thief to steal. A strict interpretation of the law was adopted, but in fact it was rarely, if ever, applied — mainly because of the many exemptions and qualifications held to be imposed by the *sharia* itself. For example, if a thief had been forced to steal to feed his starving family, or if he truly repented of his crime, retaliatory amputation would not be carried out.[28]

The population of Libya now stands at about 5.7 million people, a figure that includes half a million sub–Saharan Africans living there. Some 97 percent of the population is Sunni Muslim. Maliki law is preferred. Article I of the Libyan Civil Code describes the sources of Libyan law as the *sharia*, legislative provisions, custom, principles of natural law, and rules of equity. A Constitutional Proclamation, as amended in 1977, declares Islam to be the state religion.

There are four levels of courts: Summary Courts, located in small towns; Courts of First Instance, which have personal status divisions; Courts of Appeal; and the Supreme Court, which has five chambers, one of which deals with *sharia* issues. The secular Courts of Appeal now employ the *sharia* judges who would formerly have sat in the *Sharia* Court of Appeals. Article 72 of the Family Law of 1984 directs recourse to the sources of the *sharia* as a residual source of law in the absence of specific provisions in Libyan legislation.

Malaysia

Just over 60 percent of Malaysia's 25 million people are Muslims. The majority are Shafi'i, with Hanafi minorities. Formerly a British colony, Malaya (as it was then known) became independent in 1957. In 1963, Malaya, Sabah, Sarawak, and Singapore formed the new state of Malaysia; Singapore became an independent country itself in 1965. By constitutional definition, all Malays, who form half of the population, are Muslims. About one quarter of the people is Chinese. They have played the dominant role in trade and business. Malaysia is a constitutional monarchy, nominally headed by a traditional "paramount ruler," or king, who is also the leader of the Islamic faith.

The Malaysian legal system is based on English common law but both Islamic law and traditional law play significant roles in matters of personal status. The Federal Court, whose judges are appointed by the paramount ruler on the advice of the prime minister, reviews decisions referred from the Court of Appeals. It has jurisdiction in constitutional matters and in disputes between states or between the federal government and a state. The federal government has legal authority in most fields, including criminal law. An exception is civil law cases among Malays or other Muslims, which are adjudicated under Islamic law. There are three levels of *sharia* courts: *Sharia* Subordinate Courts, the *Sharia* High Court, and the *Sharia* Appeal Court.

Article 3(1) of the constitution, adopted in 1957, declares Islam to be the official state religion and guarantees religious freedom. Articles 3(3) and (5) provide that the Muslim ruler of each state is the head of Islam in that state. Where there is no Muslim ruler, the paramount chief of Malaysia is the head of Islam there. The states are empowered to make personal status laws governing Muslims and to establish and regulate *sharia* courts. Clarification of points of Islamic law is provided by the Council of Religion and Malay Custom of each state. The Councils usually issue *fatwas* in keeping with Shafi'i tenets. Should these rulings conflict with the public interest, the Councils may follow other Islamic legal doctrines instead.

Between 1952 and 1978, in the 11 Muslim-majority states of Malaysia and Sabah, the Administration of Islamic/Muslim Law Enactments covered the official determination of Islamic law, explanations of substantive law, and jurisdictions of the *sharia* courts. New laws relating to personal status were passed by most states between 1983 and 1987.

Taken as a whole, Malaysia has traditionally been an exemplar of a modernized and moderate Islam. For more than a decade, on the other hand, the Muslim state of Kelantan had ambitions of becoming a strictly Islamic state. In 1993, it tried to pass a *Sharia* Criminal Code Enactment, which would have applied the very severe *hadd* penalties to criminal acts. This effort resulted in a standoff between the federal and state governments: constitutionally, criminal matters fall under the jurisdiction of the federal government, not that of the states. The Kelantan state legislature did pass a *hadd* bill but this law was never brought into force because the federal government refused to approve it.[29] Since then, the Islamic party, Parti Islam se–Malaysia, has suffered reversals at the polls and has shelved any further plans to implement the *sharia* more rigorously.[30]

Mali

The Mali Federation was formed in 1960 when the Sudanese Republic and Senegal became independent of France. After Senegal withdrew from the federation, what was formerly the Sudanese Republic was renamed Mali. Beginning in 1990, armed attacks by the Tuaregs, a tribe of desert nomads who opposed the central government, led to clashes with the military. A peace settlement of this conflict was celebrated in 1996 at a colorful ceremony in Timbuktu known as *Flamme de la Paix*—"Peace Flame."

Mali is one of the poorest countries of the world. About 90 percent of its 11 million people are Sunni Muslims. While the 1992 constitution calls for independent judiciary, the government (through the Ministry of Justice) not only appoints the judges but also supervises both law enforcement and judicial functions. The Supreme Court has both judicial and administrative powers. Under the constitution, a separate constitutional court and a high court of justice can try senior government officials in cases of treason.

The constitution provides for freedom of religion. There is no state religion: the constitution defines Mali as a secular state. Its legal system is based on a mixture of the *sharia*, customary law, and codes inherited at independence from France. Some new laws have been enacted, but any French colonial laws that have not been abrogated still have the force of law. Family law, including laws pertaining to divorce, marriage, and inheritance, is based on a mixture of local tradition and Islamic law and practice. There is a large case backlog in the judicial system; this results in long periods of pretrial detention and lengthy delays in trials.

Mauritania

Reflecting its official name of the Islamic Republic of Mauritania, 99.9% of this country's 3 million people are Muslims. Mauritania became independent from France in 1960 and inherited the French legal and judicial system. A bloodless coup in 2005 brought a military council to power, which claimed that it will rule for only two years and will prepare the country for democratic institutions. At present, however, Mauritania remains a one-party state.

The constitution says that the country is an Islamic republic and that Islam is the religion of its citizens and of the state itself. The judiciary consists of a single system of courts (the Supreme Court, the Court of Appeals, and the lower courts), with a legal system based on the *sharia*. There is a cabinet-level Ministry of Culture and Islamic Orientation, as well as a High Council of Islam. This latter organization consists of six religious scholars, who make sure that proposed legislation conforms to Islamic precepts. Some observers feel that Islam is the major cohesive element unifying the country's otherwise disparate ethnic groups, i.e., the black population and the Maur (Arab-Berber) population.

One legal problem in Mauritania, inherited from its French colonial past, has been that no one is presumed to be entirely innocent. Thus, any failure by a defendant to persuade the judge that the Mauritanian government's charges are erroneous can in itself be seen as proof of guilt. First-hand testimony by a witness or codefendant can also lead to a verdict of guilty. Circumstantial evidence is inadmissible as proof of guilt. Perhaps as a result, plea bargaining became common, as were long pre-trail detentions. It seems doubtful that the new military council will be able to do much about this situation.

Morocco

More than 98 percent of Morocco's 32 million people are Muslims. Most of them are Sunnis. There are also about 4,000 Jews and less than 1,000 Christians in this country. Independent from France since 1956, Morocco is a constitutional monarchy. Karaouine University, located in the religious and cultural city of Fes, has been a center for Islamic studies for more than 1,000 years.

Morocco's legal system is based on Islamic law and on French and Spanish civil law.[31] Under French and Spanish rule, colonial systems developed outside the traditional sphere of family law. During the first half of the twentieth century, *sharia* courts applied Maliki jurisprudence. After independence in 1956, a Law Reform Commission drafted a code of personal status, which became law the next year. Article 82 of this Code states that "with regard to anything not covered by this law, reference shall be made to the most appropriate or accepted opinion or prevailing practice of the school of Imam Malik."

Article 6 of Morocco's constitution, first adopted in 1972, declared Islam to be the official state religion. It guarantees freedom of worship for all citizens. There are four levels of courts. The first level consists of courts of first instance for Muslim and Jewish personal law. Regional courts form the second level. Courts on these two levels are divided into four sections, which address, respectively, *sharia*, rabbinical, civil, commercial and administrative, and penal matters. *Sharia* sections of the regional courts also hear all matters of Islamic law affecting Moroccan Muslims. At the third level are the courts of appeal. The highest level consists of the Supreme Court in Rabat.

In 2004, the Morocco enacted numerous reforms to the *Mudawana*, the country's only code still based on the *sharia*.[32] An entirely new law was passed to replace the old one. This new personal status law governs marriage, divorce, parentage, inheritance, child custody and guardianship. A colorful trilingual poster created by Moroccan women artists highlights nine aspects of this new family law. A literal translation of its captions runs as follows:

Women Design the New Mudawana

- Age of marriage: both parties must be at least 18.
- Polygamy: permitted only with the approval of a judge and the wife.
- Conjugal home: both parties have the right to live there.
- Marriage without a contract: a delay of 5 years is needed to prove it.
- The guardian of the children, i.e., the wife, has right to food and lodging.
- Division of goods [in the event of divorce]: to be determined by a written contract between husband and wife.
- Matrimonial guardianship: An adult woman may now arrange her own marriage.
- Obedience of the wife towards her husband: eliminated!
- Divorce: only before a judge.[33]

Moroccan liberals initially hailed these reforms as a major victory for women and, more broadly, for the democratic process. Conservatives, however, had blocked several previous attempts to modernize the *Mudawana*. They failed in 2004 only because of the changed political environment following terrorist attacks in Casablanca in 2003. The king himself enforced the new law in his capacity as the highest Islamic authority in the country and as a descendent of Muhammad himself.

After the attacks, the government repressed Islamic extremists, which effectively muted opposition to these potentially far-reaching reforms. The conservatives have not given up, however, and whether the new law will advance women's rights in practice remains to be seen.

Nigeria

The most populous country in Africa, Nigeria is composed of more than 250 ethnic groups living in 36 states. It accounts for about 20 percent of West Africa's people. The country as a whole has a population of 128 million people, about half of them Muslims. The dominant ethnic group in northern two-thirds of the country is the Hausa-Fulani, most of whom are Muslim.

Nigeria became independent from Britain in 1960. The current constitution dates from 1999 and is based on English constitutional law, the *sharia* (in 12 northern states), and traditional law.[34] The judicial branch includes the Supreme Court and the Federal Court of Appeal. The judicial system is often incapable of providing criminal suspects with speedy and fair trials. State courts and the local judiciary are influenced by political leaders and suffer from more corruption and inefficiency than the federal court system.

Nigeria allows its states the option of applying aspects of the *sharia* if they so wish. The *sharia* has been in force in northern Nigeria for many years but until 2000, its scope was limited to personal status and civil law alone. Since 2000, however, 12 states in northern Nigeria have added criminal law to its jurisdiction.

The humanitarian organization Human Rights Watch reported that "Since 2000, at least 10 people have been sentenced to death by *sharia* courts; dozens have been sentenced to retaliatory amputation; and floggings are a regular occurrence in many locations in the north."[35] This organization also found that "there is little doubt that most of the governors who introduced *Sharia* into their states did so primarily for political reasons, in order to secure votes and increase their popularity."[36] Another persuasive reason was to get financial support from Saudi Arabia and other Gulf states.

On a more positive note, however, Human Rights Watch found a silver lining in this cloud:

> A study of the outcome of a number of trials, combined with comments made by state government officials, shows a reluctance to carry out some of the harsher aspects of the system, such as death sentences and amputations, and a desire to avoid further controversy ... the combination of external pressure and domestic disillusion with the manner in which the *Sharia* has been implemented has had the effect of dampening the politicians' zeal: they have realized that their strategy of using *Sharia* as a quick way to boost their popularity is not longer politically viable, particularly because it has made them unpopular among the constituencies upon whom they had relied for support.[37]

Oman

Contact with Europe dates from 1508, when the Portuguese temporarily occupied parts of Oman's coastal region. When the Portuguese were expelled in 1650, the country became fully independent. Today the hereditary sultanate of Oman is a vital transit point for crude oil transiting the Strait of Hormuz en route to world markets. In 1970, Sultan Qaboos ousted his father in a bloodless coup supported by the British and assumed power himself. He opened Oman to the outside world and preserved good relations with the West and with most other states.

The population of Oman is about 2.4 million, an estimate that includes around 600,000 foreigners, most of them guest workers from South Asia, Egypt, Jordan, and the Philippines. Some 99 percent of the Omanis are Muslims, most of them Ibadis. Ibadism, known for its moderate conservatism, is a branch of Islam distinct from orthodox Sunnism and Shiism. Oman is the only country in the Islamic world with a majority Ibadi population. There are also Sunni and Shiite minorities.

The legal system is based on French law (as transmitted via Napoleon and Egypt) and on the *sharia* (used only for family law). The sultan is the court of last appeal. In 1996, Sultan Qaboos caused the Basic Statute of the State to be drafted. Article 2 declares Islam to be the official state religion and provides that the *sharia* is "the basis for legislation." This Basic Statute has served as Oman's first written constitution and calls for the independence of the judiciary. However, it also gives the sultan the right to appoint and dismiss judges, as well as to overturn judicial decisions on appeal.

Oman's Ministry of Information describes the role of the *sharia* as follows:

> The principles derived from the Sharia law are the basis for all laws in Oman, but in recent years, separate bodies have been established to deal with matters like arbitration in civil and commercial cases to which Sharia law cannot always be applied. In June 1997, the Personal Status Law was promulgated ... with the aim of unifying judgments on matters like marriage and divorce, which had been open to differing interpretations under the existing customary laws. The Personal Status Law stipulates that no man or woman under the age of 18 shall be forced to marry without his or her consent and that having reached that age there is freedom of choice in marriage subject to certain conditions.[38]

In 1999, royal decrees put the entire court system, i.e., magistrates, commercial courts, *sharia* courts, and civil courts, under the financial supervision of the Ministry of Justice. A supreme court has been created. There are plans for regional court complexes to house the courts of first instance for criminal cases and for *sharia* cases (family law and inheritance).

Omani students can study law at the College of Sharia and Jurisprudence, which runs a three-year course. After completing it, they can either look for jobs in the government ministries or in the court system itself. Alternatively, they can go on to specialize in Sharia jurisprudence and thus qualify as a deputy judge in one of the courts.[39]

Pakistan

About 97 percent of Pakistan's 162 million people are Muslims, the majority of them belonging to the Hanafi school of jurisprudence. Pakistan became independent due to the partition of British (and largely Hindu) India in 1947. At that time, it consisted of two parts. The first was West Pakistan, which consisted of the provinces of Punjab, Sindh, Balochistan, and the Northwest Frontier Province. The second was East Pakistan, which was formed from the province of Bengal. These two entities were separated by more than 1,000 miles of Indian territory.

Over the years, Pakistan has experienced considerable unrest on both the international and the domestic fronts. It has fought three wars with India — in 1947, 1965, and 1971. Because of the last war, East Pakistan became the independent nation of Bangladesh in 1971. At home, political instability has been the norm. In 1999, for example, the former Chief of Army Staff, General Pervez Musharraf, seized power; in 2001, he named himself president of Pakistan. The Supreme Court, whose justices are appointed by the president, upheld the 1999 *coup d'état* and granted Musharraf full executive and legislative authority. Now both chief of the Pakistani Army and president of the country, he has shown no sign of wanting to relinquish either position.

After the 11 September 2001 terrorist attacks on the World Trade Center and the Pentagon, Musharraf had little choice but to accede to American demands that Pakistan work closely with the United States to deal with terrorism, e.g., by cracking down on Islamic extremist groups within Pakistan itself and by withdrawing Pakistani support for the Taliban regime in neighboring Afghanistan. This policy decision forced Musharraf to walk a tightrope.

On the one hand, he needed the external support provided by the Americans. Their price, however, was high: they wanted him to demolish Pakistan's conservative religious establishment — which the Pakistani army had nurtured and supported to keep itself in power. Faced with this insoluble problem, Musharraf temporized. He did take some cosmetic steps to curb religious extremism but, since he wanted to stay in power, he could not risk acting decisively against the conservative religious establishment as a whole.

Pakistan's legal system is based on English common law and on the *sharia*. The former has been more influential in commercial law; the latter, in personal status law. Article 227(1) of the constitution states that "All existing laws shall be brought into conformity with the injunctions of Islam as laid down in the Holy Quran and sunna ... and no law shall be enacted which is repugnant to such injunctions." This is the so-called "repugnancy" clause, which has always been part of the constitution. The constitution explains that, with respect to personal status, the expressions "Quran" and "*sunna*" mean the laws of any sect, as interpreted by that sect.

Pakistan's judicial branch includes the Supreme Court; the provincial high courts; and the Federal Sharia Court, which was established by Presidential Order in 1980. The Enforcement of *Sharia* Act of 1991 gave legal status to the *sharia*. Although declared to be the law of the land, it did not replace the existing codes. The harsh *hadd* punishments (e.g., retaliatory amputation or death by stoning) prescribed by the Quran for certain "crimes against God" are, in theory, legal but they do not appear to be used extensively in Pakistan today, except conceivably in the tribal areas which lie outside the effective control of the national government.

Qatar

Qatar (the pronunciation of its name falls somewhere between the English words "cutter" and "gutter") has been long ruled by the Al Thani family, beginning in the mid–1800s. Since independence in 1971, it has transformed itself from a poor British protectorate based on pearling and fishing into a constitutional emirate based on oil and natural gas. In a bloodless coup in 1995, the current emir, Hamad bin Khalifa Al Thani, overthrew his father, who had been crippling Qatar's economy by siphoning off petroleum revenues for his own use.

Qatar served as the headquarters and one of the main launching sites of the U.S. invasion of Iraq in 2003. The population is about 8.6 million people, 95 percent of whom are Muslims, mainly Wahhabis. There are also Indian, Pakistani, Iranian, and other ethnic groups living in Qatar. Because so many of Qatar's workers are expatriate males who have temporary resident status and are working in the petrochemical sector, Qatar now has the most heavily skewed sex ratio in the world: there are 1.88 males per female.

Qatar's jurisprudence is based on the *sharia* and has been influenced by Egyptian law. In 2003, Qatar's previously dual judicial structure (Sharia and Civil Courts) was merged under the umbrella of the Supreme Judicial Council. There is at present, however, no extensive body of codified law. In comparison with other Wahhabi states, i.e., Saudi Arabia, Qatar's laws are quite liberal. For example, women can drive in Qatar. Qatari women, however, must first have permission from their male guardian to receive a driver's license. Although Qatari women are usually shrouded in a black abaya (cloak), this full-length robe is not required for foreign women.

Saudi Arabia

Saudi Arabia was never colonized, though from the sixteenth century on parts of it were sometimes under nominal Ottoman control. The British did have nearby colonial interests in the Persian Gulf and in Oman and Yemen, but aside from occasional forays by British soldiers (e.g., T.E. Lawrence, better known as Lawrence of Arabia), diplomats and explorers, Westerners usually did not penetrate very far into the interior of the Arabian peninsula before oil was discovered there in 1938.

One reason was a conscious effort by the ruling Saud dynasty to make sure that Saudi Arabia remained a country which — as King Abdul Aziz ibn Saud (1876–1953), the founder and first king of Saudi Arabia, is said to have joked — would be very difficult for foreigners to enter and which they would want to leave as soon as possible once their business was finished. Perhaps as a result, the kingdom has never experienced the Western colonization that transformed so dramatically the traditional legal systems of most other Islamic countries.

It is virtually impossible for foreigners living outside Saudi Arabia to get extensive, accurate, up-to-date information on how the *sharia* is used there today. The Saudis are very sensitive on this point and do not want to encourage further international criticism of their human rights practices, which the U.S. Department of State described in its 2005 human rights report as "poor overall with continuing serious problems, despite some progress."[40] For this reason, it is important to discuss the *sharia* here in as much detail as can be mustered without moving to Saudi Arabia itself. As Frank Vogel, a modern American scholar who has written definitive works on law in Saudi Arabia, put it in 2000,

> Saudi Arabia is the most traditionalist Islamic legal system in the world today. Islamic law is constitutionally the law of the land, the general jurisdiction is held by traditionally trained judges who apply exclusively the Islamic law, and traditional Islamic legal learning is still good professional training for practice.... Again, this is not to claim that Saudi Arabia's legal system is the ideal Islamic law or legal system. Saudi Arabia does not perfectly apply Islamic law.... It is indisputable, however, that it does apply at least a traditionalist Islamic law in many spheres; and it does this, again, with certain notable successes relative to Islamic antecedents.[41]

We mentioned earlier that in 1749 a chieftain of the Saud tribe, Muhammad ibn Saud (d. 1765), and a very conservative Sunni reformer, Muhammad ibn Abd al-Wahhab (1703–1792), forged a unique and long-lasting alliance in the desert. They agreed that Muhammad ibn Saud would wield all the political power, while Muhammad Ibn Abd al-Wahhab would wield all the religious power. This remarkable alliance eventually led to the founding of the highly conservative Kingdom of Saudi Arabia in 1932 and is still the dominant fact of life there today.

Saudi Arabia is a Sunni monarchy based on the *sharia*. The king is both the chief of state and the head of government. His powers, however, are limited: he must follow the *sharia* and Saudi customs and must retain the support of other members of the royal family, the *ulama* (religious leaders), the tribes, and other important elements of Saudi society.

The population of Saudi Arabia today totals some 27 million people, a figure that includes about 7 million resident foreigners, whose entry and behavior is very carefully regulated. These men and women are mainly Indians, Bangladeshis, Pakistanis, Filipinos, Egyptians, Palestinians, Lebanese, Sri Lankans, Eritreans, Americans, and Europeans. Indeed, more than 35 percent of the working population consists of such foreigners, who do the hard work that the Saudis are unable or unwilling to do themselves. Each year, Saudi Arabia also hosts approximately 2 million Muslim pilgrims from around the world, and from all branches of Islam, for the Hajj.

Saudi Arabia has no formal, written constitution: the Wahhabi religious establishment strongly opposes such man-made laws as constitutions. Instead, the Basic Law (or Regulation), issued by King Fahd in 1992, reaffirms that the legal foundations of the country are exclusively religious. Here are some of its key provisions:

- Article 1 states that "The religion [of Saudi Arabia] is Islam, its constitution is the Book of God Most High [the Quran] and the Sunna of His Prophet, may God bless him and give him peace."
- Article 7 provides that "Rule in the Kingdom of Saudi Arabia draws its authority from the Book of God Most High and the Sunna of His Prophet. These two are sovereign over this Regulation and all regulations of the state."
- Article 48 decrees that "The courts shall apply in cases brought before them the rules of the Islamic *sharia* in agreement with the indications [or proofs] in the Book and the Sunna and the regulations issued by the ruler that do not contradict the Book or the Sunna."
- Article 55 establishes that "The King shall undertake the adjudication and governing of the nation in accordance with the *sharia* in fulfillment of the rules of Islam."[42]
- Two other articles are of interest here as well. Article 9 tells us that "the family is the kernel of Saudi society, and its members shall be brought up on the basis of the Islamic faith." Article 26 says that the government will protect human rights "in accordance with the Islamic *sharia*."[43]

Saudi Arabia is the birthplace of Islam. As custodian of Islam's two holiest sites (Mecca and Medina), the government understands full well that its legitimacy — and, indeed, its very survival — rests on its publicly strict enforcement and interpretation of the *sharia*. This responsibility is taken very seriously indeed. Here are three cases to the point:

- In 1979, armed Islamic extremists seized the Grand Mosque of Mecca, taking hundreds of Muslim pilgrims hostage. The Saudi dynasty was shaken to its foundations. The insurgent leader condemned the Al Saud family for corruption. Far more important, he also declared that the royal family unfit to rule Saudi Arabia any longer because its members had forsaken the primary tenets of Islam. It took Saudi forces 14 days of heavy fighting to oust the insurgents. Many people were killed in the process. The occupation of the Grand Mosque led to riots and demonstrations by Shiite dissidents. The ringleaders of the attack who survived the fighting were publicly executed by decapitation with a sword. Since then, the Al Saud family has made great efforts to depict itself as powerful and truly Islamic, e.g., by lavishly supporting Wahhabi schools and charitable foundations abroad.
- In about 1999, three men who beat up a young boy, frightened him and then raped him, were spared the death penalty or retaliatory amputation only when they changed their plea by withdrawing their confessions. They had admitted to this crime, which, according to the *sharia* as practiced in Saudi Arabia, would normally have been treated as a *hadd* crime of banditry and would have incurred the drastic punishments mentioned above. During their trial, the men withdrew their confessions, claiming that they were illiterate and therefore could not understand the papers that they had been forced to sign. The result was that the judge dropped the charge of banditry and, using his discretionary powers, sentenced each of them instead to five years in prison and 500 lashes, the latter to be administered in five installments at two-month intervals.[44]
- In 2004, a Muslim schoolteacher was tried for apostasy (a crime punishable by death under the *sharia*). He was lucky: the court declined to convict him of apostasy. He got off very lightly — with a sentence of only three years in prison and 300 lashes.[45]

Saudi law requires that all Saudi citizens must be Muslims. The public practice of non–Muslim religions is officially prohibited, but the government tacitly permits non–Muslims to worship in private — provided that they do so quietly and discreetly, e.g., only in private homes. No churches or other buildings visibly designed for non–Muslim faiths are permitted in the kingdom. The very strict dress codes and other social requirements of Wahhabism are enforced in public places by the Mutawwa'in (religious police). This official institution, formally known as the "Committee to Promote Virtue and Prevent Vice," takes its name from the Quranic injunction which orders the faithful to do precisely this. The 2 million Shiites in Saudi Arabia, who live in the oil-rich Eastern Province, often face officially-sanctioned political and economic discrimination. Saudi Shiites, like their co-religionists elsewhere, adhere to the Ja'fari school of law.

The Ministry of Justice is responsible for administering the country's more than 300 *sharia* courts.[46] The minister of justice, chosen by the king from the Council of Senior Religious Scholars (an advisory body of 20 senior jurists), serves as the chief justice. A Supreme Judicial Council supervises the work of the courts and approves all sentences of death, retaliatory amputation (of fingers and hands as punishment for theft), and stoning (for adultery).

There are four levels of *sharia*-related legal bodies: Minor Courts, General Courts, the Cassation Court and the Supreme Judicial Council. There are also a number of specialized tribunals dealing with commercial or labor law. Other spheres of law, e.g., corporate, tax, oil and gas, immigration law, etc., are regulated by royal decrees, state regulations, or codes and bylaws. The highest appellate tribunal is the Board of Grievances, which is directly responsible to the King. The king himself is the court of last appeal and the ultimate dispenser of justice.

One interesting aspect of modern Saudi jurisprudence is the importance attached to reconciliation, i.e., the agreed settlement of legal disputes. In this process, Saudi law tries to follow the lead set by the Hanbali jurist Ibn al-Qayyim (d. 1350), who was Ibn Taymiyya's pupil and successor. Ibn al-Qayyim recommends that the *qadi* (judge) use his judicial discernment and his intimate knowledge of the people to achieve sound, practical justice. A rightful judge, he tells us, is one who "knows the facts, recognizes what is obligatory, and intends justice."[47]

A good example of reconciliation in practice is a case brought before the Great *Sharia* Court of Riyadh in 1983.[48] It involved a claim for four months' unpaid rent on a shop. The amount at stake was about SR (Saudi riyals) 14,000, i.e., roughly equivalent to US$4,000. The plaintiff was described as an obstinate, ignorant, and elderly landlord; the defendant, as an articulate, reasonable-sounding tenant who had rented the shop. The tenant claimed that he had left the shop four months earlier and had given the keys back to the landlord. He said that he could call witnesses to prove he had vacated the premises and could show, by means of documents from the utility companies, that the electricity and telephone had been disconnected for the last four months.

Despite several adjournments, however, all that the tenant could actually produce was a receipt from the landlord showing part payment of past rent. The judge — his patience apparently wearing thin — then announced that it was time for the case to come to "proof or oath." He thereupon proposed a settlement, splitting the claimed rent. Both parties opposed this solution; the tenant again threatened to call witnesses. The judge then sternly lectured both men on the virtues of reconciliation. The tenant finally offered to pay SR5,000. The judge suggested to the landlord that he accept SR6,000 instead, but the landlord insisted on the full rent of SR14,000. At this point, the judge ruled that the payment would be SR5,000 and, after a final burst of argument, got the landlord to agree to this lower figure. Both parties signed the record to this effect and the case was closed.

Somalia

Independent from British and Italian rule since 1960, Somalia has been without a functioning central government since 1991, when the regime of Mohammad Siad Barre fell from power. Much of this impoverished desert land has been engulfed in civil war. An ineffective interim government was drawn up in 2004, but numerous warlords and factions are still vying for control of the capital city of Mogadishu and other areas. Northern clans have proclaimed an independent "Republic of Somaliland"; other Somalis have established a neighboring autonomous state called "Puntland."

Accurate information on judicial and other conditions in Somalia today is not readily available. More than 99 percent of the population of about 9 million people is Sunni Muslim. At independence, Somalia had four separate legal traditions: English common law, Italian law, the *sharia*, and Somali customary law. In 1973, then President Siad Barre introduced a unified civil code that sharply curtailed both the *sharia* and customary law. No constitution or national legal system is now in force. Consequently, both these traditional legal codes have resurfaced since the central government disintegrated in 1991.

Clan or lineage councils now administer customary law in the areas they control. Since 1977, religious leaders have also set up local *sharia* courts in Mogadishu and a few other cities. These are funded by wealthy contributors from the Gulf states. *Sharia* court rulings are enforced by local militiamen who are devout Muslims, e.g., they do not smoke, drink, or chew the local stimulant, a narcotic leaf known as *qat*.[49] These courts have the power of life and death. The case of a Somali murderer named Omar Hussein is instructive here.

In the spring of 2006, a *sharia* court in the capital, Mogadishu, convicted Hussein of killing a teacher, Sheik Osman Moallim, after a dispute over the education of Hussein's son. The court ordered that Moallim's teenage son should execute his father's killer in the same manner in which his father had been murdered. The sentence was duly carried out. According to a news account from Reuters, "Hundreds of people watched the teenager stab Hussein several times in the chest and throat at the Korean school where his father had worked."[50]

The two main protagonists in Somalia's long-running civil war now call themselves, respectively, the "Islamic Court Union" (a grouping of Islamic fundamentalists who want the *sharia* to be the law of the land) and the "Alliance for Restoration of Peace and Counterterrorism" (a coalition of secular warlords.) Prospects for a lasting peace are not good.

Sudan

Independent from Britain since 1956, Sudan is the largest country in Africa and now has about 40 million people, 70 percent of whom are Sunni Muslims. There are two distinct and major cultures in Sudan — "Arabs" (mainly Muslims) in the north, and black Africans (mainly Christians and animists) in the south. The northerners, who have traditionally controlled the country, have long tried to unify it along Islamic lines, despite the violent opposition of the non–Muslims in the south and elsewhere. The resulting civil wars have killed more than 2 million people and have displaced more than 4 million.

An Interim National Constitution, adopted in 2005 as part of a Comprehensive Peace Agreement, provided for power sharing with the former southern rebels and for national elections later. It declared Sudan to be a "democratic, multi-cultural, multi-ethnic, multi-religious, and multi-lingual state." The precise role of the *sharia* in this still-to-be-formed national government is unclear. We can only speculate that while the "Arabs" will never agree to abandon the *sharia* entirely, in the interests of avoiding further civil wars they may not insist that the new government apply rigorously the severe *hadd* penalties prescribed by the Quran for apostasy and other transgressions.

Syria

About 74 percent of the Syrian population of 18.5 million people are Sunnis. Alawite, Druze, and other Muslim sects account for some 10 percent; Christians and some small Jewish communities make up the remainder.

After the breakup of the Ottoman Empire during World War I, France created and administered Syria until its independence in 1946. In the 1967 Arab-Israeli war, Syria lost the Golan Heights to Israel. In 1970, Hafiz al-Asad seized power in a bloodless coup and brought an authoritarian political stability to the country until his death in 2000. His son, Bashar al-Asad, immediately succeeded him, running for office unopposed and garnering, according to Syrian government statistics, more than 97 percent of the popular vote. Syrian troops, stationed in Lebanon since the end of a civil war there in 1976, were withdrawn in 2005.

The Syrian constitution was adopted in 1973. Article 3 (1) states that the religion of the President of the country shall be Islam. Article 3 (2) declares that the *sharia* is a main source of legislation. The legal system is based on a combination of French and Ottoman civil law; the *sharia* is used in the family court system. The judicial branch includes the Supreme Constitutional Court; High Judicial Council; Court of Cassation; State Security Courts; Personal Status Courts, which hear cases related to marriage and divorce (there are separate courts for Sunnis, Shiites, Druze, Christians, and Jews); and Courts of First Instance, e.g., magistrate, summary, and peace courts.

The Ottoman Law of Family Rights continued to govern Syria on matters of personal status until 1953. It was then replaced by the Syrian Law of Personal Status of 1953, which covers matters of personal status, family relations, and intestate and testamentary succession. This law also directs that, for legal matters not otherwise covered, resort shall be had to the most authoritative doctrine of the Hanafi school. Major amendments to this law, made in 1975, relate to polygamy, dower, maintenance, *mut'a* (the temporary marriage permitted by Shiite law), cost of nursing, custody of children, and guardianship.

Tunisia

Present-day Tunisia was already a center of Arab culture and learning when it was assimilated into the Turkish Ottoman Empire in 1574 as an autonomous province. It was a French protectorate from 1881 until independence and still retains close ties to France. President Habib Bourguiba ruled the country with an iron hand for 31 years, suppressing Islamic fundamentalism and granting women rights that were unmatched by any other Arab nation. President Ben Ali, who led a bloodless coup against Bourguiba in 1987, has been in office ever since then and has continued his predecessor's moderate policies. The only Islamic fundamentalist party, Al-Nahda ("Renaissance"), is outlawed today. Its leaders now live in exile in London.

Ninety-eight percent of the 10 million people of Tunisia are Sunni Muslims. The constitution, amended in 2002, gives the president a central role in the life of the country. It declares that Islam is the state religion and that the religion of the president must be Islam. It provides for an independent judiciary, but the president and executive branch can nevertheless strongly influence judicial processes, especially in political cases. Tunisia has a legal system based on French civil law, except for matters of personal status, which are judged according to the *sharia*. The judicial branch includes District Courts; Courts of First Instance, which have social and personal status sections; Courts of Appeal; and the Court of Cassation.

Tunisia does not have separate *sharia* courts today. They were abolished in 1956; specialized sections of the civil courts now rule in personal status cases.[51] A Personal Status Law, drawing from both Hanafi and Maliki jurisprudence, was adopted shortly after independence in 1956. It gives women full legal status, thus allowing them to run their own businesses, have bank accounts, and obtain passports under their own authority. It also banned polygamy and extra-judicial divorce. Parents are required to send their children to school; today more than 50 percent of university students are women. Legislation enacted 1998 improved women's rights in matters of divorce and property ownership.

This Personal Status Law governs personal status issues for all Tunisians, regardless of their own religious affiliation. Although Tunisian family and inheritance law is codified based on the Napoleonic code, civil law judges sometimes apply *sharia* law in family cases when the French and the Islamic law systems come into conflict, especially where child custody is involved,.

Turkey

Modern Turkey is a constitutional republic with a multiparty parliamentary system and a president who has limited powers. It was initially forged in 1923 by the national hero Mustafa Kemal (1881–1938) from the remains of the 600-year-old Ottoman Empire, which had been destroyed by World War I. For this achievement, Kemal was later honored with the title of Ataturk, or "Father of the Turks." Under his authoritarian leadership, Turkey adopted a variety of legal, political, and social reforms.

For our purposes here, by far the most important of these was that the entire structure of the *sharia*—its legal documents, its tribunals and its judges — was officially abolished in 1926. It was replaced by a purely secular legal system drawn from Western models. Advocating the use of the *sharia* even became an offense under Turkey's new laws.[52]

The demise of the *sharia* began with the system of Capitulations, which dates from 1536 and which ensured that Westerners living in Turkey would be tried by their own laws. Legal changes gathered pace with the Tanzimat reforms, which began in 1839. These changes included the Commercial Code of 1850, which was a direct translation of the French Commercial Code, including payment of interest; the Penal Code of 1858, a translation of the French Penal Code, which abolished the severe *hadd* punishments prescribed by the Quran, except the death penalty for apostasy; the Codes of Commercial Procedure (1861) and Maritime Commerce (1863), both of which were basically French law; the basic law of obligations, codified between 1869 and 1876; and later legal documents.

To apply all these new codes, a new system of secular courts was established, which handled all cases except those involving personal status. Subsequently, Turkey promulgated a Criminal Code based on Italian law in 1926; a code of family law, based on the Swiss Civil Code, in 1927; and a Code of Criminal Procedure, drawn from German law, in 1928.[53] The change from the *sharia* to secular law was thereby essentially complete. Unless there is a fundamentalist Islamic revolution in Turkey, the *sharia* will not be used there again.

Today, more than 99 percent of Turkey's 69 million people are Muslims, mostly Sunnis. The civil law system is derived from various European continental legal systems. The judicial system consists of numerous secular entities. These include the general law courts; specialized courts empowered to impose long prison sentences; military courts; the Constitutional Court, the nation's highest court; and three other high courts. The High Court of Appeals hears appeals for criminal cases. The Council of State deals with appeals of administrative cases and cases between government entities. The Audit Court supervises government institutions. Most cases are prosecuted in the general law courts, which include civil, administrative, and criminal courts. To relieve the workload of the High Court of Appeals, regional appeals courts are being established.[54]

As part of its campaign to join the European Union, Parliament adopted a new Penal Code in 2004 and approved a package of constitutional amendments. Among other legal steps, so-called "honor killings" were defined as aggravated homicides and are now punishable as such. Despite this new prohibition, however, such killings are still socially accepted and still occur in the countryside of Anatolia — and even in Turkish families living in Europe.

In April 2006, for example, a German court sentenced a man of Turkish origin to more than nine years in prison for the honor killing of Hatun Surucu, his 23-year-old sister. Forced as a young girl to marry a cousin in Turkey, she had later broken up with her Turkish-Kurdish family in Berlin and then lived there independently with her 5-year-old son. Her brother, Ayhan Surucu, shot her down while she was standing at a bus stop in a Berlin suburb. The outrage of the German public over this murder was exacerbated because boys at a nearby school applauded the killing shortly afterward. They did so because the victim had "lived like a German," they said, abandoning her headscarf, wearing makeup and studying to become an electrical engineer.[55]

United Arab Emirates

Under the terms of nineteenth century treaties, the Trucial States of the Persian Gulf gave Britain control of their defense and foreign policies in order to suppress the corsairs who were infesting the "pirate coast." Six of these little states — Abu Dhabi, Ajman, Dubai, Fujairah, Sharjah, and Umm al-Qaiwain — merged in 1971 to form a loose federation known as the United Arab Emirates (UAE). They were joined by a seventh emirate — Ras al-Khaimah — the next year. The Supreme Council consists of the individual rules of the seven emirates.

Today, the UAE's strategic location along the southern approaches to the Strait of Hormuz makes it a vital transit point for crude oil. Thanks to its extensive oil and gas revenues and its position as a major financial center, the UAE now enjoys a Gross Domestic Product approaching that of some leading Western European countries. The population of the UAE is about 4 million, but only about 15 to 20 percent consists of UAE citizens. The other residents are non-nationals, e.g., Indians, Pakistanis, Bangladeshis, Egyptians, Jordanians, Iranians, Filipinos, and Westerners. Ninety-six percent of the population is Muslim. The majority is Sunni; Shiites account for 16 percent of the total.

A federal court system, introduced in 1971, applies to five of the seven emirates (the last two are not fully integrated into the federal judicial system). All the emirates, however, have secular courts for criminal, civil, and commercial disputes, plus *sharia* courts for personal status issues. The highest court is the Union Supreme Court, established in 1973. The Union Law of 1978 established the Union Courts of First Instance and Appeal and transferred jurisdiction from some tribunals to these courts. The Union Courts of First Instance deal with all civil, commercial, and administrative disputes, as well as with personal status cases, which arise in the capital, Abu Dhabi.

Article 7 of the Provisional Constitution of 1971, which was made permanent in 1996, states that Islam is the official state religion of the UAE and affirms that the *sharia* shall be a principal source of legislation. The Abu Dhabi Courts

Law of 1968 regulates the jurisdiction of the *sharia* courts, but Abu Dhabi's personal status law has not been codified. The six other emirates do not have legislation or organized judiciaries; the *sharia* courts there are not regulated. Important civil and criminal cases must be brought before the ruler in person.[56]

One *sharia* case from the UAE can be mentioned here. In 1997, the Dhobi Court of Cassation held that a divorced mother who had remarried still retained her custody rights over the children from her first marriage — due to a written agreement whereby their father had agreed not to claim custody even if she remarried.[57]

On balance, however, the UAE courts are still extremely conservative. Flogging with leather straps and canes is imposed as punishment for defamation of character, and drug or alcohol abuse. In 2006, a court sentenced 26 men, who included UAE citizens, an Indian, and three nationals of neighboring Arab countries, each to five years in prison after they were discovered getting ready for a gay wedding. The men, dressed in women's clothes and wearing make-up, were arrested in 2005 in a hotel in a UAE desert resort. The public prosecutor had charged them with homosexuality, which from an Islamic point of view is both a sin and a crime.[58]

Yemen

The British established the Aden Protectorate in 1839 and made a series of treaties with local rulers, which extended their influence into southern Yemen. In 1918, North Yemen became independent of the Ottoman Empire. A military coup in 1962 established the Yemen Arab Republic in the north and ushered in a period of civil war. Guerrilla fighting prompted the British to withdraw from Aden in 1967. This lead to the establishment of the People's Republic of South Yemen (later the People's Democratic Republic of Yemen), an Arab Marxist state. After two decades of hostility, the two Yemens were formally unified in 1990 as the Republic of Yemen.

Yemen today is a republic with a bicameral legislature. It is one of the poorest countries in the Arab world: more than 40 percent of the population lives in poverty. Some 99 percent of its 20 million people are Muslims, either Sunnis of the Shafi'i school, who live in the south and southeast, or Shiites of the Zaida sect, who live in the north and northwest. Despite its poverty and lack of exploitable resources, Yemen's location on the eastern side of Bab al-Mandab, the narrow strait linking the Red Sea and the Gulf of Aden, makes it strategically important to the Western world. Bab al-Mandab is the chokepoint of one of the world's most active shipping lanes, and all vessels bound for or coming from the Suez Canal must pass through it.

Today, Yemen's legal system is based on four sets of laws: the *sharia*, Turkish law, English common law, and local customary law. The constitution, amended in 1994, calls for an independent judiciary but the judiciary remains weak and is dependent on the executive branch. Article 2 of the constitution states that the "Islamic *sharia* shall be the source of all legislation." Article 23 provides that inheritance is regulated by the *sharia*, while Article 26 holds that "the family is the basis of society and its pillars are religion, custom and love of the homeland." Article 31 states that women have rights and duties, which are guaranteed and assigned by *sharia* and stipulated by law."

The legal codes of the former northern and southern parts of the country have been unified. Courts of first instance have jurisdiction in each district over personal status, criminal, and commercial cases. Appeals go to the Courts of Appeal. The Supreme Court has nine divisions: Constitutional, Appeals, Scrutiny, Criminal, Military, Civil, Family, Commercial, and Administrative. Due process is undermined, however, by prolonged pretrial detention, judicial corruption, and interference from the executive branch.

8

Islamic Banking

After beginning on a very modest scale in Egypt in 1971, Islamic banking has become an increasingly visible part of world banking today. Its unique and most interesting feature is that Islamic banks must adhere strictly to the requirements of the *sharia*. Toward this end, all Islamic banks must have a *fatwa* approving their activities. Most also have their own *sharia* boards or *sharia* advisers. Here is a very brief and highly generalized glimpse at Islamic banking.

What Is Islamic Banking?

As explained earlier in this book, Islamic law prohibits the charging and payment of interest (*riba*) on loans or deposits. There seem to have been two reasons for this.[1]

First, in Muhammad's time the well-developed trading system of Mecca included many transactions with a fixed time limit and with payment of interest, as well as speculation of all kinds. The custom was that if a debtor could not repay on time the money or goods he owed — together with the accumulated interest then due — he was given more time in which to pay. The bad news was that the sum due was thereupon doubled. Muhammad found this practice to be unfair. The Quran instructs the faithful: "Believers, do not live on usury, doubling your wealth many times over. Have fear of God, that you may prosper" (*sura* 3:130).

The second reason for prohibiting interest was that Muhammad was familiar with the commercial practices of the Jews in Medina and objected to their use of interest. Indeed, the Quran reproaches the Jews "because they practice usury — although they were forbidden it — and cheat others of their possessions. Woeful punishment have We prepared for those that disbelieve" (*sura* 4:161).

A reasonable question is: what forms of business fall under the Quranic prohibition of *riba*? According to the *Encyclopaedia of Islam*, Islamic traditions give varying answers to this question, but none of them can be regarded as authentic.[2] The correct understanding of *riba* passages therefore remains a matter of learned interpretation.

The Quran itself outlaws not only gambling, i.e., games of chance involving money, but also trading in substantial financial risk (*gharar fahish*). This is held to be a form of gambling; a small degree of risk (*gharar yasir*), however, is permitted. Islamic law also prohibits investing in businesses that trade in products forbidden to Muslims, e.g., alcohol, pork, armaments, tobacco, pornography, and non–Islamic banking or finance.

Islamic banking actively encourages participatory arrangements between capital and labor. This reflects the Islamic doctrine that the recipient of funds from an Islamic bank should not bear the full cost of failure alone. Muslims believe that it is God who determines any such failure and that He wants the losses to be shared by all the parties involved. Similarly, profits must be shared as well. *Sharia*-based property investment funds typically prefer offices and industrial properties. These can generate high returns and are likely to be approved by *sharia* boards and advisers.

During the earliest years of the Islamic world, most of the trade, which was based on camel caravans, was financed by two traditional commercial principles: (1) mobilizing funds on a profit-sharing basis and then extending these funds to users on the same basis, and (2) money transfer.[3] Islamic scholars assured the faithful that earning profits from such subsidiary roles in the production and exchange of real goods and services was a fully legitimate undertaking. This is still the case today.

Although details of how an Islamic bank functions are complex, in overview the outlines are clear enough. Munawar Iqbal and Philip Molyneux in their introductory survey, *Thirty Years of Islamic Banking* (2005), have summarized them.[4] These authors define an Islamic bank as a deposit-taking institution whose scope of activities includes most of the activities of non–Islamic banks — with the one important exception that borrowing and lending based on interest is not allowed.

On the liabilities side, the bank mobilizes funds, either based on a contract between two parties (financiers and an investment manager) or by a contract with an agent. It can also accept demand deposits, which are treated as interest-free loans from the clients to the bank and which are guaranteed.

On the asset side, it does not advance funds directly but rather buys the assets and then sells them to the customer, either directly as a "mark up" or over time, on a profit-and-loss or a debt-creating basis, in accordance with *sharia* principles. The bank acts as an investment manager for the owners of time deposits, usually called investment deposits. In addition, equity holding, as well as commodity and asset trading, constitute and integral part of Islamic banking operations. An Islamic bank shares its net earnings with its depositors in a manner that reflects the size and date-to-maturity of each deposit. Depositors must be informed beforehand of the exact formula that will be used for sharing the net earnings with the bank.[5]

Iqbal and Molyneux assert that Islamic banking can offer its clients several advantages compared with conventional banking. A great deal more could be said, pro or con, on each of the following points but the interests of brevity we will list here only some of the key advantages claimed by these two authors[6]:

- *Risk sharing*: The most important feature of Islamic banking, in the eyes of Iqbal and Molyneux, is that it promotes risk sharing between the provider of funds (the investor) and the user of funds (the entrepreneur). Both parties share the results of a project. If there is a profit, both share it in pre-agreed proportions. If there is a loss, it is borne both by the provider of funds, who loses his capital, and by the entrepreneur, who loses his labor.
- *An emphasis on productivity*: Since an Islamic bank profits only if the project itself succeeds and produces a profit, Iqbal and Molyneux argue that an Islamic bank will be very attentive to the soundness of the project and the managerial skills of the entrepreneur.
- *A moral dimension*: Conventional banking is secular in its orientation: in principle, it can finance any project which is both legal and economically feasible. Islamic banking, in contrast, must work within the confines value system of Islam. It cannot finance any project, e.g., a nightclub, which conflicts with this value system.
- *More economic growth*: Iqbal and Molyneux claim that Islamic banks can offer a variety of innovative profit sharing financing techniques that can help to stimulate economic growth.

To present a balanced picture of Islamic banking, two things should be noted here. The first is that although Islamic economic institutions are said to operate on the basis of "zero interest," some critics have disputed this assertion. They claim that the fundamental characteristic of charging interest, that is, charging a premium on the principal amount of a loan for the time value of the loaned money, is not truly eliminated in Islamic banking. According to these critics, the interest is merely hidden and relabeled — along the lines of the traditional and technically *sharia*-compliant legal stratagems known as "devices" or "legal tricks" (*hiyal*), which were discussed in an earlier chapter.

A rebuttal to this charge draws a clear distinction between money, which the non–Islamic bank loans to its customer, and an asset, which the Islamic bank owns on behalf of its customer. This rebuttal runs as follows[7]:

- Under interest based finance, a non–Islamic bank provides money to invest in a business at a fixed rate of return or margin over an agreed period. The money may be for a specific purpose, e.g., buying a building, and the bank will arrange security to protect its finance, e.g., by means of a mortgage or a charge over the company's assets (a debenture).
- In Islamic finance, in contrast, the bank purchases a specific physical asset on behalf of the customer. The asset is then either sold to the customer at a markup to cover the bank's profit over a period of time, or the customer enters into an agreement whereby the use of the asset is made available to him against a program of monthly step payments and ongoing rent while the asset is owned by the bank.

The second thing that must be noted is there are not enough qualified *sharia* scholars to fill all the appropriate openings in Islamic banks. Moreover, there is no standardized approach to Islamic banking, so the rulings these scholars provide are not always consistent. Moves are afoot now to introduce some standardization into this process.

Prospects for the Future

Compared with older well-developed financial institutions, Islamic banking still occupies only a niche market but its long-term prospects are good.

According to a report by the International Organization of Securities Commission, as of mid–2004 the Islamic financial market comprised 265 banks with assets of more than US$262 billion and investments of more than US$400 billion. The Commission estimated that although Islamic banking, insurance, and capital markets still form only a small part of the global industry, this "Islamic sector" has been growing at 10 percent to 20 percent a year for a decade. Within 8 to 10 years, the Commission forecast, as much as half the savings of the world's 1.5 billion Muslims will be in Islamic banks.[8]

In 2005, the wealth of high-net-worth individuals in the Middle East alone was estimated by the financial advisory firms of Merrill Lynch and Capgemini at more than US1.1 trillion — not including the assets of their counterparts in Asian Muslim countries, such as Malaysia and Indonesia.

Indeed, Singapore hopes to overtake Malaysia as the leader in developing Islamic financial products for Muslim customers in Southeast Asia.[9]

Major international banks — e.g., Lloyds TSB, Citigroup, HSBC, Standard Chartered, Paribas, Deutsche Bank, and Natwest — all have Islamic units now. In 2005, Deloitte, a New York-based business and consultancy group, decided to enter this market too. The first Islamic bank in Britain, known as the Islamic Bank of Britain, opened its first branch in London in 2004. It now has some 10 offices, located chiefly in the Muslim areas of British cities. There are also a number of other Islamic banks in the UK, mainly subsidiaries of Middle Eastern and Pakistani banks. These include ABC International, AHLI United, and Habib. Factors driving greater interest in Islamic banking including historically high oil prices, leaving the Middle East literally awash with cash; a wider choice of *sharia*-based products; and greater consciousness among wealthy Muslim investors of their religious duties.[10]

Islamic banking has been active on the multilateral front as well. The Islamic Development Bank (IDB), founded in Jeddah, Saudi Arabia, in 1975 and headquartered there, is a multilateral bank serving Muslim countries. Now consisting of 56 member states, the IDB is designed to foster economic development and social progress in accordance with the *sharia*. It has regional offices in Morocco, Malaysia, and Kazakhstan, as well as field representatives in eleven other member states. In one recent year, the authorized capital of the IDB stood at over US$20 billion; its subscribed capital at over US$11 billion; its paid-up capital at over US$3 billion; and its ordinary resources (members' subscriptions, i.e., paid-up capital, reserves and retained profits) at nearly US$6 billion.[11]

9

The Future of Islamic Law: Reform or Retrenchment?

We noted at the beginning of this book that Islamic culture is a legal culture. This fact brought great stability to Islamic life but it also became an enormous liability when the rise and expansion of the West made legal reform imperative for the Islamic world. The need for such reform has long been evident to most Western specialists on Islam and to many liberal Muslims as well. As a result, in most Islamic countries today the *sharia* is usually confined to personal status law. For a variety of political, religious and personal reasons, however, conservative Islamic governments and clerics still shy away from any far-reaching reforms in the *sharia* itself. As the British scholar J.N.D. Anderson explained with a nice turn of phrase, "In Islam ... it has always been a far more heinous offense to deny or question the divine law than to accept it in principle but disobey it in practice: so the path of the would-be reformer was difficult indeed.[1]

This brief survey of the *sharia's* long history suggests that the rivalry between Islam's reformers and its fundamentalists, which first surfaced in the nineteenth century, will be a continuing theme throughout the remainder of our own century — and probably long thereafter. As Khaled Abou El Fadl, a professor of law at the School of Law at the University of California in Los Angeles, put it in a recent book about Islam, there is a basic schism in the religion today between "Puritans" and "moderates."[2]

The most important current issue in Islamic law is how the *sharia* can be adapted to meet new circumstances without doing great violence to its traditional teachings. Because the *sharia* is considered to express the direct will of God, it does not lend itself easily to radical changes What *can be changed*, however, is the system of legal reasoning which is used to interpret the *sharia* in daily life.

Islamic countries can now, if they so wish, modernize their traditional legal systems. The new family law (*Mudawana*) in Morocco and the civil marriage discussions in Lebanon point in this direction. As Muhammad Abduh and other reformers have urged, Islamic jurists can also "piece together" (*talfiq*) judgments from the four Sunni legal schools to make new laws relevant to modern times. A good example of such an amalgamated selection (*takhayyur*) was the Ottoman Law of Family Rights of 1917.

Modernization of the *sharia* should ideally arise from within a given society. Reforms of this type are likely to be the most solidly based, the most widely accepted and the most enduring. Perhaps the most sensible approach that can be recommended for non–Muslims is to encourage the Islamic world to look for the most liberal and most modern interpretations of the *sharia*, including more rights for women.

To have the best chance of success, proposed reforms must be seen by devout Muslims as falling within the limits imposed by the Quran and the *sunna*. In a classic example of a reform derived from the Quran, when Tunisian legislators decided in 1956 to abolish polygamy, they based their justification squarely on the Quranic verse which sanctioned polygamy in the first place. This is *sura* 4:3, which reads in part,

> ... you may marry other women who seem good to you: two, three, or four of them. But if you fear than you cannot maintain equality among them, marry one only.... This will make it easier for you to avoid injustice.

The Tunisian reformers emphasized the second sentence of this verse, arguing that no one, except Muhammad himself, could treat two or more wives with complete equality and justice. They therefore concluded that this part of the verse abrogates the earlier permission to marry more than one wife. If so, it followed that polygamy was not legal.[3]

Today, liberal movements within Islam aim at reform, not schism. They often embrace these five tenets:

- Increased reliance on independent reasoning (*ijtihad*), leading to greater freedom for the individual to interpret the Quran and *hadith*.
- Critical analysis of religious texts and traditional Islamic practices.
- Better treatment of women.
- Greater tolerance for the customs, dress and patterns of behavior of non–Muslim peoples.

Reform may be difficult but it is not impossible. Islam has a surprising degree of flexibility. Modern Islamic states, for example, quickly concluded that the time-honored Islamic tradition of slavery (the index to Dawood's translation of the Quran contains 15 entries under "slaves") runs contrary to the ethos of modern life and thus had to be abandoned. It is also conceivable that some other traditions, e.g., the status of women, will eventually be considered inappropriate for modern times and will thus lend themselves to reform.

Despite the numerous possibilities for reform and modernization of the *sharia*, since 1972 seven countries have drafted legislation to reintroduce Islamic criminal law. Only in five cases, however, have such proposed laws actually become effective. These five countries are Libya, Pakistan, Iran, Sudan, and the northern part of Nigeria. In the other two cases, the legislation never became effective. A law was passed in the UAE in 1978 ordering *sharia* courts to hear cases of homicide and wounding, but this law does not appear to have been implemented. In 1993, Kelantan, one of the federal states of Malaysia, passed a similar a law but the government of Malaysia never approved it.[4]

Thus in recent years there has not been any groundswell abroad in favor of *sharia*-based criminal laws. Perhaps of greater concern is the fact that some highly conservative and often well-organized forces are now at work in the Muslim world today. They are trying hard to retrench Islam — by trying to steer the *sharia* away from any modernizing tendencies and return it to the fundamentalist purity which they allege was its hallmark during the days of the prophet and his Companions.

The views of these radical conservatives are too well known to need repeating here in any detail. Perhaps we can summarize them by quoting Osama bin Laden again. In so doing, we must never forget that he is not an Islamic scholar and that, legally speaking, he does not represent any Islamic state or people.[5] Nevertheless, his views have in fact had a major impact on the world scene. For more than 10 years, here is what he has pleaded with Islamic scholars to do:

> Come and lead your *umma* [the Muslim community], and call her to God, and return her to religion in order to correct beliefs, spread knowledge, enjoin good and forbid evil. Call her to *jihad* for the sake of God Almighty and call her to motivate people for it.[6]

This is his consistent theme: to encourage Muslim religious leaders all over the world to promote *jihad* by word and by deed. In his "letter to the American people," which was cited in an earlier chapter, he asked rhetorically, "What are we calling you do?" Here is part of his answer:

> The first thing that we are calling you to is Islam. The religion of the Unification of God; of freedom from associating partners [i.e., other divinities] with Him, and rejection of this; of complete love of Him, the Exalted; of complete submis-

sion to His Laws; and of the discarding of all the opinions, orders, theories and religions which contract with the religion he sent down to His Prophet Muhammad.... It is the religion of *Jihad* in the way of Allah so that Allah's Word and religion reign Supreme....[7]

The rivalry between those Muslims who want to reform the *sharia* and those who want it to revert to an earlier alleged purity will not be settled in the foreseeable future. Moreover, this low key but protracted contest will not have any clear winners or losers either. Both sides — and all the subtle gradations of opinion which lie between these two extremes — will be able to point to occasional victories.

All that seems safe to say at this point is that while radical fundamentalist doctrines can have an enormous emotional appeal to traditionalists, they are necessarily based on a tradition-bound faith, not on a more flexible religious rationalism. For this reason, it is unlikely they will ever be the sole basis on which a modern country can be governed successfully. It will indeed be interesting to see whether, in the years ahead, the *sharia* will evolve toward reform or toward retrenchment.

Appendix 1:
Al-Shafi'i's Views on
Legal Knowledge

This appendix is taken from pp. 81–82 of Majid Khadduri's translation of al-Shafi'i's treatise, Al-Risala. It has been lightly edited.

Someone asked [al-Shafi'i]: What is [legal] knowledge and how much should men know of it? He replied: Legal knowledge is of two kinds: one is for the general public, and no sober and mature person should be ignorant of it.

The questioner then asked: For example? Al-Shafi'i replied: For example, that the daily prayers are five, that men owe it to God to fast the month of Ramadan, to make the pilgrimage to the House [i.e., to the Ka'ba, a cubic stone structure located in the Grand Mosque of Mecca] whenever they are able, and to [pay] the legal alms in their estate; that He [God] has prohibited usury, adultery, homicide, theft, [drinking] wine, and [everything of that sort which He has obligated men to comprehend, to perform, to pay in their property, and to abstain from [because] He has forbidden it to them.

This kind of knowledge may be found textually in the Book of God [the Quran] or may be found generally among the people of Islam. The public relates it from the preceding public and ascribes it to the Apostle of God [Muhammad], nobody ever questioning its ascription or its binding force upon them. It is the kind of knowledge which admits of error neither in its narrative nor in its interpretation; it is not permissible to question it.

The questioner then asked: What is the second kind? Al-Shafi'i replied: It consists of the detailed duties and rules obligatory on men, concerning which there exists neither a text in the Book of God, nor regarding most of them, a *sunna*. Whenever a *sunna* exists [in this case], it is of the kind related by few authori-

179

ties, not by the public, and is subject to different interpretations arrived at by analogy.

The questioner asked: Is there a third kind [of knowledge], drawn from a narrative or analogy? Al-Shafi'i replied: There is a third kind. The public is incapable of knowing this kind of knowledge, nor can all specialists obtain it. But those who do obtain it should not all neglect it. If some can obtain it, the others are relieved of the duty [of obtaining it], but those who do so will be rewarded. [This third kind of knowledge involves *jihad*, which al-Shafi'i discusses at some length.]

Appendix 2: Translating the Concept of Jihad

Here are 10 different translations of the Arabic concept of *jihad* as it is used in *sura* 22:78. It can variously mean either "striving," "fighting" (as in fighting a war against the infidels), or something else. The names of the translators, all of them well known, are given in parentheses. Except for the first citation, which is from Dawood, these citations come from the Quran Browser (see bibliography), pp. 15–16. The modern scholar Wael B. Hallaq explains that "the translations are all, in a sense, inaccurate [because no translation can hope to convey precisely the full flavor of the original text]; but the first two — by Dawood and Pickthall — are the most precise."[1]

- "Fight for the cause of God with the devotion due to Him." (Dawood)
- "And strive for Allah with the endeavour which is His right." (Pickthall)
- "And strive in his cause as you ought to strive (with sincerity and under discipline)." (Yusuf Ali)
- "And strive hard in the way of Allah, (such a striving) is due to Him." (Shakir)
- "And strive in the cause of ALLAH as it behooves you to strive for it." (Sher Ali)
- "You shall strive for the cause of GOD as you should strive for His cause." (Khalifa)
- "...and struggle for God as is His due." (Arberry)
- "...and fight strenuously for God, as is His due." (Palmer)
- "And do valiantly in the cause of God as it behooveth you to do for Him." (Rodwell)
- "And fight in defense of God's true religion, as it behooveth [you] to fight for the same." (Sale)

Appendix 3:
The Sharia *in 29* *Selected Countries Today*

The estimated percentage of Muslims in each country is shown in parentheses. These figures refer to citizens of the state, not to resident foreigners.

Afghanistan (99%)	Mauritania (99%)
Algeria (99%)	Morocco (99%)
Bahrain (98%)	Nigeria (50%)
Bangladesh (88%)	Oman (99%)
Egypt (91%)	Pakistan (97%)
India (13%)	Qatar (95%)
Indonesia (88%)	Saudi Arabia (100%)
Iran (99%)	Somalia (99%)
Iraq (97%)	Sudan (70%)
Jordan (92%)	Syria (84%)
Kuwait (85%)	Tunisia (98%)
Lebanon (60%)	Turkey (99%)
Libya (97%)	United Arab Emirates (96%)
Malaysia (60%)	Yemen (99%)
Mali (90%)	

Appendix 4:
Selected Chronology,
c. 570–2001

This chronology expresses most dates according to both the Islamic and the Gregorian calendar. An Islamic date is signified by the abbreviation "H" for "Hijra year." See "A Note on Calendar Dates" in the Introduction for more details.

Because the Islamic calendar only began in the Gregorian year 622, dates before then cannot be expressed in terms of this calendar. Also, some dates in the chronology are not sufficiently precise to justify converting them into Islamic dates; others (for example, September 11, 2001) are so closely associated with Western history that only the Western date has been provided.

c. 570CE	Birth of the prophet Muhammad.
620 CE	Muhammad's Night Journey (*isra*) from Mecca to Jerusalem.
622 CE/1 H	Muhammad's "emigration" (*hijra*) from Mecca to Medina and the inter-clan agreement known as the Constitution of Medina. This agreement results in the formation of the first Muslim community (*umma*).
632 CE/11 H	Death of Muhammad.
d. 765 CE/148 H	Ja'far al-Sidiq, the sixth Shiite imam, founds the Ja'afari school of law.
d. 767 CE/150 H	Silk trader Abu Hanifah becomes a jurist and founds the Hanafi school of law.

d. 795 CE/179 H	Malik bin Anas bridges the gap between different authorities and founds the Maliki school of law.
d. 804 CE/198 H	Muhammad al-Shaybani determines the proper basis for legal rulings.
d. 820 CE/204 H	Muhammad ibn Idris al-Shafi'i, hailed as the "renewer" of Islam, is revered as the founder of the Shafi'i school of law.
d. 855 CE/241 H	Ahmad ibn Hanbal, founder of the Hanbali school of law, demonstrates personal courage and legal orthodoxy.
d. 875 CE/261 H	Muslim ibn al-Hajjah's advice on choices for the enemy and the role of women in battle.
c. 900 CE	Contemporary Islamic scholars agree that all the essential questions of the *sharia* have by this date been finally settled. This "closing of the door of *ijtihad* [independent reasoning] amounts to an unquestioning imitation of orthodox Sunni schools and authorities (*taqlid*).
975 CE	Chief Justice Abu El-Hassan begins the tradition of teaching the *sharia* at Al-Azhar University in Cairo, now the oldest and most important Islamic university in the world.
d. 1064 CE/456 H	Ibn Hazm, founder of the Zahiri school of law, insists that the holy scriptures of Islam must be interpreted and applied literally.
d. 1111 CE/505 H	Abu Hamidal-Ghazali urges the faithful "To promote what is right and to prevent what is wrong."
d. 1198 CE/595 H	Ibn Rushd defends the use of reason in implementing the *sharia*.
d. 1277 CE/676 H	Even the sultan Ibn Abd al-Zahir is subject to the *sharia*.
d. 1277 CE/676 H	Muhyi al-Din al-Nawawi tries to regulate the whole range of human activities.
d. 1325 CE/726 H	Allama al-Hilli becomes the first Ayatollah.
d. 1328 CE/728 H	Ibn Taymiyya's "kink in the brain" infuriates some of his fellow jurists.
d. 1388 CE/790 H	Abu Ishaq al-Shatibi looks for a normative basis for the *sharia*.
r. 1520–1566 CE	Ottoman sultan Süleyman is known as the "Lawgiver" in the East and as the "Magnificent" in the West.
1749 CE	Conservative reformer Muhammad ibn Abd al-Wahhab and tribal chieftain Muhammad ibn Saud agree to

	share religious and political power, respectively. This unique agreement will eventually result in the founding of the Kingdom of Saudi Arabia in 1932.
d. 1792 CE	Muhammad ibn Abd al-Wahhab's fundamentalist reforms will later greatly influence Saudi Arabia and other Islamic states.
1798 CE	Napoleon invades Egypt.
d. 1817 CE	Uthman Dan Fodio and the doctrine of the "double *jihad*" in West Africa.
1839 CE	Tanzimat ("reforms") policy of the Ottoman Empire begins.
d. 1897 CE	Jamal al-Din al-Afghani offers a way to deal with incursions by the West.
d. 1898 CE	Sayyid Ahmad Khan defines *jihad* as a pacifist creed.
d. 1905 CE	Muhammad Abduh, legal reformer and Grand Mufti of Egypt, tries to modernize Islam.
1924 CE	Turkish caliphate is abolished in the wake of World War I.
1926 CE	Turkey replaces the *sharia* with Western law.
1932 CE	Founding of Saudi Arabia, today one of the countries based solely on the *sharia*.
d. 1935 CE	Rashid Rida tries to make the *sharia* fit modern times.
d. 1963 CE	Mahmud Shaltut gives *jihad* a modernist interpretation.
d. 1966 CE	Sayyid Qutb founds modern Islamic fundamentalism.
1979 CE	Armed Islamic extremists seize the Grand Mosque of Mecca and proclaim that the Saud family is no longer fit to rule because it is un-Islamic.
d. 1979 CE	Sayyid Abdul-Ala Mawdudi calls for a worldwide *jihad*.
1978–1979 CE	Islamic revolution in Iran.
1983 CE	Suicide bomb attack against the American Embassy in Beirut marks the beginning of such attacks against Western targets.
1996 CE	The intense humiliation at the hands of the West felt by some Muslims is well expressed by Osama bin Laden's 1996 "Declaration of War Against the Americans Occupying the Land of the Two Holy Places," i.e., Saudi Arabia.
2001 CE	11 September 2001 suicide terrorist attacks on New York and Washington, D.C. kill more at least 2,986 people, including the 19 hijackers themselves.

Glossary

ahl al-tawhid: The "People of Unity," i.e., the name preferred by followers of the eighteenth century fundamentalist reformer Muhammad ibn Abd al-Wahhab. Opponents of this sect and non–Muslims in general usually refer to them as Wahhabis. See *tawhid*.

bedouin: Nomads.

bismillah: A traditional invocation, i.e., "In the Name of God, the Compassionate, the Merciful."

Dar al-Harb: The "House of War," i.e., the non–Muslim world.

Dar al-Islam: The "House of Islam," i.e., the Islamic world itself.

dhimmi: "Protected minorities," i.e., the semi-autonomous status given to Christians and Jews in return for tax payments to their Muslim rulers. See *jizya*.

faqih: *Sharia* jurist.

fara'id: "Succession," i.e., Quranic verses that give specific portions of an estate to relatives.

fatiha: "Opening," i.e., the short prayer that begins the first *sura* of the Quran.

fatwa: An authoritative legal opinion issued by a *mufti*, i.e., a highly qualified scholar of the *sharia*.

fiqh: Islamic jurisprudence in general.

firmans: Royal Ottoman edicts.

"Five Pillars of Islam": The Islamic profession of faith (*shahada*); five obligatory prayers (*salat*) a day; paying annual alms (*zakat*); fasting during the lunar month of Ramadan (*sawm*); and making the pilgrimage to Mecca (*hajj*).

gharar: "Uncertainty," i.e., the doctrinal requirement of Islamic law that the profit or loss of any proposed transaction must be known to both parties in advance. If it is not, the transition is void.

ghaybah: Occultation, referring to the Shiites' Twelfth Imam, who vanished from human sight in 878 and who is expected to return at some future point.

187

hadd: Severe punishment prescribed by the Quran for offenses against "God's law."

hadith: The traditions, habits and sayings of the prophet Muhammad, as preserved and transmitted by his favored Companions. (See *sunna*.)

haqq: adami Legal claims made by human beings.

haqq: Allah "God's law." See *hadd*.

hijra: Muhammad's "emigration" from Mecca to Medina in 622. This marks the start of the Islamic era and is the first year of the Muslim calendar today.

hisba: "Accountability," i.e., "the duty [of every Muslim] to promote what is right and to prevent what is wrong." The official market inspector was known as *muhtasib*, i.e., one who practices *hisba*.

hiyal: "Legal tricks," i.e., stratagems which permit Muslims to charge and receive interest legally.

ibadat: Ritual acts of worship.

idda: A three-menstruation waiting period before a divorced woman can remarry. The purpose is to see whether she is or is not pregnant.

ijma: The scholarly consensus of the Muslim community.

ijtihad: Independent reasoning by a qualified Islamic jurist.

islam: "To surrender," i.e., believers must surrender themselves totally to the will of God.

isnad: "Chain of transmission," i.e., a test of the reliability of *hadith*.

isra: Muhammad's Night Journey from Mecca to Jerusalem.

jahiliyya: The state of pagan ignorance and barbarism said to have prevailed in Arabia before the coming of Islam.

jihad: "To exert effort." The best translation is not "holy war" but "holy struggle." This can be either external struggle, e.g., by warfare, or internal struggle, e.g., by subduing one's own desires.

jihad al-nafs: "Fighting one's own desires," i.e., internal *jihad*. (See *jihad*.)

jizya: Poll tax paid by Christians and Jews to receive protection from their Muslim rulers.

kanun: A parallel, extensive system of administrative laws designed by the Ottomans to augment the *sharia*.

kufar: A perjorative term for non–Muslims.

madhab: A school of law. The four doctrinal schools of Sunni law are the Hanafi, the Maliki, the Shafi'i, and the Hanbali. The major Shiite school is the Ja'-fari.

madrasas: Islamic theological colleges; today, as in Pakistan, they are often of an extreme fundamentalist orientation.

mahdi: The messiah awaited by Shiites.

mahr: Dower.

maslaha: The public interest.

mu'amalat: Regulations governing relations between human beings.

mujaddid: "Renewer of Islam," i.e., the title of an Islamic scholar thought to fulfill a *hadith* promise that God will send one such renewer into the world every 100 years.

mujahidin: "Those that do *jihad*," i.e., Muslim soldiers fighting to expel foreign invaders, such as the Soviets in Afghanistan, or, by extension, Western expansionism in general.

mujtahid: A highly qualified scholar of Islamic thought who is permitted to use independent reasoning on doctrinal issues. See *ijtihad*.

mushrikun: Polytheists.

mut'a: A marriage contract for a fixed period of time, permitted under Shiite law.

Mutawwa'in: Religious police charged with enforcing, in public places in Saudi Arabia and in Iran, the strict dress codes and other social requirements of fundamentalist Wahabbi Islam. This institution is formally known as the "Committee to Promote Virtue and Prevent Vice."

naskh: "Repeal," i.e., the abrogation of earlier Quranic texts by later Quranic texts.

normative acts: Islam holds that all acts are normative and must be placed into one of five legal categories: the obligatory (*wajib*), the recommended (*mandub*), the permissible or the indifferent (*mubah*), the prohibited (*haram*), or the repugnant (*makruh*).

qadi: Islamic judge.

qiyas: Legal reasoning by analogy.

Quran: "Recitation," i.e., the holy book of Islam.

ra'y: "Juristic speculation," i.e., the personal opinion of an Islamic scholar.

riba: Usury, i.e., interest, prohibited by the Quran.

ribat: Staying at the frontiers of Islam to defend its territory against enemies.

sharia: The religious law of Islam.

shirk: Idolatry.

sunna: The whole body of customary social and legal traditions and obligations of the Muslim community, based authoritatively on the life, teachings and practices of Muhammad.

sura: A chapter of the Quran.

tafsir: Exegesis, i.e., a learned explanation or critical interpretation of a text, especially the Quran.

talaq: Divorce by the husband's unilateral repudiation of a wife. When uttered three times (the triple *talaq*), it constitutes an irrevocable divorce.

tanzimat: "Reforms," i.e., the Ottoman reform program of 1839–1876.

taqlid: "Tradition," i.e., unquestioning imitation of the doctrines of established Sunni schools and authorities.

tawhid: The singularity or absolute "oneness" of God.

ta'zir: Punishing a criminal by eye-for-an-eye retaliation, or, more broadly, the corrective discretionary punishment imposed by a jurist.

ulama: Islamic religious scholars.

umma: The Islamic community, i.e., the community of believers first formed by the Constitution of Medina (622).

usul al-fiqh: The "roots" or principles of Islamic jurisprudence, which crystallized early in the tenth century.

waqf: Islamic religious endowment.

zahir: "Literal interpretation," e.g., Ibn Hazm's inflexible interpretations of the Quran and *hadith*.

zina: Illicit sexual intercourse, a capital crime under the *sharia*.

Chapter Notes

Introduction

1. After Hallaq, *Islamic Legal Theories*, p. 209.
2. Coulson, *History of Islamic Law*, p. 85.
3. Gibb, "The *Sharia*," p. 5.
4. After Schacht, *Islamic Law*, p. 201.
5. After Peters, *Crime and Punishment*, p. 19.
6. Vikør, "The *Sharia*," p. 2. Italics added.
7. Slackman, "Islamic group flaunts its clout in Egypt," p. 8.
8. Council on Foreign Relations, "Islam," p. 2.
9. Shiyin, "Religion doesn't hamper returns," p. 22.
10. Quoted in Zubaida, *Law and Power*, p. 35.
11. After Coulson, *History of Islamic Law*, p. 81.
12. After Zubaida, *Law and Power*, p. 44. Zubaida adds, on pp. 46–47, that the *qadi* had many duties other than merely hearing cases in court. Some of these responsibilities may have been delegated to deputy *qadis*. They included protection of minors and the incapable, execution of wills and testaments, supervision of charitable foundations, guardianship of unmarried women without guardians, application of punishments mandated by the Quran, and dealing with complaints about immoral activities in particular neighborhoods.
13. Anderson, "The Role of Personal Statutes," p. 8.
14. The Ottomans were good record-keepers. For example, during a 25-year period alone (1746–1771), more than 50,000 cases were recorded in the *sharia* court in the city of Aleppo (Syria). After Marcus, *Middle East on the Eve of Modernity*, p. 11.
15. After Peters, *Crime and Punishment*, p. 187.
16. Quoted in Janin, *Pursuit of Learning*, p. 172.

Chapter 1

1. Schacht, *Islamic Law*, p. 17. Italics added.
2. Doughty, *Arabia Deserta*, pp. 96–97.
3. This translation is from Abdul AliHamid, *Moral Teachings of Islam*, p. 1.
4. After Lings, *Muhammad*, p. 43.
5. This evocative account follows Lings, *Muhammad*, pp. 43–44. Lings is an extremely useful reference work because he relies extensively on the earliest primary sources — al-Bukhari, Ibn Ishaq, and the Quran. These give the full flavor of local traditions. In his book, however, Lings does not always distinguish clearly between these sources and his own views. The two sometimes run together.
6. Lings, *Muhammad*, p. 44.
7. "Medina Charter," p. 1.
8. "Medina Charter," p. 1.
9. After Hallaq, *Islamic Legal Theories*, p. 4.
10. After Nasir, *Islamic Law of Personal Status*, p. 1. We believe that, although somewhat dated, this is the best single source in English on the details and complexities of Islamic personal status law.
11. Adapted from Gerber, *Islamic Law and Culture*, p. 43.
12. Calder and Hooker, *Encyclopaedia of Islam*, "*Sharia*," p. 8.
13. Quoted by Ringgren, "Quran," p. 3.
14. This example is taken from Hallaq, *Origins and Evolution of Islamic Law*, p. 33.

15. After Peters, *Crime and Punishment*, pp. 35–36.

16. The following section is drawn from Kamali, "Law and Society," pp. 119–120.

17. Coulson, "*Shariah*," p. 2.

18. Dawood, *Koran*, pp. 446, 440, 443.

19. After Lapidus, *History of Islamic Societies*, p. 26.

20. Ringgren, "Qur'an," p. 8.

21. In Arabic, the plural of *sunna* is *sunan* but it is rarely used in English.

22. Quoted in Janin, *Pursuit of Learning*, p. 18.

23. Hallaq, *Origins and Evolution of Islamic Law*, p. 104.

24. Coulson, *History of Islamic Law*, p. 80.

25. The following examples are taken from Hallaq, *Origins and Evolution of Islamic Law*, p. 115.

26. The following section is drawn selectively from Hallaq, *Islamic Legal Theories*, pp. 40–81.

27. The following section is adapted from Mitchell's views, which can be found in his book, *Colonising Egypt* (Cambridge: Cambridge University Press, 1988, pp. 83–84). They are quoted in Brown, *Sharia and State*, p. 364.

28. Adapted from Zubaida, *Law and Power*, p. 184.

29. After Halm, *Shi'ism*, Foreword (no page number).

30. Schacht, *Islamic Law*, p. 16.

31. Coulson *History of Islamic Law*, p. 105.

32. After Coulson, *History of Islamic Law*, pp. 106–118.

Chapter 2

1. After Calder and Hooker, *Encyclopaedia of Islam*, "*Sharia*," p. 1.

2. After Calder and Hooker, *Encyclopaedia of Islam*, "*Sharia*," p. 1.

3. After Calder and Hooker, *Encyclopaedia of Islam*, "Sharia," p. 5.

4. The "vertical" and "horizontal" categories mentioned here come from a private communication of 16 August 2005 from Dr. Ulrika Mårtensson.

5. After Calder and Hooker, *Encyclopaedia of* Islam, "*Sharia*," p. 6.

6. Hallaq, *Origins and Evolution of Islamic Law*, p. 1.

7. The classic introductory survey to Islamic law is Joseph Schacht's *Introduction to Islamic Law* (1964). Schacht is authoritative but this book is so dense and scholarly that it is very difficult for a beginner to use easily. More reader-friendly choices are N.J. Coulson's *A History of Islamic Law* (1964) and two more recent books by Wael B. Hallaq: *A History of Islamic Legal Theories: An*

introduction to Sunni usul al-fiqh (2004), and *The Origins and Evolution of Islamic Law* (2005).

8. After Melchert, "The Hanbali Law of *Gihad*," p. 31.

9. After Calder and Hooker, *Encyclopaedia of Islam*, "*Sharia*," p. 5.

10. After Hallaq, *Origins and Evolution of Islamic Law*, p. 20.

11. After Hallaq, *Origins and Evolution of Islamic Law*, p. 21.

12. Some of the following section is drawn from Zubaida, *Law and Power*, pp. 68–73.

13. The medieval era in Europe was also characterized by the orality of knowledge. As Manlio Bellomo put it in *The Common Legal Past of Europe: 1000–1800*, "Throughout the later Middle Ages both the formation and the transmission of knowledge were typically oral.... 'From what one hears,' Humbert de Romans stated as early as the thirteenth century, 'one obtains an excellent result, which is *sapientia* [wisdom]. In no other way, in fact, can man make himself more wise than by what he listens to'" (pp. 126, 127).

14. Quoted in Spectorsky, *Marriage and Divorce*, p. 3.

15. Marcus, *Middle East on the Eve of Modernity*, p. 101. Some of the other points in this section are drawn from pp. 101–120 of this book.

16. Marcus, *Middle East on the Eve of Modernity*, p. 102.

17. Quoted in Marcus, *Middle East on the Eve of Modernity*, p. 104.

18. After Marcus, *Middle East on the Eve of Modernity*, p. 112.

19. After Marcus, *Middle East on the Eve of Modernity*, p. 112.

20. After Marcus, *Middle East on the Eve of Modernity*, p. 113.

21. Marcus, *Middle East on the Eve of Modernity*, pp. 113–114.

22. After Schacht, *Islamic Law*, p. 76, and Coulson, "*Shariah*," pp. 6–11.

23. Zyzik, "Personal Status Law in the Arab States," p. 30.

24. Quoted in Nasir, *Islamic Law of Personal Status*, p. 35.

25. After Schacht, *Islamic Law*, p. 161.

26. Quoted in Tucker, *House of the Law*, p. 39.

27. After Peters, *Jihad*, p. 106.

28. Quoted in Tucker, *House of the Law*, pp. 1–2.

29. Quoted in Tucker, *House of the Law*, p. 65.

30. Quoted in Tucker, *House of the Law*, p. 78.

31. Schacht, *Islamic Law*, p. 171.

32. Quoted in Schacht, *Islamic Law*, p. 188.

33. After Schacht, *Islamic Law*, p. 194.

34. Quoted in Peters, *Crime and Punishment*, p. 107.

35. After Peters, *Crime and Punishment*, p. 107.
36. This case is taken from Peters, *Crime and Punishment*, pp. 12–13.
37. Adapted from Schacht, *Islamic Law*, p. 196.
38. After Schacht, *Islamic Law*, p. 145.
39. Adapted from Zubaida (quoting Heyd), *Law and Power*, p. 112.
40. After Schacht, *Islamic Law*, p. 94.
41. After Schacht, *Islamic Law*, p. 176.
42. After Coulson, *History of Islamic Law*, p. 124.
43. Adapted from Peters, *Crime and Punishment*, p. 187.
44. Quoted in Peters, *Crime and Punishment*, p. 55.
45. Adapted from Peters, *Crime and Punishment*, p. 55.
46. These comments are adapted from Coulson, *History of Islamic Law*, pp. 126–127.
47. Quoted in Zubaida, *Law and Power*, p. 35.
48. After COPress, "Jihad," p. 1.

Chapter 3

1. Some of the points made here are drawn from Hallaq, *Origins and Evolution of Islamic Law*, p. 31.
2. These examples come from Hallaq, *Origins and Evolution of Islamic Law*, pp. 34–35.
3. After Hallaq, *Origins and Evolution of Islamic Law*, p. 51.
4. Macdonald and Schacht, *Encyclopaedia of Islam*, "Idjtihad," p. 1026.
5. After Melchert, "The Hanbali Law of Gihad," p. 23.
6. Adapted from Lapidus, *History of Islamic Societies*, p. 85.
7. After Gerber, *Islamic Law and Culture*, p. 72.
8. Gerber, *Islamic Law and Culture*, p. 123.
9. After USC-MSA Compendium, "*Shariah* and *fiqh*," p. 1.
10. Hallaq, *Origins and Evolution of Islamic Law*, p. 151. The rest of this section is adapted from the same source, pp. 150–151.
11. After Coulson, *History of Islamic Law*, p. 79.
12. This example is drawn from Coulson, *History of Islamic Law*, p. 139.
13. After Coulson, *History of Islamic Law*, p. 81.
14. After Coulson, *History of Islamic Law*, p. 88.
15. Some of this section has been drawn from Janin, *Pursuit of Learning*, pp. 47–48.
16. After Hallaq, *Origins and Evolution of Islamic Law*, p. 170.

17. Quoted in Coulson, *History of Islamic Law*, pp. 51–52.
18. Quoted in Janin, *Pursuit of Learning*, p. 47. This citation has been lightly edited.
19. Ansari, "Abu Hanifah," p. 2.
20. Schacht, *Islamic Law*, p. 44.
21. This section is drawn from Coulson, *History of Islamic Law*, p. 46.
22. This section is drawn from Coulson, *History of Islamic Law*, pp. 44–46.
23. This section is drawn from Coulson, *History of Islamic Law*, p. 47.
24. After Bloom and Blair, *Islam*, p. 56.
25. After Peters, *Jihad*, p. 137.
26. After Hallaq, *Islamic Legal Theories*, p. 20.
27. After Hallaq, *Islamic Legal Theories*, p. 18.
28. Adapted from Chaumont, *Encyclopaedia of Islam*, "al-Shaybani," p. 2.
29. Khadduri, *al-Risala*, p. 4.
30. After Schacht, *Islamic Law*, p. 48.
31. After Schacht, *Islamic Law*, p. 48, and Coulson, *History of Islamic Law*, p. 56.
32. Quoted in Janin, *Pursuit of Learning*, p. 54.
33. Quoted in Robinson, *Islamic World*, p. 208.
34. After Khadduri, *al-Risala*, p. 21.
35. Esposito, *Oxford Encyclopedia*, vol. 2, "Shafi'i," p. 451.
36. After Chaumont, *Encyclopaedia of Islam*, "al-Shafii," p. 5.
37. Coulson, *History of Islamic Law*, p. 55. Some of the other points in this section are drawn from his chapter on al-Shafi'i (pp. 53–61).
38. This section on abrogation closely follows Coulson, *History of Islamic Law*, pp. 58–59.
39. Coulson does not specifically identify these texts.
40. After Hallaq, *Origins and Evolution of Islamic Law*, p. 139.
41. Quoted in Coulson, *History of Islamic Law*, p. 60.
42. After Coulson, *History of Islamic Law*, p. 71.
43. Laoust, *Encyclopaedia of Islam*, "Ahmad b. Hanbal," p. 1.
44. Quoted in Zubaida, *Law and Power*, p. 87.
45. After Hallaq, *Origins of Islamic Law*, p. 125.
46. After Spectorsky, *Marriage and Divorce*, p. 2.
47. Quoted in Janin, *Pursuit of Learning*, p. 18.
48. This section is drawn from Coulson, *History of Islamic Law*, pp. 189–191.
49. Laoust, *Encyclopaedia of Islam*, "Ahmad b. Hanbal," p. 3.
50. The quotations in this section come from Peters, *Jihad*, pp. 10–17.
51. After "Ibn Hazm," p. 1.

52. These points are drawn from Janin, *Pursuit of Learning*, p. 81.

53. After Watt, *Encyclopaedia of Islam*, "Al-Ghazali," p. 4.

54. Quoted in Janin, *Pursuit of Learning*, p. 87.

55. This section is drawn from Musallam, "Ordering of Muslim Societies," pp. 173–186.

56. Musallam, "Ordering of Muslim Societies," p. 173.

57. This section follows Musallam, "Ordering of Muslim Societies," pp. 173–186.

58. After Musallam, "Ordering of Muslim Societies," p. 185.

59. Quoted in Musallam, "Ordering of Muslim Societies," p. 186.

60. Quoted in Hourani, *Arabic Thought*, p. 13. Some of the other points made in this section are also drawn from this book (pp. 13–15).

61. Quoted in Zubaida, *Law and Power*, pp. 91–92.

62. "Ghazali on Jihad al-Nafs," p. 2.

63. Watt, *Encyclopaedia of Islam*, "al-Ghazali," p. 5.

64. Some of this section is drawn from Janin, *Pursuit of Learning*, pp. 92–94.

65. Quoted in Janin, *Pursuit of Learning*, p. 93.

66. After Hallaq, *Islamic Legal Theories*, p. 86.

67. After Hallaq, *Islamic Legal Theories*, pp. 157–160.

68. Quoted in Tucker, *House of the Law*, pp. 15–16.

69. Quoted in Janin, *Pursuit of Learning*, p. 92.

70. This account is adapted from Kunt and Woodhead, *Süleyman*," pp. 129–133.

71. After *Encyclopedia Britannica*, "Baybars I," pp. 2, 4.

72. This account is drawn from Kunt and Woodhead, *Süleyman*, p. 132.

73. This section is drawn from Zubaida, *Law and Power*, pp. 32–35.

74. Adapted from Zubaida, *Law and Power*, p. 33.

75. After Zubaida, *Law and Power*, p. 34.

76. This section is drawn from Halm, *Shi'ism*, pp. 63–67.

77. Quoted in Halm, *Shi'ism*, p. 66.

78. Quoted in Halm, *Shi'ism*, p. 66.

79. Quoted in Janin, *Pursuit of Learning*, p. 103.

80. Quoted in Janin, *Pursuit of Learning*, p. 102.

81. Quoted in Janin, *Pursuit of Learning*, pp. 103–104.

82. Quoted in Janin, *Pursuit of Learning*, p. 103.

83. After Peters, *Jihad*, p. 180.

84. Quoted in Zubaida, *Law and Power*, p. 92.

85. Robinson, *Islamic World*, p. 237.

86. Masud, "Muslim Jurists' Quest," p. 8. Some of this section is drawn from pp. 8–9 of this same work.

87. For a good presentation of al-Shatibi's thought, see Hallaq, *Islamic Legal Theories*, Chapter 5, "Social Reality and the Response of Theory," pp. 162–206.

88. After Hallaq, *Islamic Legal Theories*, p. 163. In other parts of this section we have drawn selectively on Chapter 5 of this book as well.

89. Hallaq, *Islamic Legal Theories*, p. 166.

90. Thirteen other modern reformers of Islam are discussed briefly in Janin's earlier book, *Pursuit of Learning*, but chiefly in terms of Islamic learning, not the *sharia* itself. They are: Muhammad Iqbal (1878–1938), Mustafa Kemal Ataturk (1881–1938), Ali Shariati (1933–1977), Sayyid Abdul-Ala Mawdudi (1903–1979), Sayyid Qutb (1906–1966), Fazlur Rahman (1911–1988), Ayatollah Ruholla Khomeini (1902–1989), Edward W. Said (1935–2003), Mohammad Arkoun (1928-), Seyyed Hossein Nasr (1933-), Abdolkarim Soroush (1945-), Aziz al-Azmeh (c. 1949-), and Osama bin Laden (1957-). The specific views on *jihad* held by some of these men are covered in the present volume.

Chapter 4

1. After Johansen, "Islamic Law on Land Tax and Rent," p. 2.

2. After Gerber, *State, Society, and Law*, p. 43.

3. After Gerber, *State, Society, and Law*, p. 14.

4. Kavalcioglu, "Süleyman the Magnificent," p. 1.

5. Imber, "Ideals and legitimation," p. 149.

6. Quoted in Janin, *Pursuit of Learning*, p. 118.

7. Quoted in Peters, *Crime and Punishment*, p. 71.

8. After Gerber, *Islamic Law and Culture*, p. 29.

9. Quoted in Gerber, *Islamic Law and Culture*, p. 59. Italics added.

10. This account is adapted from Peirce, *Morality Tales*, pp. 351–352, 375.

11. Quoted in Peirce, *Morality Tales*, p. 352.

12. Quoted in Peters, "The Enforcement of God's Law," p. 109.

13. After Peters, "The Enforcement of God's Law," p. 112.

14. This discussion follows Schacht, *Islamic Law*, pp. 89–93.

15. Quoted in Imber, "Ideals and legitimation," p. 149.

16. Quoted in Imber, "Ideals and legitimation," p. 152.

17. After Gerber, *State, Society and Law*, pp. 90–91.

18. After Gerber, *State, Society, and Law*, p. 93.

19. After Zubaida, *Law and Power*, p. 110.

20. This account follows Zubaida, *Law and Power*, pp. 110–111.

21. Quoted in Johansen, "Islamic Law on Land Tax and Rent," p. 7.

22. Quoted in Imber, "Ideals and legitimation," p. 152.

23. After Gerber, *Islamic Law and Culture*, p. 64.

24. After Schacht, *Islamic Law*, p. 106.

25. Schacht, *Islamic Law*, p. 92.

26. After Dale, "Islamic World in the Age of European Expansion," p.

Chapter 5

1. *Modern History Sourcebook*, "Sir William Eton," p. 1.

2. Quoted in Ignatenko, "Wahhabism," p.

3. "Kitaab At-Tawheed, Chapter 36," p. 1.

4. Quoted in Ignatenko, "Wahhabism," pp. 2–3.

5. "Kitaab At-Tawheed," p. 1.

6. "Kitaab At-Tawheed," p. 1.

7. "Kitaab At-Tawheed," p. 1.

8. Robinson, *Islamic World*, p. 239.

9. After Thornton, "Wahhabi Movement," p. 1.

10. Prosperous Saudis and expatriates often live in big houses screened by high walls. What goes on behind those walls is considered to be a private, not a public, matter. Only when private matters literally spill out into the street do they attract official attention. A good example here is someone who has been drinking alcohol in a private house and then has an automobile accident on his way home.

11. This section is drawn from Delong-Bas, *Wahhabi Islam*, pp. 118–119.

12. Quoted in Delong-Bas, *Wahhabi Islam*, p. 119.

13. After Coulson, *Islamic Law*, p. 149.

14. After Janin, *Pursuit of Learning*, pp. 128–129.

15. Robinson, *Islamic World*, p. x.

16. After "Napoleon in Egypt," p. 1.

17. After "Egypt — the French Invasion," p. 1.

18. Quoted in Peters, "The Enforcement of God's Law," p. 114.

19. These points are adapted from *Encyclopedia of the Orient*, pp. 1–2, and Coulson, *Islamic Law*, pp. 151–152.

20. After Brown, "*Sharia* and State," pp. 360, 362.

21. After Coulson, *Islamic Law*, p. 14.

22. This section is drawn from Janin, *Pursuit of Learning*, pp. 138–140.

23. This section is drawn from Janin, *Pursuit of Learning*, pp. 142–144.

24. See Peters, *Jihad*, p. 156.

25. Quoted in Janin, *Pursuit of Learning*, p. 143.

26. After "Abduh, Muhammad," p. 2.

27. Thornton, "Muhammad Abduh," pp. 1–2. Italics added.

28. Excerpted from Hourani, *Arabic Thought*, pp. 228–230.

29. Quoted in Janin, *Pursuit of Learning*, p. 145.

30. Hourani, *Arabic Thought*, p. 238.

31. The following section relies heavily on Hallaq's *Islamic Legal Theories*, pp. 214–220.

32. Hallaq, *Islamic Legal Theories*, p. 215.

33. Hallaq, *Islamic Legal Theories*, p. 215.

34. After Hallaq, *Islamic Legal Theories*, p. 219.

Chapter 6

1. After *Encyclopaedia of Islam*, "Djihad," p. 1, and a private communication of 21 December 2005 from Dr. Rudolph Peters.

2. After *Encyclopaedia of Islam*, "Djihad," p. 1.

3. After *Encyclopaedia of Islam*, "Djihad," pp. 1–2. The source of this quote is not given but it is probably from a *hadith* rather than the Quran.

4. After *Encyclopaedia of Islam*, "Djihad," pp. 2–3.

5. Private communication of 21 December 2005 from Dr. Rudolph Peters.

6. The following section has been drawn from CQPress, "Jihad," p. 2.

7. Private communication of 1 December 2005 from Dr. Wael B. Hallaq.

8. Private communication of 2 December 2005 from Dr. Noga Hartmann.

9. After Lewis, [*Wall Street*] OpinionJournal, p. 1.

10. After CQPress, "Jihad," p. 1.

11. After a private communication of 21 December 2005 from Dr. Rudolph Peters. In support of this thesis, one should note Osama bin Laden's "Letter to America," which was published in the *Guardian* on 24 November 2002. In it, bin Laden asks, rhetorically, why American crimes against Islam justify Muslim retaliation against innocent American civilians. His answer makes several points (for the text, see Bin Laden, Osama, in the bibliography):

- "...the American people are the ones who choose their government by way of their own free will; a choice which stems from their agreement to its policies.... The American people have the ability and choice to refuse the policies of their Government and even to change it if they want."

- "...the American people are the ones who fund the attacks against us, and they are the ones who oversee the expenditure of these monies in the way they wish, through their elected candidates."

- "...the American army is part of the American people."
- "The American people are the ones who employ both their men and their women in the American Forces which attack us."
- "This is why the American people cannot be innocent of all the crimes committed by the Americans and the Jews against us.'"

12. These citations are drawn, selectively, from Peters, *Jihad*, pp. 19–26.

13. The quotations in this section are drawn selectively from Khadduri, *al-Risala*, pp. 81–87.

14. The Quranic verses used in this section come from Dawood's translation.

15. This is Dawood's translation.

16. Khadduri, *al-Risala*, p. 84.

17. Quoted in Janin, *Pursuit of Learning*, p. 81.

18. This section and the quotations in it are drawn from Melchert, "The Hambali Law of *Gihad*," pp. 24–32.

19. This quotation is from Dawood.

20. Watt, "al-Ghazali," p. 5.

21. This Quranic translation is from Dawood.

22. This section and the quotations in it are drawn from Peters, *Jihad*, pp. 27–42.

23. This section is drawn from Peters, *Jihad*, pp. 43–54. For another good discussion of Ibn Taymiyya's views, see Zubaida, *Law and Power*, pp. 93–103.

24. Zubaida, *Law and Power*, pp. 102–103. This quotation has been very lightly edited.

25. "Doctrine of Ahl Al-Sunna," p. 2.

26. "Wahhabi Menace," pp. 1–2.

27. This section is drawn from Lapidus, *History of Islamic Societies*, pp. 416–424.

28. "What Does Jihad Mean," p. 1.

29. Quoted in Peters, *Jihad p. 123*.

30. Quoted in Janin, *Pursuit of Learning*, p. 141.

31. Quoted in Peters, *Jihad*, p. 125.

32. Adapted from Lapidus, *History of Islamic Societies*, p. 581.

33. This section is drawn from Peters, *Jihad*, pp. 59–101.

34. The quotations from the Quran used in this section are from Dawood's translation.

35. Quoted in Peters, *Jihad*, p. 79.

36. Quoted in Peters, *Jihad*, p. 80.

37. Unless otherwise noted, this section is drawn from Janin, *Pursuit of Learning*, pp. 158–160.

38. After Wurmser, "The Roots of Islamic Revolution," p. 2.

39. Quoted in Peters, *Jihad*, p. 129.

40. This section is drawn from Janin, *Pursuit of Learning*, pp. 151–152.

41. Quoted in Peters, *Jihad*, p. 128.

42. Quoted in Janin, *Pursuit of Learning*, p. 171.

43. Quoted in Janin, *Pursuit of Learning*, p. 172.

44. Quoted in Janin, *Pursuit of Learning*, p. 173.

45. Quoted in Janin, *Pursuit of Learning*, p. 174.

46. Quoted in Bin Laden, "Letter to America," pp. 1–11.

47. Falk, "Big little stories," p. 6.

Chapter 7

1. After "West Africa," p. 2.

2. After *International Herald Tribune*, "Apostasy charges dropped," and Thier, "Balancing religion and rights."

3. U.S. Department of State, "Background Note: Afghanistan," p. 6.

4. Central Intelligence Agency, "The World Factbook: Afghanistan," p. 1.

5. Central Intelligence Agency, "The World Factbook: Afghanistan," p. 4.

6. Much of this section is drawn from U.S. Department of State, "Background Note: Bahrain," pp. 1–5.

7. Central Intelligence Agency, "The World Factbook: Bangladesh," p. 6.

8. After "Bangladesh, People's Republic of," p. 1.

9. These cases are drawn from "Bangladesh," pp. 5–7.

10. This account is drawn from Norton, "Activism and Reform," p. 381.

11. Some of the information in this section is drawn from "India, Republic of."

12. After "India, Republic of," p. 5.

13. Bilimoria, "Muslim Personal Law in India," p. 11.

14. After Bilimoria, "Muslim Persona Law in India," p. 13.

15. This section is drawn from "Indonesia, Republic of," pp. 1–6.

16. U.S. Department of State, "Country Reports on Human Rights Practices — Iran," p. 15.

17. Quoted in Peters, "The Enforcement of God's Law," p. 126.

18. Quoted in U.S. Department of State, "Country Reports on Human Rights Practices — Iran," p. 18.

19. After Zubaida, *Law and Power*, pp. 199–200.

20. Amnesty International, "Iran: Report 2004," p. 1.

21. U.S. Department of State, "Country Reports on Human Rights Practices — Iran," p. 2.

22. Cockburn, "Diary," pp. 34, 35.

23. After "Jordan," p. 5.

24. After "Jordan," p. 6.

25. After "Jordan, Hashemite Kingdom of," pp. 4–5.

26. This section is drawn from "Kuwait, State of," pp. 1–5.
27. This section is drawn from "Lebanon," pp. 1–5.
28. "Libya — Law and the Judiciary," p.p. 1–2.
29. "Malaysia," p. 5.
30. After Mydans, "Islamic rule faces a test."
31. This section is drawn from "Morocco, Kingdom of," pp. 1–5.
32. The section is drawn from Bordat and Kouzzi, "Challenge of Implementing Morocco's New Personal Status Law," pp. 1–2.
33. The poster was printed and distributed in Morocco by the human rights organization Global Rights.
34. These comments are drawn from "Political Sharf'a?," pp. 1–4.
35. "Political Sharia?," p. 1.
36. "Political Sharia?," p. 3.
37. "Political Sharia?," p. 3.
38. Ministry of Information — Oman 2000, "The Rule of Law," p. 2.
39. Ministry of Information — Oman 2000, "The Rule of Law," pp. 2–3.
40. U.S. Department of State, "Country Reports on Human Rights Practices — 2005: Saudi Arabia," p. 1.
41. Vogel, *Islamic Law and Legal System*, p. xiv, xv.
42. After Vogel, *Islamic Law and Legal System*, pp. 3, 169.
43. Adapted from "Saudi Arabia, Kingdom of," p. 3.
44. Adapted from Peters, *Crime and Punishment*, p. 150.
45. U.S. Department of State, "Saudi Arabia," p. 3.
46. This section is drawn from "Saudi Arabia: The Legal System," pp. 1–2.
47. This section and the quotation are drawn from Vogel, *Islamic Law and Legal System*, p. 158.
48. This case is drawn from Vogel, *Islamic Law and Legal System*, pp. 158–159.
49. After "Horn of Africa," p. 2.
50. *International Herald Tribune*, 3 May 2006, "Mogadishu: Teenager slays killer in a public execution," p. 7.
51. Some of this information is drawn from Carnegie Endowment, "Tunisia," pp. 1–19.
52. After Zubaida, *Law and Power*, p. 158.
53. After Coulson, *Islamic Law*, pp. 150–152.
54. These comments are drawn from the U.S. Department of State's "Country Reports on Human Rights Practices — Turkey."
55. *International Herald Tribune*, "'Honor killer,'" p. 3.
56. After "United Arab Emirates," p. 1.
57. After "United Arab Emirates," p. 2.
58. *International Herald Tribune*, 13 February 2006 citing the UAE newspaper *Emirates Today*.

Chapter 8

1. The following section is drawn from the *Encylopaedia of Islam*, "*Riba*," p. 1.
2. After *Encyclopaedia of Islam*, "Riba," p. 1.
3. This discussion of Islamic banking draws heavily on Iqbal and Molyneux, *Thirty Years of Islamic Banking*, pp. 18–105.
4. Iqbal is chief of the Islamic Banking and finance Division of the Islamic Development Bank in Jeddah, Saudi Arabia. Molyneux is Professor of Banking and finance at the University of Wales in Bangor, UK.
5. Adapted from Iqbal and Molyneux, *Thirty Years of Islamic Banking*, p. 27.
6. Adapted from Iqbal and Molyneux, *Thirty Years of Islamic Banking*, pp. 28–31.
7. After a private communication of 13 March 2006 from Paul Sherrin.
8. Greenlees, "Banking by the Koran," p. 1.
9. Kolesnikov-Jessop, "Islamic banking," p. 13.
10. Greenlees, "Banking by the Koran," p. 8.
11. After Iqbal and Molyneux, *Thirty Years of Islamic Banking*, p. 60.

Chapter 9

1. Anderson, "The Role of Personal Statutes," p. 8.
2. Shapiro, "The telegenic face of conservative Islam," p. 2.
3. After Hallaq, Islamic Legal Theories, p. 211.
4. After Peters, Crime and Punishment, p. 153.
5. Adapted from a private communication of 26 March 2006 from Dr. Wael B. Hallaq.
6. Quoted in Glass, "Cyber-Jihad," p. 16. Bin Laden made this plea throughout 1994 and 1995.
7. Quoted in bin Laden, "Letter to America," p. 5.

Appendix 2

1. Private communication of 21 December 2005 from Dr. Wael B. Hallaq.

Appendix 4

1. Quoted in Spectorsky, *Marriage and Divorce*, p. 10.

Bibliography

"Abduh, Muhammad." http://www.bookrags.com/biography-abduh-muammad-eorl-01/. Accessed 20 November 2005.

Abdul Ali Hamid, trans. and ed. *Moral Teachings of Islam: Prophetic Traditions from al-Adab al-mufrad by Imam al-Bukari.* Walnut Creek CA: Altamira Press, 2003.

Al-Omar, Fuad, and Mohammed Abdel-Haq. *Islamic Banking: Theory, Practice & Challenges.* Karachi: Oxford University Press, 1996.

Amnesty International. "Iran: Report 2004." http://web.amnesty.org/report2004/irn-summary-eng. Accessed 8 January 2006.

Anderson, J.N.D. "The Role of Personal Statutes in Social Development in Islamic Countries" *Comparative Studies in Society and History* (Cambridge University Press), vol. 13, no. 1., January 1971, pp. 16–43.

Ansari, Zafar Ishaq. "Abu Hanifah." http://www.britannica.com/eb/print?articleId=3423& fullArticle=true&tocId=9003423. Accessed 30 August 2005.

Armstrong, Karen. *Islam: A Short History.* London: Phoenix Press, 2002.

"Bangladesh, People's Republic of." http://www.law.emory.edu/IFL/legal/bangladesh.htm. Accessed 3 February 2006.

Bellomo, Manlio. *The Common Legal Past of Europe: 1000–1800.* Washington, D.C.: Catholic University Press, 1995.

Bilimoria, Purushottam. "Muslim Personal Law in India: Colonial Legacy and Current Debates." http://www.law.emory.edu/IFL/cases/India.htm. Accessed 6 February 2006.

bin Laden, Osama. "Letter to America." http://observer.guardian.co.uk/worldview/story/ 0,11581,845725,00.html. Accessed 8 March 2006.

Bloom, Jonathan, and Sheila Blair. *Islam: Empire of Faith.* London: BBC Worldwide Ltd., 2001.

Bordat, Stephanie Wilman, and Saida Kouzzi. "The Challenge of Implementing Morocco's New Personal Status Law." In the Carnegie Endowment for International Peace's *Arab Reform Bulletin*, vol. 2, no. 8. www.ceip.org/arabreform. Accessed 13 January 2006.

Brown, Nathan J. "*Sharia* and State in the Modern Muslim Middle East" *International Journal of Middle East Studies.* Cambridge: Cambridge University Press, 1997, pp. 359–376.

Calder, N., and M.B. Hooker. "*Shariah.*" http://www.britannica.com/eb/print?arti cleId=105857&fullArticle=true&tocId=9105857. Accessed 22 April 2005.

_____. "*Sharia*" *Encyclopaedia of Islam*, WebCD edition. Leiden: Brill, 2003.

Carnegie Endowment. "Tunisia." www.carnegieendowment.org/arabpolitical systems. Accessed 5 February 2005.

Central Intelligence Agency. "The World Factbook: Afghanistan." http://www.cia.gov/ cia/publications/factbook/print/af.html. Accessed 2 January 2006.

_____. "The World Factbook: Bangladesh." http://www.cia.gov/cia/publications/factbook/print/bg.html. Accessed 3 February 2006.

Chaumont, E. Article "al-Shafi'i" *Encyclopaedia of Islam*, WebCD edition. Leiden: Brill, 2003.

Cockburn, Patrick. "Diary." *London Review of Books*, vol. 28, no. 7, 6 April 2006, pp. 34–35.

Coulson, N.J. *A History of Islamic Law*. Edinburgh: Edinburgh University Press, 2004.

Council on Foreign Relations. "Islam: Governing Under Sharia." http://www.cfr.org/publication.html?id=8034. Accessed 3 January 2006.

CQPress in Context. "Jihad." http://www.cqpress.com/context/articles/epr_jihad.html. Accessed 5 December 2005.

_____. "al-Shaybani." In *Encyclopaedia of Islam*. WebCD edition. Leiden: Brill, 2003.

Dale, Stephen E. "The Islamic World in the Age of European Expansion." In Robinson, Francis, ed. *The Cambridge Illustrated History of the Islamic World*. Cambridge: Cambridge University Press, 1998, pp. 62–89.

Dawood, N.J., trans. and ed. *The Koran*. London: Penguin, 1999.

Delong-Bas, Natana J. *Wahhabi Islam: From Revival and Reform to Global Terrorism*. Oxford: Oxford University Press, 2004.

"The Doctrine of Ahl Al-Sunna." http://www.sunnah.org/publication/fajr/fajr.htm. Accessed 26 December 2005.

Doughty, Charles Montague. *Passages from Arabia Deserta*. Harmondsworth: Penguin, 1983.

"Draft Iraqi Constitution." http://news.bbc.co.uk/1/shared/bsp/hi/pdgs/24_08_05.pdf. Accessed 9 January 2006.

"Egypt — the French Invasion and Occupation, 1798–1801." http://countrystudies.us/egypt/20.htm. Accessed 17 November 2005.

Encyclopedia Britannica. "Baybars I." http://www.britannica.com/eb/print?tocId=9013863&fullArticle=false. Accessed 14 January 2006.

Encyclopaedia of Islam. "Riba." WebCD edition. Leiden: Brill, 2003.

Encyclopedia of the Orient. "Tanzimat." http://i-cias.com/e.o/tanzimat.htm. Accessed 20 November 2005.

Ergene, B. *Local Court, Provincial Society and Justice in the Ottoman Empire: Legal Practice and Dispute Resolution in Çankiri and Kastamonu (1652–1744)*. Leiden: Brill, 2003.

Esposito, John L., ed. *The Oxford Encyclopedia of the Modern Islamic World*. Oxford: Oxford University Press, 1995.

Falk, William. "Big little stories you might have missed [in 2005]." *International Herald Tribune*, 31 December 2005, p. 6.

Gerber, Haim. *Islamic Law and Culture, 1600–1840*. Leiden: Brill, 1999.

_____. *State, Society, and Law in Islam: Ottoman Law in Comparative Perspective*. Albany: State University of New York, 1994.

"Ghazali on Jihad al-Nafs [Fighting the Ego]." http://www.sunah.org/tasawwuf/jihad002.html. Accessed 7 December 2005.

Gibb, H.A.R. "The *Sharia*." http://answering-islam.org.uk/Books/Gibb.sharia.htm. Accessed 28 November 2005.

Glass, Charles. "Cyber-Jihad." *London Review of Books*, vol. 28, no. 5, 9 March 2006, pp. 14–18.

Greenlees, Donald. "Banking by the Koran: Islamic finance surges." *International Herald Tribune*, 2 June 2005, p. 1.

Hallaq, Wael B. *A History of Islamic Legal Theories: An Introduction to Sunni* usul al-fiqh. Cambridge: Cambridge University Press, 2004.

_____. *The Origins and Evolution of Islamic Law*. Cambridge: Cambridge University Press, 2005.

Halm, Heinz. *Shi'ism*. Trans. Janet Watson and Marian Hill. 2nd ed. Edinburgh: Edinburgh University Press, 2004.

"Horn of Africa." http://www.law.emory.edu/IFL/region/hornofafrica.html. Accessed 4 February 2006.

Hourani, Albert. *Arabic Thought in the Liberal Age, 1789–1939.* Cambridge: Cambridge University Press, 1986.
"Ibn Hazm (384–456/994–1064 CE) Muslim theologian and man of letters." http://www. muslimphilosophy.com/hazm/ibnhazm.htm. Accessed 8 December 2005.
Ignatenko, Alexander. "Ordinary Wahhabism, Part 2." http:www.islamistwatch.org/ intro/wahhabism/wahhabism_2.html. Accessed 12 November 2005.
Imber, Colin. "Ideals and legitimation in early Ottoman history." In Kunt and Woodhead, *Süleyman the Magnificent.* London and New York: Longman, 1995, pp. 138–153.
_____, ed. *Studies in Ottoman History and Law.* Istanbul: Isis Press, 1996.
"India, Republic of." http://www.law.emory.edu/IFL/legal/india.htm. Accessed 5 January 2006.
"Indonesia, Republic of." http://www.law.emory.edu/IFL/legal/indonesia.htm. Accessed 6 January 2006.
International Herald Tribune. "Apostasy charges dropped," 27 March 2006, p. 4.
_____. "'Honor killer' of sister sentenced in Germany," 14 April 2006.
_____. "Mogadishu: Teenager slays killer in a public execution," 3 May 2006, p. 7.
Iqbal, Munawar, and Philip Molyneux. *Thirty Years of Islamic Banking: History, Performance and Prospects.* Basingstoke: Palgrave MacMillan, 2005.
Janin, Hunt. *Cultures of the World: Saudi Arabia.* Singapore: Times Books International, 1992.
_____. *The Pursuit of Learning in the Islamic World, 610–2003.* Jefferson, NC: McFarland, 2005.
Johansen, Baber. *The Islamic Law on Land Tax and Rent: The Peasants' Loss of Property Rights as Interpreted in the Hanafite Legal Literature of the Mamluk and Ottoman Periods.* London: Croom Helm, 1998.
"Jordan." www.carnegieendowment.org/arabpolitical systems. Accessed 6 February 2006.
"Jordan, Hashemite Kingdom of." http:www.law.emory.edu/IFL/legal/jordan.htm. Accessed 6 February 2006.
Kamali, Mohammed Hashim. "Law and Society: The Interplay of Reason and Revelation in the Shariah." In Esposito, John L., ed., *The Oxford History of Islam.* Oxford: Oxford University Press, 1999, pp. 107–153.
Kavalcioglu, Tülay. "Süleyman the Magnificent." http://www.byegm.gov/tr/yayinlarimiz/ NEWSPOT/1997/2/N9.htm. Accessed 12 October 2005.
Khadduri, Majid, trans. and ed. *Al-Imam Muhammad ibn Idris al-Shafi'i's al-Risala: Treatise on the Foundations of Islamic Jurisprudence.* 2nd ed. Cambridge: Islamic Texts Society, 1997.
"Kitaab At-Tawheed: Chapter 36: Whoever obeys a scholar or a ruler...." http://islamicweb. com/beliefs/creed/abdulwahab/KT1-chap-36.htm. Accessed 12 November 2005.
Kolesnikov-Jessop, Sonia. "Islamic banking seeks new customers as wealth expands." *International Herald Tribune,* 24 May 2006, p. 13.
Kunt, Metin, and Christine Woodhead. *Süleyman the Magnificent and His Age: The Ottoman Empire in the Early Modern World.* London: Longman, 1995.
"Kuwait, State of." http:www.law.emory.edu/IFL/legal/kuwait.htm. Accessed 7 February 2006.
Laoust, H. "Ahmad b. Hanbal." *Encyclopaedia of Islam.* WebCD edition. Leiden: Brill, 2003.
Lapidus, Ira M. *A History of Islamic Societies.* 2nd ed. Cambridge: Cambridge University Press, 2002.
"Lebanon (Lebanese Republic)." http:www.law.emory.edu/IFL/legal/lebanon.htm. Accessed 10 January 2006.
Lewis, Bernard. *Wall Street Journal* article on *Jihad,* 27 September 2003. http://www.opin ionjournal.com/extra/?id=95001224. Accessed 2 December 2005.
"Libya — Law and the Judiciary." http: countrystudies.us/libya/75.htm. Accessed 5 February 2006.
Lings, Martin. *Muhammad: His Life Based on the Earliest Sources.* Cambridge: Islamic Texts Society, 2002.
"Malaysia." http://www.law.emory.edu/IFL/legal/malaysia.htm. Accessed 10 January 2006.

Marcus, Abraham. *The Middle East on the Eve of Modernity: Aleppo in the Eighteenth Century*. New York: Columbia University Press, 1989.

Masud, Muhammad Khalid. "Muslim Jurists' Quest for the Normative Basis of the *Sharia*." Leiden: ISIM, 2001. http://www.isim.nl/files/inaugural_masud.pdf. Accessed 1 October 2005.

"Mauritania — Legal System." http://countrystudies.us/mauritania/57.htm. Accessed 13 January 2006.

"The Medina Charter." http://www.constitution.org/cons/medina/con_medina.htm. Accessed 12 February 2006.

Melchert, Christopher. "The Hanbali Law of *Gihad*." *The Maghreb Review*, Vol. 29, 1–4, pp. 22–32, 2004.

Ministry of Information — Oman 2000. "The Rule of Law." http://www.omanet.om/english/oman2000.sec5/1.asp. Accessed 5 June 2006.

Modern History Sourcebook. "Sir William Eton: A Survey of the Turkish Empire, 1799." http://www.fordham.edu/halsall/mod/1799Ottomans.html. Accessed 12 November 2005.

"Morocco, Kingdom of (& Western Sahara)." http://www.law.emory.edu/IFL/legal/morocco.htm. Accessed 12 January 2006.

Musallam, Basim. "The Ordering of Muslim Societies." In Robinson, Francis, ed. *The Cambridge Illustrated History of the Islamic World*. Cambridge: Cambridge University Press, 1998, pp. 164–207.

Mydans, Seth. "Islamic rule faces a test in Malaysia." *International Herald Tribune*, 6 December 2005.

"Napoleon in Egypt: A Short Account." http://www.geocities.com/athens/styx/3776/Nap.html?200516. Accessed 16 November 2005.

Nasir, Jamal J. *The Islamic Law of Personal Status*. 3rd ed. The Hague: Kluwer Law International, 2002.

Norton, Augustus Richard. "Activism and Reform in Islam." *Current History*, November 2002. http://www.currenthistory.com/org_pdf_files/101/658/101_658_377.pdf. Accessed 5 January 2006.

Peirce, Leslie. *Morality Tales: Law and Gender in the Ottoman Court of Aintab*. Berkeley: University of California Press, 2003.

Peters, Rudolph. *Crime and Punishment in Islamic Law: Theory and Practice from the Sixteenth to the Twenty-first Century*. Cambridge: Cambridge University Press, 2005.

_____. "The Enforcement of God's Law: The *Shariah* in the Present World of Islam." In Ostien, Philip, Jamila Nasir, and Franz Kogelmann, eds. *Comparative Perspectives on Shariah in Nigeria*. Ibadan: Spectrum, 2005, pp. 107–143.

_____. *Jihad in Classical and Modern Islam: A Reader*. Princeton: Markus Wiener, 1996.

"Political *Sharia*? Human Rights and Islamic Law in Northern Nigeria. I. Summary." http://www.hrw.org/reports/2004/nigeria0904/1.htm. Accessed 17 January 2006.

Quran Browser: search for translations of the Quran where *jihad*-related words appear. http://qb.gomen.org/Quranbrowser/cgi/bin/retrieve.cgi. Accessed 2 December 2005.

Rentz, George S. *The Birth of the Islamic Reform Movement in Saudi Arabia: Muhammad b. Abd al-Wahhab (1703/4–1792) and the Beginnings of Unitarian Empire in Arabia*. London: Arabian Publishing, 2004.

Ringgren, Helmer. "Qur'an." http://www.britannica.com/eb/print?articleId=105854&fullArticle=true&tocId=9105854. Accessed 10 August 2005.

Robinson, Francis, ed. *The Cambridge Illustrated History of the Islamic World*. Cambridge: Cambridge University Press, 1998.

Rosen, Lawrence. *The Anthropology of Justice: Law as Culture in Islamic Society*. Cambridge: Cambridge University Press, 1998.

"Saudi Arabia, Kingdom of." http://www.law.emory.edu/IFL/legal/saudiarabia.htm. Accessed 19 November 2006.

"Saudi Arabia: The Legal System." http://countrystudies.us/saudi-arabia/5.1.htm. Accessed 5 November 2005.

Schacht, Joseph. *An Introduction to Islamic Law.* Oxford: Clarendon, 1996.

_____. "Idjtihad." *Encyclopaedia of Islam.* 2nd ed. Vol. 3, p. 1026. Leiden: Brill, 1997.

Shapiro, Semantha M. "The telegenic face of conservative Islam." *International Herald Tribune,* 29–30 April 2006, pp. 1–2.

Shiyin, Chen. "Religion doesn't hamper returns." *International Herald Tribune,* 13 April 2006, p. 22.

Slackman, Michael. "Islamic group flaunts its clout in Egypt." *International Herald Tribune,* 17 August 2005, pp. 1, 8.

Spectorsky, Susan A., trans. and ed. *Chapters on Marriage and Divorce: Responses of Ibn Hanbal and Ibn Rahwayh.* Austin: University of Texas Press, 1993.

"Striving hard in God's cause." http://qb.gomen.org/Quranbrowser.cgi/bin/retrieve.cgi. Accessed 2 December 2005.

Thier, J. Alexander. "Balancing religion and rights." *International Herald Tribune,* 27 March 2006, p. 8.

Thornton, Ted. "Muhammad Abduh." http://www.nmhschool.org/tthornton/muhammad_abduh.htm. Accessed 18 November 2005.

_____. "The Wahhabi Movement, Eighteenth Century Arabia." http://www.nmhschool.org/tthornton/wahhabi_movement.htm. Accessed 16 November 2005.

Tucker, Judith E. *In the House of the Law: Gender and Islamic Law in Ottoman Syria and Palestine.* Berkeley: University of California Press, 2000.

Tyan, E. "Djihad," *Encyclopaedia of Islam.* WebCD edition. Leiden: Brill, 2003.

"United Arab Emirates." http:www.law.emory/IFL/legal/UAE.htm. Accessed 8 February 2006.

U.S. Department of State. "Background Note: Afghanistan." http://www.state.gov/r/pa/ei/bgn/5380.htm. Accessed 2 January 2006.

_____. "Background Note: Bahrain." http://www.state.gov/r/pa/ei/bgn/26414.htm. Accessed 9 February 2006.

_____. "Background Note: Egypt." http://www.state.gov/r/pa/ei/bgn/5309.htm. Accessed 4 January 2006.

_____. "Country Reports on Human Rights Practices — 2004: Egypt." http://www.state.gov/g/drl/rls/hrrpt/2004/41720. htm. Accessed 3 January 2006.

_____. "Country Reports on Human Rights Practices — 2005: Iran." http://www.state.gov/g/drl/rls/hrrpt/2005/61688.htm. Accessed 30 April 2006.

_____. "Country Reports on Human Rights Practices — 2005: Saudi Arabia." http://www.state/gov/g/drl/rls/2005/61698.htm. Accessed 9 March 2006.

_____. "Country Reports on Human Rights Practices — 2005: Turkey." http://www.state.gove/g/drl/rls/hrrpt/2005/61680.html. Accessed 23 March 2005.

_____. "International Religious Freedom Report 2005: Saudi Arabia." http://www.state.gov/g/drl/rls/irf/2005/51609.htm. Accessed 14 December 2005.

USC-MSA Compendium of Muslim Texts. "*Shariah* and *Fiqh.*" http://www.usc.edu/dept/MSA/law/shariaintroduction.html. Accessed 1 December 2005.

Vikør, Knut. "The *Sharia* and the nation state: who can codify the divine law?" http://www.hf.uib.no/smi/pao/vikor.html. Accessed 20 September 2005.

Vogel, Frank E. *Islamic Law and Legal System: Studies of Saudi Arabia.* Leiden, Boston and Köln: Brill, 2000.

"Wahhabi menace comes to the Cape." http://sunnah.org/aqida/cape_town_wahabi/wahabi_menace_capetown.htm. Accessed 26 December 2005.

Watt, W. Montgomery. "al-Ghazali." *Encyclopaedia of Islam.* WebCD edition. Leiden: Brill, 2003.

_____. "Muhammad." *Encyclopedia Britannica.* http://www.britannica.com/eb/print?articleId=1058533&fullArticle=true&tocId=9105853. Accessed 7 June 2005.

"West Africa." http://www.law.emory.edu/IFL/region/westafrica.html. Accessed 7 February 2006.

"What Does Jihad Mean." http://www.ict.org.il/articles/jjihad/htm. Accessed 27 December 2005.

"Why You Should Poison Your Husband: A Note on Liability in Hanafi Law in the Ottoman Period." *Islamic Law and Society.* 1/2: 1994, pp. 206–16. Reprinted in Imber, Colin. *Studies in Ottoman History and Law.* Istanbul: Isis Press, 1996, pp. 253–261.

Wurmser, Meyrav. "The Roots of Islamic Radicalism." http://www.americanoutlook.org/index.cfm?fuseaction=article_detail&id=1084. Accessed 19 January 2006.

Zubaida, Sami. *Law and Power in the Islamic World.* London: Tauris, 2005.

Zyzik, Marlena. "Personal Status Law in the Arab States, Process of Codification," in *Studia Arabistyczne i Islamistyczne* (Uniwersytet Warszawski Zaklad Arabistyki i Islamistyki, 2001), pp. 29–43.

Index

205